Environmental Geopolitics

Shannon O'Lear
University of Kansas

ROWMAN & LITTLEFIELD
Lanham • Boulder • New York • London

Executive Editor: Susan McEachern
Editorial Assistant: Katelyn Turner
Senior Marketing Manager: Kim Lyons

Published by Rowman & Littlefield
An imprint of The Rowman & Littlefield Publishing Group, Inc.
4501 Forbes Boulevard, Suite 200, Lanham, Maryland 20706
www.rowman.com

Unit A, Whitacre Mews, 26-34 Stannary Street, London SE11 4AB, United Kingdom

Copyright © 2018 by The Rowman & Littlefield Publishing Group, Inc.

All rights reserved. No part of this book may be reproduced in any form or by any electronic or mechanical means, including information storage and retrieval systems, without written permission from the publisher, except by a reviewer who may quote passages in a review.

British Library Cataloguing in Publication Information Available

Library of Congress Cataloging-in-Publication Data
Names: O'Lear, Shannon, author.
Title: Environmental geopolitics / Shannon O'Lear.
Description: Lanham : Rowman & Littlefield, [2018] | Series: Human geography in the twenty-first century issues and applications | Includes bibliographical references and index.
Identifiers: LCCN 2017058547 (print) | LCCN 2018002704 (ebook) | ISBN 9781442265820 (electronic) | ISBN 9781442265806 (hardcover : alk. paper) | ISBN 9781442265813 (pbk. : alk. paper)
Subjects: LCSH: Political ecology.
Classification: LCC JA75.8 (ebook) | LCC JA75.8 .O638 2018 (print) | DDC 304.2—dc23
LC record available at https://lccn.loc.gov/2017058547

∞™ The paper used in this publication meets the minimum requirements of American National Standard for Information Sciences—Permanence of Paper for Printed Library Materials, ANSI/NISO Z39.48-1992.

Printed in the United States of America

This book is dedicated to those willing to read it with an open mind.

Contents

	List of Illustrations	vii
	Acknowledgments	ix
Chapter 1	Introduction to Environmental Geopolitics	1
Chapter 2	Population and Environment	27
Chapter 3	Resource Conflict and Slow Violence	65
Chapter 4	Climate Change and Security	103
Chapter 5	Science, Imagery, and Understanding the Environment	135
Chapter 6	Building from Here	165
	References	179
	Index	197
	About the Author	205

Illustrations

Figures

2.1	Thomas Malthus's Famous Projection	33
2.2	Hubbert's Projection	56

Maps

2.1	World Freshwater Resources	53
2.2	World Water Use	54
3.1	U.S. Continental Earthquakes	88
3.2	Largest Oil Spills Affecting US Waters since 1969	97
5.1	Newly Accessible Ocean due to Arctic Ice Melt	157

Photos

The 2014 People's Climate March in New York City	4
Warning sign in Centralia, Pennsylvania	8
Nepalese group participating in the 2014 People's Climate March in New York City	17
Green tea plantation	20
Apollo 17 image of earth from space, December 1972	22
Cemetery in Dargavs, North Ossetia	29
Bridge spanning the Ganges riverbed in Allahabad, India	44
Satellite image of the remaining Aral Sea	46

Krabi, Thailand	67
Palm oil plantation in Sulawesi, Indonesia	68
National Ice Core Lab, Denver, Colorado	78
Christopher Columbus and the International Monetary Fund	90
Sign at the Reluctant Fisherman Inn in Cordova, Alaska	96
Activist artists of the Brandalism project created posters to challenge corporate sponsorship of the UN COP 21 Climate Conference in Paris	107
The Svalbard Global Seed Vault, Norway	114
Climate change graffiti	120
Flooding in Bangkok, Thailand, October 2008	128
Air-conditioning units on a backstreet in Little India, Singapore	143
Wind turbine foundations	146
Paper or plastic?	151
Nam Ngum Dam, Laos	154
Vertical forest buildings, Milan, Italy	167
Gulf of the Farallones National Marine Sanctuary	175
Wunderland in Kalkar, Germany	176

Acknowledgments

The ideas in this book are the fruits of both focused pursuit and unplanned, intellectual adventures. I am grateful for my interactions with people over the years who have been part of both of these tracks: teachers, professors, mentors, tormentors, colleagues, friends, and family. Many thanks to the students, both undergraduate and graduate, with whom I've worked over the years for your questions, your effort, your resistance, and your perspective. I am fortunate to have appointments and thoughtful colleagues in the Geography and Atmospheric Sciences Department and in the Environmental Studies Program here at the University of Kansas. Thanks are due to Susan McEachern at Rowman & Littlefield for shepherding this project forward, and to Barney Warf, also with Rowman & Littlefield and next door in Lindley Hall, for his unwavering support and hearty good humor.

CHAPTER ONE

Introduction to Environmental Geopolitics

Look at the cover of this book again. Is the image familiar to you? You may recognize the lines of a well-known graphic showing how scientific projections for increased greenhouse gas emissions are associated with anticipated increases in global temperature. In this image, do you see reason to be concerned about the well-being of the planet? Or do you wonder how society might alter its course? How do we know if we are even using the *right* kinds of science to ask and answer questions that could affect not just us but other people and ecosystems around the planet?

An artistic interpretation of scientific information is a useful analogy for a central question of this book: What kinds of evidence and assumptions serve to stabilize our view of the world and, in particular, our understanding of human-environment relationships? When we think about ways in which we are connected to the environment, how do we imbue those relationships with power? That is, in what ways do we portray certain environmental features as posing a risk to our well-being? Or, at the other end of the spectrum, how do we understand some aspects of the environment as worth preserving or as providing some form of security?

Indeed, environmental issues often seem to be at the heart of both conflicts and security these days. In popular media and scholarly research, environmental aspects of political tension issues are a frequent focus and concern. Many armed conflicts are understood to be linked to resources, such as diamonds, oil, or water; there are ongoing debates over various benefits or costs of energy systems based on oil, coal, wind, and solar energy; supplies of natural resources are thought to be dwindling under the demand of a growing human population; predictions of unstable water supplies and agricultural systems due to climate change are made; and the environment—whether in terms of pollution, water and food availability, oil supply, and more—is increasingly portrayed as a security concern. On the flip side, environmental features are also discussed as being fraught with risk and posing threats to our well-being. People, including scholars, often perpetuate broad assumptions about environmental concerns. For instance, the presence of a resource (such as oil or diamonds) or a scarcity of a resource (such as food or water) at a particular location is often assumed to drive violence or conflict in that place. Poverty may be singled out as the reason why people make environmentally destructive decisions. An influx of people to a certain place may be assumed to have only negative consequences for the environment. These kinds of assumptions or discourses about human-environment relationships tend to be universalizing. That is, they are often assumed to be *truths* that fit all situations and may be used to justify certain actions. Such discourses may serve to maintain an unjust status quo instead of questioning the arrangements of power that have contributed to current circumstances. Discourses—what they are and how we can examine them—are discussed in more detail later in this chapter.

An initial definition of environmental geopolitics is that it is an approach to examining how environmental themes are used to support geopolitical arguments and realities. It asks how *the environment* is brought into narratives, practices, and physical realities of power and place. Geographers study places, patterns, and processes across human and physical realms. Political geographers examine dimensions of power as it shapes and is shaped by place and spatial patterns and processes. As a subfield of political geography, environmental geopolitics encourages reflection on how particular aspects of the nonhuman environment—mineral resources, weather patterns, arable land, ecosystem services, and more—are understood, represented, and portrayed in terms of spatial aspects of risk or security. Instead of taking arguments about food shortages, resource conflicts, or climate security, for instance, at face value, environmental geopolitics investigates how food, resources, and climate are identified, made distinct, measured, and portrayed as something, somewhere, to be secured or that pose a particular threat requiring a response. It is a practice of clarification and examining how alternative interpretations and realities could also be viable. In this way, environmental geopolitics is a project to think otherwise about the kinds of power shaping the places, patterns, and spatial processes of the world today. Of course, this definition of environmental geopolitics offers an introduction to the approach and contents of this book, but it is also a starting point for further dialogue about what we mean by environment, what we think of as geopolitics, and how we can usefully understand relationships connecting them.

An environmental geopolitics approach is particularly useful in understanding how environmental issues are associated with security or risk. A traditional approach to security studies focuses on military threats to the territorial state. However, a growing body of work known as critical security studies has expanded the understanding of security to objects beyond the state as well as beyond the military sector. Scholars in this field have considered how particular environmental or economic issues move from being nonpolitical to political (or part of public policy debates) to being securitized (Buzan et al. 1998). Once an issue is labeled as a *security* issue, it is prioritized and "justifies responses that go beyond normal political processes" (Peoples and Vaughan-Williams 2015, 94). A key part of this securitization process is the acceptance of the security label by the intended audience. Therefore, an attempt to move an issue into the realm of a security concern must convincingly link the issue to some form of well-being or effectively demonstrate how inaction will lead to the increase of a perceived threat. The knowledge presented about the issue must be persuasive, and the authority to take action must be established for it to be accepted as a security concern. In addition to examining the process of how issues are securitized, it is also important to consider *why* a particular issue is being securitized and who will benefit from that arrangement (Walker 1987).

Tied up with how we understand security is the notion of risk. Ulrich Beck's seminal book *Risk Society* (1992) considered how the technologies of modern society are not only an indication of scientific progress but also bring about new kinds of unintended and uncontrollable risk. Nuclear power, for instance, or widespread use of chemicals in industrial-scale agriculture, make life in a modern society in some ways more comfortable and convenient; however, these technologies are also fraught with uncertainties in terms of safety, human health, and ecosystemic resilience. In his more recent work, Beck (2009, 9–10) describes the influence of risk:

> The moment risks become real, when a nuclear power station explodes or a terrorist attack occurs, they become catastrophes. Risks are always *future* events that *may* occur, that *threaten* us. But because this constant danger shapes our expectations, lodges in our heads and guides our actions, it becomes a political force that transforms the world.

This view of risk as future events raises the question: How do we conceptualize and discuss risk? In the interest of avoiding catastrophe, modern

Sign from the 2014 People's Climate March in New York City. In what ways are environmental resources linked to violence?
Source: iStock

society aims to minimize risk. Immediately, risk becomes something that may be studied, measured, calculated, and modeled through scientific and mathematical methods. Such a technical approach to risk can serve to increase or diminish our perceptions of risk. Even more important, perhaps, is that culture has a significant influence on how risk is perceived. Media coverage, for instance, can greatly amplify the public perception of risk and heighten the anticipation that similar but worse events will follow. The accidents at Three Mile Island and Fukushima nuclear facilities, the tampering with and poisoning of Tylenol in 1982, and the British beef scare resulting from mad cow disease are all examples of events with high *signal value* that had ripple effects well beyond their initial, direct damages (Slovic 2016).

Security and risk are therefore slippery yet powerful concepts, and this book looks at how notions of security and risk are developed and promoted within specific discourses about environmental issues. It is important to examine environmental risk and security if we want to assess, for example, how science is used to make political arguments, how consumers are encouraged to make choices, and how environmental features are viewed as threat multipliers from a military perspective. To provide structure for this investigation, this book presents an analytical approach of environmental geopolitics as a way to analyze and understand how human-environment relations are securitized or portrayed as risks and why that matters.

This book focuses on four dominant topics in which we find discourses associated with environmental risk and security: (1) human population and the environment; (2) resource conflict and slow violence; (3) climate change and security; and (4) science and imagery as ways of understanding and responding to environmental issues. While these four topics by no means capture the full spectrum of human-environment relationships, they are worth considering because they are both familiar and widely misunderstood. An analysis of these four topics shows how an environmental geopolitical approach questions universal assumptions about resources, draws our attention to spatial nuance and context, and brings power dynamics and human agency into sharper relief. Rather than promising concrete, universal answers, this approach raises deeper questions and helps us to think more clearly about complex human and environmental systems and ways in which interpretations of these systems are used to serve particular interests.

Three Observations of Environmental Geopolitics

Environmental geopolitical analyses make three overarching observations about popular and scholarly discourses on the environment:

1. The role and meaning of the environment are rarely specified.

    The key topics examined in this book reflect many different understandings of the environment. For climate security, for instance, we may understand that a warming atmosphere contributes to melting ice sheets and rising sea levels that will have an impact on coastal areas. Here, the environment might be thought of as global-scale atmospheric and oceanic circulation patterns that are shifting, resulting in more chaotic weather. Yet when we hear news stories about resource-related conflict, such as disputes over freshwater supplies or violent control of diamond-producing areas in Sierra Leone, the environment seems to be more local and something that can be controlled militarily or politically. Overuse or misuse of the environment may be linked to environmental degradation such as soil erosion, declines in crop output, or polluted air and water supplies. The decline of ecosystem services—benefits of a resilient and healthy ecosystem—is yet another dimension or different way of looking at the environment. As discussed in this book, these different aspects of "the" environment can hardly be grouped into a single, uniform category. In some cases, the environment is understood to mean commodity resources that may be extracted, grown, refined, packaged, and traded or sold. In other instances, such as concerns over the rate and level of acidification of the world's oceans, the environment is understood more like a commons to be shared by everyone. Later in this chapter, the issue of the environment label is discussed in greater detail. The problem with not clarifying what exactly is being referred to as the environment is that a great deal of specificity is lost or overlooked. It is important to understand the nuance of the spatial scale of an environmental feature (e.g., local, national, global, or aligned with the boundaries of an ecosystem, etc.); in what ways that environmental feature is understood, valued, and used by people; and how that environmental feature is associated with political, economic, or social systems in different places. Thus, it is important to be clear on the role and meaning of the environment as we investigate topics such as climate security and resource conflict.

2. Humans' role or agency in these situations tends to be considered selectively. In particular, dynamics of power remain invisible and uninvestigated.

    Carrying over from the previous point, almost any aspect of the environment that you might think of is in some way linked to political, economic, or social systems created by people. How did oil become a dominant fuel source? How do subsidies of food crops influence food prices and consumer demand for certain foods? How does our understanding of pollution lead to the establishment of environmental standards? Who has the power to implement (or disregard) these standards? Often, in news stories or discussions about environmental issues, we do not hear about how the current situation came to be, who is benefitting from how things are arranged or valued, or what other alternative configurations or valuations might be possible. Without this context, environmental situations—for example, the drought in Syria, the expansion of hydraulic fracturing (fracking) for natural gas in the United States, the decline of bees in North America due to colony collapse—become crystalized and are portrayed as inevitable. The situation, then, is postpolitical (Swyngedouw 2010a) in that dissent, debate, and opportunities for alternative trajectories are shut down or sidelined. Examining notions of risk and security can highlight how dynamics of power are woven into presentations and discussions of environmental issues.

3. Insufficient attention is paid to spatial dimensions of human-environment relationships that occur unevenly in different places and are intertwined with local, political, and cultural geographies.

Interactions between people and environmental features have spatial dimensions that are often overlooked. Our impact on resource supplies, such as forests, fish stocks, and the various minerals and metals used to make the things that we consume, happens in particular places. Often the environmental impacts of our consumption and waste generation are distanced from us, and we do not experience them directly. The demand for diamonds as a symbol of love in North America, Europe, and Japan is linked to negative and violent impacts in diamond-producing, former European colonies of West Africa. Similarly, although we may fault China for its unabated greenhouse gas emissions, the industrial productivity there, enabled in part by low environmental standards, provides inexpensive goods to consumers around the world. Consumption in richer parts of the world is often both spatially and cognitively distant from its negative impacts, whether it is the mining of materials for batteries in hybrid cars or the dumping of toxic electronic waste in poor countries desperate for a source of income. If we can't see it, we don't think about it.

It is also important to understand spatial dimensions of particular ecosystems and aspects of the environment. International agreements on fishing must address not only the lateral area of oceans to be negotiated as open or closed to certain kinds of capture, but they must also address the fact that different species of fish live at different depths of the ocean (*Economist* 2015). Increasingly, political geographers are turning their attention to this kind of space-as-volume and geometrics of space (Elden 2013) related to environmental features, such as rising sea levels and volumes of carbon dioxide related to climate change (Dalby 2013), or calculations of oil reserves and energy security (Bridge 2015). Thinking spatially about environmental features in terms of connections and disconnections, and in terms of areas and volumes, is critical to understanding nuances of human-environment interactions.

These three observations provide a starting point for an environmental geopolitical analysis of the topics we will explore in this book. Dominant discourses or understandings of human population and the environment, resource conflict and slow violence, climate security, and science and imagery as ways of understanding and responding to environmental issues

Warning sign in Centralia, Pennsylvania. An underground coal fire has been burning since 1962. The town of Centralia, Pennsylvania, was condemned due to this ongoing, subterranean environmental catastrophe.
Source: JohnDS/Wikimedia

will be identified and critiqued. But why is this important? The goal is to demonstrate how mainstream, Western discourses on these environmental topics can perpetuate misguided generalizations about the environment, obscure value judgments, and limit more thoughtful approaches to human-environment relationships. An environmental geopolitical analysis helps us to identify hidden complexities in seemingly simple relationships portrayed in dominant understandings of these topics.

The critical approach demonstrated in this book is easily transferable to other studies. Taking a critical view means to question common understandings and assumptions in order to examine how certain pieces of information are used—and how other pieces of information are hidden—to promote a particular view or agenda. How an issue is presented or framed, so to speak, influences how we see and understand the issue, thus highlighting why it is useful to identify and examine particular discourses. Additionally, it is helpful to ask: Whose interests are served by a particular framing, and what other perspectives or possibilities are obscured from view? The connections and critiques in the pages that follow offer insightful perspectives on current events as well as on the way our society understands and conceptualizes environment-related risk, security, and stability. Environmental geopolitical analysis is an approach that encourages careful and spatially attentive consideration of how environmental features are described, promoted, bounded, and attached to human values and concerns or portrayed as threats requiring action. Within the context of political geography, my objective is to investigate and question the status quo so that we may create the possibility for intelligent dissent and the development of alternative responses.

First, however, it is important to clarify the environmental geopolitics approach as used in this book. The label itself is imperfect and incomplete, which is an intentional reminder to maintain an inquisitive mind. As an analytical approach, environmental geopolitics takes cues from critical geopolitics. In order to understand critical geopolitics, it is necessary to understand what classical geopolitics is and how a critical stance is useful.

A Brief Overview of Classical Geopolitics

We start with geopolitics. Although the word *geopolitics* may be familiar, most people are unclear as to what it actually means other than some systematic way to explain current events. My aim is to describe geopolitics not as providing a form of objective explanation or *truth* of how the world *is*, but as a way of representing and projecting a particular *understanding* of the world and spatial relationships.

Swedish political scientist Rudolph Kjellén coined the word *geopolitics* in 1899. He wanted a label to describe how knowledge of state-level geography—including knowledge about topography, population, natural resources, and physical relationships to other states—could be used in competition with other states or territories (Smith 2003). Around that time, Western European powers were ramping up their imperial efforts to expand and take control of distant territories and peoples. Such imperial expansion contradicted the notion of the national, territorial state that was defined through the long-standing occupation of a particular territory by a relatively homogenous group of people. The idea of taking over nontraditional territories and peoples not only contradicted the notion of the established, national state, but it also challenged the idea of a community of equal states that had been emerging in Western Europe. Expending valuable resources in the drive toward expansion and the acquisition of unfamiliar territories and peoples required justification to gain popular support.

It is in this context that Friedrich Ratzel, a German geographer in the late 1800s, advanced his organic theory of the state, portraying the state as a biological organism that needed to expand in order to survive (Bassin 1987). Ratzel's conceptualization of *Lebensraum*, or living space, was one of biological reductionism. It took the then-popular practice of applying an analogy from the plant and animal world directly to human activity as a way to explain, scientifically, why territorial expansion of the state made sense. Ratzel's argument also carried the assumption that territorially defined groups of people could be treated as cohesive units struggling with other groups or territorial units of people over resources. This categorizing of whole groups of people and assigning them particular attributes of weakness or success underpins the idea of Social Darwinism that was popular in the late 1800s (Kearns 2009). States were assumed to contain homogenous groups of people, or nations, which would naturally come into conflict with other homogenous groups of people, or nations.

Environmental determinism was another popular idea at the time in Western Europe. This concept, which is similar to the concept of *Lebensraum* and draws on work done in evolutionary biology in the late 1800s, argues that environmental conditions directly shape human capacity rather than seeing humans as adapting to different environments or even humans and environments adapting to each other. Based on this perspective, societies in Western Europe were seen as having developed significant innovations that allowed them to survive harsh winters, whereas societies in tropical climates, for instance, lacked the seasonal motivation to pursue such advanced forms of development. Taking the view that an environment determines human outcomes leaves no room for cultural adaptability and can result in racist views that some groups of people are more advanced than others (Jones et al. 2015). This idea of environmental determinism helped to justify the undermining or even complete destruction of other cultures in an effort to expand the territory and economic wealth of imperial powers. Combining Social Darwinism and environmental determinism with an interest in a grand strategy to expand imperial power, early theorists of geopolitics focused on state or imperial rivalry as a way to maximize gains in power measured by influence and material resources while restricting the ability of other states to expand (Dodds et al. 2013). That is, dominant geopolitical ideas and arguments put forward at the time were not mere expressions of observable "facts"; they integrated popular notions of science and current, political objectives to construct and promote particular perspectives about the world.

Geopolitical theorists took different approaches to explaining relationships between territorial spaces and power. A particularly well-known theory promoted by Sir Halford Mackinder (1861–1947) warned against the decline of British sea power and emphasized the importance of controlling large amounts of land-based territory as a measure of power. Mackinder was predominantly interested in global strategy, and he was specifically concerned with the vast landmass of Eurasia as an important indicator of global power. He observed that Russia was extending its ability to move into and draw resources from the Eurasian heartland and that Germany was also interested in the resources of that area. As a result of these observations, and out of concern for promoting British interests, in 1919 Mackinder promoted the narrative that "Who rules East Europe commands the Heartland: Who Rules the Heartland commands the World-Island: Who Rules the World-Island commands the World" (Mackinder 1919, 186). Mackinder's "Heartland Theory" depicted a threat to British power and served to justify the British colonial presence in India to keep either Germany or Russia from expanding into the Eurasian landmass and gaining access to the ocean. Some years later, taking up Ratzel's organic theory of the state and Mackinder's focus on land territory as power, Karl Haushofer (1869–1946) twisted the concept of *Lebensraum* as a means to justify the deadly Nazi effort to clear space in Eastern Europe so that the German people could expand territorially and thrive (Jones et al. 2015, 7).

Some geopolitical theoreticians explicitly recognized the impact and influence of new technologies on the control of territorial space. In his time, Mackinder acknowledged the vital role that railroad expansion played in a state's ability to bring new areas and activities into the service of the state economy (thus reiterating the significance of power in the form of control over land-based territory). Years later, after World War II, Alexander de

Seversky (1894–1974) pointed to the risk of Soviet airplanes and missiles reaching US industrial areas by way of a northern route over the Arctic Circle (de Seversky 1942). His arguments helped to generate a polar projection map, centered on the North Pole, to depict the reach not only of Soviet missile technology but also the potential of the United States to reach into Soviet industrial areas via suitably located US military bases in the far North. Such a polar view of the world, and the specified threat of Soviet missiles, illustrated the importance of air power. This view of the world was used to justify the expansion of US military presence in the northern reaches of Alaska, a move that would not have made sense without this particular spatial perspective of risk, a perspective that did not exist prior to the development of particular technologies of flight and jet propulsion (President's Air Policy Commission 1948; see also Kaplan 2006 for a contemporary and critical view of air power). However, even though many geopolitical arguments have focused on states as actors, geopolitical theorists often used world maps without political borders to explain how "natural" processes of human conflict would likely interact with topography such as rivers, mountains, plains, and coastal areas.

This brief comparison of a few classic geopolitical narratives cannot do justice to the fuller picture of the complexities of geographic thought, competing values and economic priorities, or relations among states and peoples across this timeline. However, what these classic geopolitical narratives demonstrate are efforts to describe the world in a particular way to justify a particular response. In order to generate mass appeal or to portray the intended view as obvious, classic geopolitical narratives from 1875 to 1945 were promoted through the naturalization of knowledge claims. That is, quietly embedded in these geopolitical views are assumptions about values and about society that served to bolster the strength of a particular argument. Two key maneuvers stand out in this context. The first is to naturalize knowledge claims by offering a viewpoint that is assumed to be universal and unquestionable (Agnew and Muscarà 2012). Promoting such a "view from nowhere" makes an argument seem, on one hand, as having no clear source or bias, and on the other, conveniently universal in applicability. For instance, in nineteenth-century Europe, women were widely portrayed as being motherly, nurturing, and incapable of comprehending complex political or financial issues (Hansen 2006, 19–21). This view, promoted as an "objective account of women's nature" (19), was reinforced as the natural state of things through legal and cultural practices until women's rights activists challenged this limited view of women as secondary, but necessary, to politically privileged men. That is, assumptions about the limitations and capabilities of all women were challenged by alternative views informed by different values and priorities. In a similar way, although geopolitical narratives during this period were often crafted or used in the service of particular state interests, the narratives were framed as emerging from "obvious" elements of global strategy. When an argument is presented as being obvious and objective, it can take a shortcut around discussions of who or what the argument supports. This "god trick" (Haraway 1988, 581) of objectivity hides from view other possible interpretations of events as well as diverse cultural interpretations of places.

A second maneuver in the naturalization of knowledge claims is to apply scientific understandings of natural phenomena to explain social and political activity. We have seen how Ratzel and other early geopolitical theorists applied biological concepts to political, economic, social, and demographic aspects of a state as if these concepts could be transferred directly from the category of natural science to the social realm. Pointing to scientific explanations or analogies to the natural world safely avoids discussion of politics, priorities, and values. Even a move so subtle as referring to "natural" boundaries of a state cuts off any discussion about what, exactly, might constitute a natural boundary when states are in fact political units constructed to serve human interests.

The classic examples of geopolitics briefly described above illustrate how a geopolitical narrative attempts to explain a particular understanding of spatial aspects of security and risk. For example, the justification to annex new territory in the interest of a state's economic wealth or the danger of losing territory to a competitor state are situations portrayed as promoting security or identifying risk. Indeed, "geopolitics was, and for many authors still is, the study of statecraft and the divination of patterns of global politics" (Dodds et al. 2013, 3). However, we can see that these narratives are not universal truths or facts but instead reflect a particular view and a specific context of place and time. Geopolitical discourses have taken different forms over time because geopolitics captures a particular interpretation about power and space under the specific conditions of that place and time. Indeed, at any time there are simultaneous, competing discourses that take different views of relationships of power and space (for a counterexample from one of Mackinder's contemporaries, see Kearns 1997). There is never a single, correct geopolitics. Rather, a geopolitical discourse summarizes political priorities and a spatial agenda from a particular perspective at a given point in time. When we step back from a geopolitical discourse and see it as an ideological move rather than an objective assertion of fact, we create the possibility to ask questions about how these narratives "limit the way in which it is possible to speak, write and act concerning issues of war, peace and security" (Dalby 1990, 167). This questioning of assumptions and assertions embedded in geopolitical narratives is the entry point for critical geopolitics.

Critical Geopolitics

Critical geopolitics is concerned with "the politics of geographical knowledge and the power of geographical representation" (Dodds 2001, 470). It examines how geographical knowledge is produced and deployed and to what effect. It asks: What kinds of places or resources are highly valued and why? What kinds of place-related trends or movements of ideas, people, or things threaten the interests of certain groups of people? The aim, and challenge, is to understand and explain how geography and place matter in political processes (Murphy et al. 2004, 626; see also Atkinson and Dodds 2000). The term *critical* does not mean an automatic rejection of an idea. Rather, to be critical is to be curious. A critical stance provides an open-ended approach to identifying and examining statements about power over space and place. There is no singular, established definition of what it means to be critical; it is an orientation rather than a precise label (Peoples and Vaughan-Williams 2015, 2). To be critical is to question assumptions embedded within a discourse as a way to examine what it tells us about a particular understanding of geography and politics. So, as noted above, much of classical geopolitics centers on global strategy from a state's perspective, or a state-centric approach. Classical geopolitics focuses on the need to dominate over territorial threats and to maximize the power of the viewer (or state) or at least maintain the status quo. Classical geopolitical discourses have tended to view space as absolute, two-dimensional (Cartesian) space that can be objectively measured, mapped, and assessed as valuable, dangerous, or empty. Critical geopolitics, on the other hand, is a response to the limitations of classical geopolitical assumptions. Critical geopolitics questions the positionality of a geopolitical discourse: Whose interests does the narrative, image, or message serve? A critical geopolitical approach questions simplifications behind arguments that *we*, here, should be secured from someone or something, *there*, that poses a threat to our power or our way of life.

A discourse does not emanate from a single person but is a representation or practice through which meaning is produced. That is, it is not just the ideas or the stated narrative that Mackinder, for example, articulated, but the way in which the political, social, and technological context at that time allowed his ideas to take root in the minds of British people and politicians in order to justify a particular worldview, set of values, and actions. Discourses "'naturalize' and often implicitly universalize a particular view of the world and position subjects differentially within it" (Johnston et al. 2000, 180–81). Much of the way in which geographers study discourses draws from the work of Michel Foucault (1926–1984). Discourses, in Foucault's work, are structures and carriers of knowledge that establish a particular way of ordering and prioritizing of the world (see Dreyfus and Rabinow 1983). Discourses serve to stabilize a particular understanding or construction of things such as identities, objects, and places. Geopolitical discourses serve to produce meaning about place and the construction of spatial relationships. The way in which geopolitical ideas, such as Mackinder's Heartland Theory or Ratzel's organic state, supported particular objectives of statecraft at a particular time are examples of geopolitical discourses because they constructed an understanding of the value of certain places and justified certain spatial actions.

Geopolitical Discourse as Narrative, Materiality, Embodiment, and Practice

Geopolitical discourses may be communicated through many different forms and genres (see Mamadouh and Dijkink 2006). They may be reflected in narratives, a term used to refer to written or spoken texts including official documents, policy statements, and speeches (such as President George Bush's "Axis of Evil" speech in 2002 following the attacks on September 11th). They may also be communicated through popular culture media. Analyses of Captain America comic books (Dittmer 2005) or political cartoons (Dodds 1996) demonstrate how particular understandings of national security and sources of risk are portrayed to the general public. Similarly, films such as the James Bond series (Dodds 2003, 2005) capture and promote certain understandings of security and risk and how they can move between places or be contained. Additionally, critical cartographers examine how maps lie (Monmonier 1996) or tell partial truths to portray a particular representation of place (Moore and Perdue 2014).

Scholars of critical geopolitics have tended to pay close attention to representations of place in verbal narratives and texts (see Ó Tuathail 1996), but critical geopolitics is increasingly relevant off the page and can be useful in assessing materiality, embodiment, and practices (Thrift 2000; Dittmer 2015), all of which are discussed below. Indeed, discourses are more than linguistic or visual narratives, and they are not mere abstract ideas or thoughts. Discourses can be evident in tangible ways in actual places: "The operations of discourse, knowledge, and power are crucially bound up with the soils of nameable places; the material contexts of particular environments and landscapes, regions and countries" (Philo 1992, 155). It is helpful to understand that "it is not the individual that structures and manipulates discourse but vice versa—discourses speak through the individual" (Müller 2008, 326). Therefore, we can study a discourse by examining how it *speaks* through materiality, embodiment, and practices as well as through textual or visual narratives that construct certain meanings of place and spatial relationships. Put another way, "It is not actions that determine discourse; the critical issue is the power of discursive formations rooted in existing geographical and geopolitical imaginations to determine patterns of action" (Murphy et al. 2004, 634). Discourses, the way we think about and discuss the world, can shape actions and outcomes.

One way of examining geographical and geopolitical imaginations is to study texts, documents, and speeches, such as Mackinder's writing on Heartland Theory or speeches by government leaders in which they outline steps to build national security and thwart risk. However, we can expand the scope of our study beyond texts to include materiality, embodiment, and practices to see how they communicate and reinforce particular geopolitical imaginations or assumptions. Additionally, by broadening our assessment to include other forms of geopolitical discourse, we can see how dominant understandings of security and risk are challenged by alternative views and geographical understandings.

First, *materiality* is evident when we look at ways in which power and understandings of place have tangible influence on infrastructures, physical networks, activities, and economies in particular places. For instance, examining the on-the-ground negotiations and forms of knowledge involved in determining the route of an oil pipeline employs a critical geopolitics approach to materiality (Barry 2013). The material aspects of an oil pipeline—how it is physically routed through villages, the details of its construction and operation, how it alters the structure and value of landscapes, such as agricultural or mudslide-prone areas along its route—are shaped by negotiations over what kinds of knowledge and what kinds of values are in a position of power and why. Focusing on materiality lends perspective to ways in which things, artifacts, and physical systems interact with and shape decisions about how physical space will be used, valued, and devalued.

Second, *embodiment* recognizes lived experiences of space and power and how bodies are represented and restricted. Identities and social categories of belonging and otherness are not merely linguistic categories but are accomplished and expressed through material and symbolic means (Atkinson et al. 2005). According to this view:

> Bodies are entwined in multiple power relations realized through space. These power relations may be differentially organized through varying relations of race, sexuality, gender and so on, but in all instances they are written on and through the bodies and spaces under discussion. Bodies cannot be snatched from the spatial relations that constitute them. (Longhurst 2005, 93)

Examining embodiment, then, aims to understand how constructions of identity (e.g., national, gendered, public/private, belonging, threatening, etc.) are experienced, situated, resisted, and intertwined with the construction of space from different perspectives. For example, a study of legal responses to the rape of civilians by UN Peacekeepers in Haiti illustrates varying degrees of acknowledgment of violence against actual bodies. Peacekeepers sent from different countries under one specific peacekeeping mission remain under the legal jurisdiction of their countries of origin, and they are immune from any prosecution by the state in which they are hosted (Reiz and O'Lear 2016). Differing national, legal guidelines determine how, or to what extent, peacekeepers will be held accountable for violations against civilians. Despite the physical violence the survivors of these crimes have endured, they often have few, if any, legal rights to make claims against their attackers who are protected by international security protocol. This example from critical legal geography considers how the embodiment of violence may or may not be legally recognized in the interest of maintaining national or international peace and security.

Third, a critical geopolitics approach can be helpful in understanding *practices* that implement spatial discourse, resist a spatial discourse, or construct

Nepalese group participating in the 2014 People's Climate March in New York City. How does identity shape a view of the world? Or does one's view of the world shape one's identity?
Source: iStock

an alternative space to foster a particular form of activity or resistance. For instance, when the Soviet Union collapsed, both overt political activism and public use of the Internet were tremendously rare. Environmental activist groups, however, found ways to use email connectivity with distant environmental activist organizations to inform their work and create spaces of activism to pursue their environmental agendas (O'Lear 1996, 1999). Even day-to-day practices such as consumption are forms of discourse. Often, we make choices about what to purchase or consume based on our associations with or understanding of place: shade-grown coffee from Ethiopia, American-made cars, or sustainably sourced goods to help save the planet. Other times we might take a stand by refusing to purchase items or support companies if we do not approve of their business policies. The environmental activist group Greenpeace has called for a boycott of bluefin tuna since it is an endangered species, yet it is still served in sushi restaurants. PETA, the animal rights activist organization, has called for a ban on Air France since the airline allegedly engages in the transportation of captured wild monkeys to animal research laboratories. Practices of consumption are also evident in where we shop: Walmart or the local farmer's market? And which one of these might actually provide more support to organic farming practices? All of these choices about what to consume have real impacts on actual places in ways that we understand well and probably in ways that remain beyond the average consumer's understanding. Such practices are a form of discourse that help us to understand power relationships and competing views of the meaning of space and place.

These examples of materiality (physical, tangible things), embodiment (personal, lived experience), and practice (actions or behaviors of individuals or groups) draw from a wider field of political geography beyond environmentally focused issues to illustrate the stance of critical geopolitics. As we focus on environmental themes, however, we can take a critical geopolitics stance to examine textual narratives, materiality, embodiment, and practice in the arena of environmental issues as a way to enrich our inquiry. This effort speaks to the second observation made earlier in this chapter: humans' role or agency in environment-related situations tends to be considered selectively. In particular, dynamics of power remain invisible and uninvestigated. By looking at how geographical assumptions and understandings of particular human-environment situations are portrayed, experienced, justified, and challenged, we can look more directly at human agency and how and why certain understandings or priorities are promoted or obscured from view. Why are some places or environmental features, such as steady commodity supplies, worth protecting, and at what cost to whom? How are other place-related features, such as site-specific water shortages, portrayed as a threat and to whom? How might we understand these human-environment relationships differently by questioning how discourses about them are stabilized or challenged?

In this book, the approach of discourse analysis draws from the work of Lene Hansen (2006). I am interested in how dominant discourses on a particular topic, such as climate security or resource conflict, are stabilized. That is, how is a particular understanding or portrayal of environmental security or risk justified as a reasonable form of knowledge, and who is understood to have authority and responsibility to take action? Since this book is a project in political geography, we will focus on spatial representations, such as the origins, movement, or containment of threats, and the representation of particular places or place-related trends as valuable or threatening. The material and data sources from which these discussions draw are necessarily varied but consistently tied to the theme of dominant environmental narratives. Sources will include: mainstream news media, prominent scholarly journals, government sources, nongovernmental organizations (NGOs), environment-related corporations, and policy documents. This broad scope will allow not only a consideration of official discourse and articulations of environmental risk and security, but it will also make room for insights into how these geographical understandings are contested.

Critical Geopolitics and Environmental Issues

Noel Castree (2003a, 427) has observed, "*There is a geopolitics to how environmental problems are represented.*" At the international scale, for instance, there are two dominant discourses about global environmental politics. One, the realist or traditional approach, sees that states will adopt ideas and rules about environmental management if doing so will preserve or increase their power relative to other states. A second discourse is a liberal/pluralist approach that sees world politics not just as an arena for states as actors, but that supranational organizations (such as the UN), nonstate organizations such as major corporations and NGOs (e.g., Greenpeace and civil society in general), and the media can all influence negotiations about ideas and rules for environmental management (Castree 2003a, 432). Both of these discourses, realist and liberal/pluralist, identify which actors are seen as legitimate and which structures are deemed appropriate for addressing environmental issues. However, both are also problem-solving approaches that "accept the prevailing order" (Cox 1981, 130) and frame issues in ways that can be addressed through established, business-as-usual methods.

Quite differently, critical theory "stands apart from the prevailing order of the world and asks how that order came about" (Cox 1981, 129). Although problem-solving approaches may claim to be value-free, they take as a given the existing order with its embedded assumptions and values. The traditional geopolitical perspectives discussed earlier in this chapter are examples of the problem-solving approach. They provide a narrow selection of response options based on a particular way of viewing or framing the world. Critical approaches, however, question the very framings and embedded assumptions of dominant discourses about global environmental issues—who gets to define the problems and determine how they should be addressed? Castree (2003a, 436) emphasizes the value of critical perspectives in contributing to "a future based on *qualitatively different* geopolitical and environmental criteria." In his work on critical environment politics, Carl Death (2014, 1) sums it up as "making the familiar appear strange and bringing the unfamiliar into clearer focus are both core functions of critical scholarship." The aim of this book is to operationalize that precept in a consideration of a few key environmental issues as part of a larger effort to not only shift our thinking about these issues but also allow us to identify meaningful action and alternative ways forward. This book does not aim to provide a comprehensive analysis of

Green tea plantation. Which aspects of this landscape are environmental, and which aspects are human? Or it is possible to separate them?
Source: iStock

environmental discourses, but it will consider materiality, embodiment, and practice as well as texts as forms of discourses to look at the construction of environmental security and risk.

What Is the Environment? "Nature Does Not Exist!"

Earlier in this chapter, we saw that popular discourses about the environment rarely specify the role and meaning of the environment. What *is* the environment? Even the substitution of the word *nature* for *environment* does not provide much clarity. Geographer Erik Swyngedouw (2010b, 299–300) has put it this way:

> Nature is indeed very difficult to pin down. Is it the physical world around and inside us, like trees, rivers, mountain ranges, HIV viruses, microbes, elephants, oil, cocoa, diamonds, clouds, neutrons, the heart, shit, etc. . . . ? Does it encompass things like roses in a botanical garden, freshly-squeezed orange juice, Adventure Island in Disneyland (one of the most bio-diverse eco-topes on earth), a Richard Rogers skyscraper, sewage flows, genetically-modified tomatoes, and a hamburger? Should we expand it to include greed, avarice, compassion, hunger, death? Or should we think about it in terms of dynamics, relations and relational processes like climate change, hurricane movements, speciation and species extinction, soil erosion, water shortages, food chains, plate tectonics, nuclear energy production, black holes, supernovas, and the like?

Such ruminations challenge the notion that nature or the environment is somehow outside of or separate from us. It highlights the many ways in which our lives and our existence are wrapped up with and indistinguishable from some external landscape or stockpile of resources neatly labeled as the environment. Swyngedouw considers how words or concepts such as nature or the environment are often used to stabilize an unstable meaning. Nature is in constant flux from the bodily to the planetary scale, and it weaves in and out of our physical being. To distinguish ourselves from nature or from the environment is to draw an artificial binary that allows us to simplify, compartmentalize, and establish a stance of management or control over a fixed, external entity. Swyngedouw (2010b, 301) cites Slavoj Žižek's assertion that "Nature does not exist!" (see also Žižek 1991, 38) to counter the idea of a stable, constant, and universal backdrop to human life. Instead, there are multiple natures and "almost infinite (socio-)ecological relations through which new natures come into being" (Swyngedouw 2010b, 303). The very assumption that there exists a stable, universal nature (or environment) depoliticizes these concepts and situates "nature outside the political, that is, outside the field of public dispute, contestation, and disagreement" (301). At the heart of this book is an interest in challenging such depoliticization by examining ways in which the role and meaning of the environment in dominant discourses are shaped to serve particular interests in different contexts. An example will help to illustrate this point. The image of Earth is everywhere—advertisements, logos, T-shirts, news programs, and more. Yet when the first photographic images of Earth were sent back from US space missions between 1966 and 1972, it was a new phenomenon to see images of the globe suspended in space. The *Apollo 17* image of the planet, with continents and oceans colorful and clearly visible, is well-known. It has been speculated that seeing this image of our planet motivated a shared sense of the planet's fragility and that this common response to images of planet Earth ignited the environmental movement and the first Earth Day in the United States (Poole 2008). From that understanding, the image of Earth from space has been linked unproblematically to a singular and widely held popular interpretation and political response: everyone saw the same thing in the image of Earth in space. This idea runs parallel to the notion of a universal nature or environment that Swyngedouw has critiqued.

Apollo 17 *image of earth from space, December 1972.*
Source: NASA

Sheila Jasanoff (2012, 78–102), a scholar of science and technology studies, points out that images of Earth from space actually evoked multiple interpretations. Yes, Earth did appear isolated, vulnerable, and in need of careful stewardship by its human inhabitants. This view of Earth as a shared, closed system did support an environmental movement in parts of the world that sought policies to limit harm to planetary systems. No longer an open frontier for speculative exploitation, this interpretation of the planet weighed in favor of economic restraint. However, the closed and limited characteristics of planetary systems also gave rise to concerns about an increasing human population and its growing demands for all kinds of resources and fears of sudden, systemic collapse. Other interpretations focused on the lack of visual evidence of state boundaries in the images of Earth from space. From this perspective, it became doubly important to emphasize state sovereignty by staking claims on limited resources rather than working toward collaborative agreements to share resources. Jasanoff (2012, 85) discusses how

> many of the themes invoked in connection with the Apollo image predated the photographs that gave them unforgettable embodiment. In particular, reflections on the earth's finiteness, its fragility, its limited resources, the interconnectedness of its physical and biological systems, and the flimsiness of its geopolitical boundaries were all current in Western thought and writing well before the astronauts of Apollo 17 brought back the most famous icon of the floating planet.

Even an image as provocative as the early photographs of Earth from space bear no meaning in and of themselves and no single meaning in particular. This observation raises two points for this introductory chapter. First, the multiplicity of responses to the images of Earth from space reminds us that there is no universal nature or environment that may be held as a constant backdrop to human activity; there are many natures and many environments. This brings us to the second point: geopolitical discourses are constructed. As Jasanoff (2012, 85) also argues:

> Whether in the history of science or in the history of art, it seems that images become persuasive only when ways of looking at them have been carefully prepared in advance, through the creation of a stylized visual idiom or an interpretive tradition that knows how to respond to particular types of images . . . The meaning of pictures is inseparable from the context that supplies the idioms of interpretation.

Here again, we can study the discourse by examining the interpretation, promotion, or explanation of an image. This point also holds for examining how discourses are embodied, practiced, or evident in the material world. How do those different interpretations of images of Earth from space—a shared sense of human responsibility versus risks of too many people and limited resource supply versus threatened national sovereignty and the need to assert control over resources—become evident? Embodiment of those discourses could be evident in the formation of questions about which people are the "too many" and *who* is at risk if national sovereignty is threatened. Looking at practices emerging from these discourses, we might see as an example President Reagan's refusal to sign the UN Convention on the Law of the Sea so as not to surrender US access to seabed mining. Material expressions of these discourses could be seen in the measurable changes in air and water quality since the introduction of the Clean Air Act and Clean Water Act that were mandated in that time period. This nuanced approach to environmental themes throughout this book, with particular attention to ways in which risk and security are spatialized, demonstrates an environmental geopolitics approach.

Enter the Anthropocene

Humans are not distinct from the environment, and our fates are, in fact, intertwined. It has been suggested (Crutzen and Stoermer 2000; Steffen, Crutzen, and McNeill 2007) that we have entered a new geologic era, the Anthropocene, brought about by human activity that has altered the planet's systems. Although a specific starting point for the Anthropocene is still debated, social scientists frequently point to the Industrial Revolution. With the expansion of a global, capitalist economy powered by fossil fuels, human activity has changed the atmosphere (air content and circulation), hydrosphere (water systems), lithosphere (rock, soil, and topography), biosphere (living matter), and even the cryosphere (ice) through the rate and reach of resource extraction, consumption, and waste generation.

The idea of the Anthropocene has garnered attention in mainstream media, but physical scientists debate the precise indicators of having made a transition beyond the Holocene (Castree 2014a). The Anthropocene has also piqued the interest of social scientists and scholars in the humanities who are concerned less about precise indicators and more about implications for society and directions for useful research (Castree 2014b). The Anthropocene is not a "'problem' of analysis and policy action waiting to be solved," but instead provides incentive to explore new perspectives on possible responses to how we live (Castree 2014c). A recent discussion among geographers (Johnson and Morehouse 2014) suggests productive ways of thinking about the Anthropocene. Rather than framing the Anthropocene as inciting a need to respond to danger, Simon Dalby (2014) suggests focusing on intentionally making the future by asking what kind of future is desirable and possible (6). Jessi Lehman and Sara Nelson (2014) encourage an "experimental orientation" to the Anthropocene "without falling into oppressive or narrowly technocratic responses" (447). Similarly, rather than assume that more technology or more of the same management approaches will fix the Anthropocene, Stephanie Wakefield (2014) argues that it is important to ask how will we move forward through "the constitution of worlds in common" (452) that take a different perspective than what has been the norm. These views all point to the value of taking a critical stance in looking at environmental themes and how they are drawn into geopolitics and discourses about power and space, security and risk. The aim is, in Castree's (2014c, 464) words, "to 're-graph the geo' imaginatively and practically."

Ahead: Environmental Geopolitics

This book demonstrates environmental geopolitics analysis as a critical approach to understanding how human-environment relationships are portrayed in mainstream, Western understanding. Specifically, this book examines how themes of security and risk are constructed within discourses on four topics: (1) human population and the environment; (2) resource conflict and slow violence; (3) climate change and security; and (4) science and imagery as ways of understanding and responding to environmental issues. Analysis of these dominant discourses will highlight ways in which the environment is often not specified or is oversimplified to develop certain notions of security or risk. We will also consider ways in which human agency is obscured as a way to underplay political motives and to assign agency to nature or otherwise blame natural processes for threatening human wellbeing. Additionally, I ask: How does the portrayal of environment-related security and risk rely on constructions of certain kinds of places, place-based trends, or groups? How are environmental themes represented as fixed or as flows of material objects and phenomena (e.g., people, consumption trends, weather cycles), or as calculations of volume and space? The method of this project is to examine dominant discourses of the four selected topics as they are evident in mainstream discussions, official statements, and popular media, as well as examples of how these discourses are embodied and how they are evident in texts, practices, and materiality. What is the point of this effort? Ultimately, this book is a project in political geography. To be political "would be to interrupt discourse, to challenge what have, through discursive practices, been constituted as normal, natural and accepted ways of carrying on" (Edkins 1999, 12). All of that, from a geographic perspective, necessitates an appreciation that discourses about human-environment relationships are not abstract ideas but are intertwined with tangible realities in particular places.

CHAPTER TWO

Population and Environment

Environmental geopolitics is a way to examine explanations about how the environment is associated with risk or security and how these views are stabilized through discourse. Discourse may take the form of textual or visual narrative, materiality, practice, embodiment, or some combination of these forms as explained in the introductory chapter. What we find is that discourses about human-environment relationships are often simplified to focus our attention on certain issues or processes. The stabilization of such a focus often serves particular interests over others; this is how power is reflected in discourse. Who benefits from a particular view of the environment or a focus on certain features or processes? What important issues are left out of such a focus? How is risk or security linked to environmental features or processes? We can learn a great deal about environmental risk or security by looking at exactly who, or what, is being secured or threatened, and what kind of response or actions are justified.

This chapter considers the theme of human population and environmental issues. We have been told for years that the human population is growing beyond Earth's ability to provide enough food for everyone. Even if we can increase food production with high-tech agriculture, there may still be parts of the world where people cannot grow or afford enough food. These conditions may lead to social unrest or even political instability—so the narratives go. Another common example in which a growing human population is linked to resource scarcity is fresh water; more people and the increased demand for domestic and agricultural water are thought to be leading us to a global crisis in freshwater supply. We hear the same arguments about fossil fuels. More people on the planet are driving cars, heating their homes with natural gas, and using any number of petroleum-based products. We are not even sure how much oil is left in the ground, so how much longer will it be possible to meet the growing demand? We hear these kinds of stories in the news about too many people or too few resources, and we can point to cases where the stories seem to be true.

The following section of this chapter examines the well-known $I = PAT$ formula, which is a shorthand statement referring to human impact on the environment as a factor of population size, wealth, and technology. This formula remains in use to explain human-environment relationships, but it is misleading. It was developed to highlight a need to control human population. Placing an emphasis on human population growth shifts attention to how to control it; the human population itself becomes a threat to a stable environment. This chapter, then, considers the roots of this persistent focus on uncontrolled population as a threat, the roots of which may be found a few hundred years ago in the work of Thomas Robert Malthus.

As we will see, Malthusian ways of thinking persist in promoting technological solutions and resource management practices that widen the gap between the "haves" of the world and the "have nots." The chapter continues the critique of Malthusian thinking by raising questions about how we measure poverty, how we define a population, and unpacking the complexity of the food supply. We will look at examples of deterministic arguments by scholars and in the news media to see how these discourses are stabilized and why they are worth dismantling. We will also look at mainstream notions about water and oil scarcity and global population trends to demonstrate the need for new ways of thinking that break out of Malthusian assumptions.

As we consider these different aspects of Malthusian arguments that persist today, we will see how the role and meaning of the environment are rarely specified, or specified in a partial way, and how that vagueness can be helpful for some groups of people or interests. We will also see how Malthusian arguments are often portrayed as an objective "view from nowhere," as if there is no human agency or intention involved. The views are presented as being natural or obvious, particularly if they are framed in scientific or mathematical terms. Finally, we will also look at the ways in which Malthusian arguments perpetuate uneven geographies in which some places (and groups of people associated with those places) are safe or responsible while people in other places are unsafe and/or contributing to the problem. We will also see how Malthusian arguments or discourses can take the form of textual narratives, practices, embodiment, and materiality. Through critical assessment of

Cemetery in Dargavs, North Ossetia. Legends of these ancient stone crypts in the village of Dargavs, located in the Russian republic of North Ossetia, tell of an eighteenth-century plague that wrought havoc on the local population. People built small houses where family members were quarantined until they died.
Source: Ahsartag/*Atlas Obscura* (public domain)

these discourses, we can begin to imagine other ways of understanding and ordering the world. It is helpful and important to identify and examine these different dimensions of Malthusian arguments because they are pervasive, persuasive, and often tied to notions of risk and security.

Roots and Limitations of $I = PAT$

We have been trained to think about growing human population as a threat to a supposedly stable environment through our exposure to discourses about human-environment relationships that we may not even recognize as such. News coverage, popular media, and introductory textbooks dealing with human geography, globalization, and demographic trends tend to offer a few familiar ways to think about human population and the environment. A well-known starting point is the work of Reverend Robert Thomas Malthus (1766–1834), who argued that human population could grow more quickly than the food supply. The point at which human population surpassed the capacity to supply food was the point of crisis that Malthus warned us all to avoid. Malthus was writing about his local context in the late 1700s. Nevertheless, his narrative persists today as a universal way to think about human population growth versus food, oil, or freshwater supply, or nearly any other environmental feature or commodity around the world. We will return to Malthusian arguments in the next section of this chapter.

This Malthusian view, linking a growing human population to resource scarcity, was reinvigorated in the 1960s in the work of biologist Paul Ehrlich. His bestselling book, *The Population Bomb* (1968), warned that the human population was growing so rapidly that it threatened to launch widespread starvation and death in the face of a lack of food to feed so many people. When that book appeared in 1968, the human population had reached 3.5 billion. An altogether different way to think about human population and the environment was forwarded by a contemporary of Ehrlich: Ester Boserup. She, followed by Julian Simon a few decades later, argued that human ingenuity would provide solutions needed to address the growing population and its demands on environmental resources. From this perspective, the problem was not having too many people; in fact, more people meant more solutions.

At about the same time, Norman Borlaug developed a disease-resistant, high-yielding strain of wheat and contributed to what became known as the Green Revolution. The Green Revolution promoted the cultivation of specially bred crops, particularly in parts of the world where rapid population growth was putting pressure on food supply. The resulting higher production levels of food crops arguably helped to stave off the humanitarian disaster predicted by Ehrlich. In his Nobel Prize acceptance speech in 1970, however, Borlaug emphasized that biotechnological advances in food production could only delay the inevitable need for humans to control their population growth (quoted in Weisman 2013, 57–58). Although *The Population Bomb* had sold millions of copies and stoked public fear about humans outstripping their food supply, the Green Revolution seemed to disprove these renewed Malthusian fears by demonstrating that food supply was a problem that could be conquered by technology. This way of thinking continues today, as we will see later in this chapter.

However, there were other concerns about the negative effects of technological advancement. Rachel Carson's book *Silent Spring*, first published in 1962, focused on the adverse effects of pesticides. Her work drew attention to the inherent risk to humans and to environmental features of chemicals such as DDT that were widely used in industrial-scale agriculture at the time. Building on these concerns, in his book *The Closing Circle: Nature, Man and Technology*, Barry Commoner (1971, 294–95) wrote about the dangers of increased pollution that had accompanied economic development: "We are in an environmental crisis because the means by which we use the ecosphere to produce wealth are destructive of the ecosphere itself." Ehrlich and his coauthor, John Holdren, took issue with Commoner's focus on faulty technology and argued that any impact humans have on the environment is determined by the size of the population. They argued that attention should be focused on per capita consumption and environmental impact. They noted that improvements made through advanced technology would likely be limited; therefore, it was particularly important to control population growth (Ehrlich and Holdren 1971). They generated a formula, $I = PAT$, to represent not only the size of human population (P) but also measures of wealth or affluence (A) and technology (T) (Ehrlich and Holdren 1972). All of these variables, they argued, work together either to increase or decrease humans' impact on the environment (I), but controlling population growth was highlighted as the most important factor. Ehrlich appeared on *The Tonight Show Starring Johnny Carson* in 1970 to talk about the formula and to promote this idea to a wider public audience.

The $I = PAT$ formula is still in circulation today as a way to think about the impact of population on the environment, and it is commonly found in introductory textbooks dealing with human-environment interactions. The relationships reflected in this equation seem clear enough, and presenting them as a mathematical formula lends a degree of legitimacy to this idea. Yet the $I = PAT$ formula has been critiqued in a number of ways. First, it is not clear how the I, impact on environment, is being measured (air quality? healthy forests? amount of plastic floating in the world's oceans?) or the geographic scale of concern (the globe? this continent? your neighborhood?). Similarly, what is meant by affluence is unclear—a topic discussed further below. Even T, technology, is barely a placeholder to represent any number of meanings. A critique of the $I = PAT$ model from 1981 observed, more broadly, that

> invoking an equation or statistic can be even more persuasive than citing a well-known authority. An argument which would be quickly disputed if stated in plain English will often acquire some momentum if accompanied by numbers and formulas, regardless of whether or not they are relevant or accurate. The threshold of expertise and self-confidence needed to challenge an argument becomes much higher if it is enshrouded in science. (Koblitz 1981, 115)

In addition to being questioned as an actual scientific measurement, the $I = PAT$ formula has also been challenged for assuming a direct relationship across all variables. If population increases by a factor of three, do the impacts of affluence and technology also increase by a factor of three? The formula offers no way of disaggregating these contributing factors to environmental impact (Chertow 2001). The underlying message of $I = PAT$ is the importance of controlling human population growth. Focusing on human population—as opposed to consumption levels—raises certain questions and concerns, but it leaves other questions unasked.

One of the reasons why the $I = PAT$ formula, or even just this way of thinking, has such staying power in our society is due to the persistence of Malthusian thinking. People may not refer to it as such, but Malthusian thinking sets population growth against food supply, or any potentially limited resource, to make one of two arguments. One is about the risk of running out of a scarce resource and implications for conflict. Another argument is about security and the necessary steps to prevent conflict. Sometimes, both arguments are made at the same time. Often these arguments are established as obvious fact—about human nature, about resources, or about inevitable relationships between the two—yet we rarely consider the assumptions underlying these arguments. Below, we look at Malthus's original writing and ideas to understand the context in which he was writing, the assumptions he made, and how his work has been misinterpreted as well as used to legitimize contemporary agendas.

Malthus and the Risk of Population Growth beyond Natural Limits

Thomas Robert Malthus was born in England in 1766, ten years before the American Revolution, but his work continues to have an impact on our thinking today. He took an honors degree in mathematics, became a parson, and taught political economy at East India College. Utopian theorists at the time viewed a robust population as a good thing. From the utopian perspective, a larger population meant more demographic strength for a state. A larger population meant greater potential for economic productivity and innovation that would allow "man" to continually improve and overcome limits imposed by nature. In contrast to his contemporaries, Malthus promoted an opposing view that a rapidly growing population was the cause of society's problems (Gallagher 1986). In his view, humans could not help but reproduce, and unchecked population growth would inevitably outstrip the food supply and likely lead to a devastating crash in human population. Malthus was not the first person to make this kind of argument. There had already been a long line of philosophers and theorists, such as Plato and Confucius, who recognized a relationship between human population growth and its environmental support system. These views observed that, in the animal world, species are able to increase their population only so far as their environment allows it. Philosophers applied these observations of the animal world to humans (Appleman 1976). Like others before him, Malthus pointed to basic postulates that humans need food and that sexual passion is a constant of human existence. He argued that population growth will likely increase more quickly than food supply and push against natural limits of the environment. The result will be famine, disease, poverty, and suffering. That is, the environment would check human population growth beyond certain limits, just as animal species are bound by an ecosystem's carrying capacity. Malthus's unique twist on this familiar idea was to use a quasi-scientific approach. He argued that food supply can only increase as more agricultural land is brought into production. The rate of change for food production, he argued, reflects a constant rate of change and can only increase arithmetically: 1, 2, 3, 4, 5, 6, and so on. On the other hand, the human population is able to increase exponentially: 1, 2, 4, 8, 16, 32, and so on. The rate of change itself, in this case, increases. Although the steam engine had been invented twenty-two years before he wrote his initial essay, the mechanical revolution in agriculture had not yet happened. The chemical and biological revolutions in agriculture that saw the large-scale adoption of pesticides, fertilizers, and genetically modified organism crops were inconceivable (Appleman 1976). His mathematical logic seemed irrefutable (figure 2.1).

Malthus was writing not about humanity as a whole or about environmental features in general, but about the situation of his own local parish

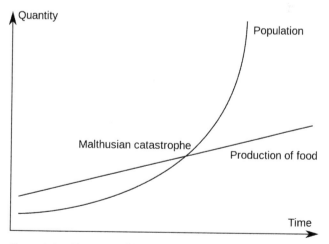

Figure 2.1. Thomas Malthus's famous projection. Malthus's misleading "science" makes for a dramatic graphic.
Source: AP Images

or county. In England at the time that Malthus was writing, there was an established welfare system administered by local parish or district authorities. Laborers who were paid under a subsistence rate could seek financial support from the district in which they lived and thereby feed their families. This support was provided by the Poor Laws that had originated in the sixteenth century (Ross 1998, 2000). To some degree, this practice reflected public support of subsistence rights: the idea that everyone has a right to basic means of subsistence. However, the Poor Laws were not charity. They were a way of dealing with people who had been uprooted and displaced when their agricultural land was privatized or enclosed (Ross 1998, 2000). These laws kept impoverished people tied to a particular parish or district in order to receive financial support. However, business entrepreneurs, with an eye on emerging industrial development in England, wanted a mobile workforce to supply labor where it was needed. They were in favor of getting rid of the Poor Laws so that people would have incentive to move to wherever labor was in demand.

Malthus argued that welfare, in the form of financial support to laborers, only delayed the inevitable. Distributing such handouts or allowing artificially low food prices would only give a false sense of well-being to families who could not otherwise support more children. He argued that with this system in place, more people would be surviving on less food, leading to a weaker and less productive population (Malthus [1798] 1993a). Malthus came to be most criticized for his views that providing welfare support for people who were struggling financially should be significantly decreased or, preferably, removed altogether. He regretted the suffering and misery that withdrawing this support would cause to the poorest people, but he argued that doing so would lead to greater human well-being in the long run. Malthus favored policies to increase food supply, such as shifting labor away from luxury goods and foreign trade toward the expansion of farmland to increase domestic food supplies. Yet a key concern underlying his writing was enabling land enclosure by wealthier people and creating a mobile labor force for growing industry (Ross 2000).

Malthus's argument relies on the assumption of two preexisting classes in society: proprietors and laborers. If the wealthy members of society, the proprietors, simply give laborers the means of survival (food or money to buy food) without requiring from them the labor to produce basic goods, society as a whole loses out on food or other items that could have been produced. This practice of handouts with no expectation of labor, he argued, gave laborers a false sense of well-being. A better way to organize society, according to Malthus, was to abolish the welfare system and allow laborers to move to wherever they could get paid the most for their labor. This is an important but often overlooked spatial aspect of Malthus's argument. He was not writing about *the* human population outstripping *the* food supply everywhere; he was writing about only one, localized place. In his mind, if people were not tied to a place to receive welfare benefits, they could be free to move to other locations and thus ease the burden of welfare payments in the place they had vacated. Adopting an idea from Adam Smith, whose work on the invisible hand of trade was popular at the time, Malthus thought it better for laborers to be able to relocate to where their labor was needed instead of being tied by subsidies to a particular place.

Proprietors, on the other hand, enjoyed excess wealth because they were concerned about maintaining their status. Therefore, according to Malthus, these wealthier people restrained themselves from having more children than they could support. Rather than spending their excess wealth raising large families, proprietors served society by bringing more land into production and investing in manufacturing. Private property rights were key. England had been in a long process of enclosing common pastures and other land with the argument that "improving" the use of these lands through private ownership would increase their efficiency and production. Such enclosure worked against the rural poor whose survival depended on these lands. A not-so-subtle argument supporting the enclosures was that land that had been held in common was always at the risk of misuse in the hands of people who could not even control their own reproduction, so it was better to put these lands under the control of the elite who were better equipped to manage it productively (Lohmann 2005). Subsistence rights, by Malthus's account, harmed the fabric of society, whereas private property rights enriched and strengthened it.

The overarching threat identified by Malthus is scarcity caused by too many people demanding too much from the environment; in this case, the environment is food supply. Notice how the focus is on the growing human population and its demands, but not on the demands themselves. Malthusian arguments do not focus on consumption or on how we might consume less or differently. It is assumed that people's demands are somehow natural, basic, and unchangeable. We do not investigate what the demands are or if there are different kinds or impacts of demands (e.g., what about the demands of the wealthier proprietors?). Our attention is guided back to population with the particular focus on how population growth is a threat. As we will see in the following critique of Malthusian arguments, the human population becomes unquestioningly divided into the part of the population that is the threat (*Them*) and the part of the population whose well-being and security is at risk from *Their* demands (*Us*).

> Ideas about environment, population, and resources are not neutral. They are political in origin and have political effects. Once, for example, connotations of absolute limits come to surround the concepts of resource, scarcity, and subsistence, then an absolute limit is set on population. And the political implications of a term like overpopulation can be devastating. Somebody, somewhere, is redundant and there is not enough to go round. Am *I* redundant? Of course not. Are *you* redundant? Of course not. So who is redundant? Of course! It must be *them*. (Harvey 1996, 148)

In the following discussion, pay attention to the ways in which the use of simple binaries, such as laborers and proprietors, reflect an uneven distribution of power and how population trends are associated with notions of security and risk.

Critiquing Malthusian Assumptions

We can critique Malthus's argument from a few directions. Questioning his assumptions helps us to see flaws in current ways of thinking about humans and the environment that draw, often implicitly, from Malthusian thinking. His starting assumption of society as a binary (proprietors and laborers) does nothing to explain how there came to be those two classes of people, and it glosses over other possible identities that people may have. Along these class lines, we see another binary in how Malthus views the distribution of benefits. He makes the case that land held in common and public welfare are forms of irresponsible freeloading. In contrast, private property regimes that benefit the already wealthy are not seen as a form of welfare that further skews the distribution of wealth (Lohmann 2005, 90).

Another binary evident in Malthus's arguments is male and female. Malthus, living before the age of the DNA or paternity test, was troubled that a man cannot actually know if a child is his but a woman most certainly knows if a child is hers. Utopian thinkers of Malthus's time were not bothered by this point because they viewed a community as raising children together regardless of a child's biological parents. Malthus was concerned that such an attitude would encourage people to have more children since the parents would not be held directly responsible for raising their own offspring. He argued that monogamous, heterosexual marriage allows men to know who their children are while keeping women from having children by other men.

In short, on a personal, embodied level, Malthus was also arguing in favor of control of women's bodies by men since, without such control, population growth would surely increase. Somehow, though, Malthus viewed wealthier people as being able to control their passions and therefore the number of children they have. As David Harvey (1996, 144) has noted about Malthus's view of population growth, "The law of population is in effect disaggregated into one law for the poor and another law for the rich." Over the years, Malthus revised his essay several times. His basic position of removing support for the poor remained the same, but he later acknowledged a role for human intervention in the form of delayed marriage. By marrying later in life and assuming no sexual activity prior to or outside of marriage, people would have fewer children and slow the rate of human population growth (Malthus [1803] 1993b).

These binaries in Malthus's arguments—wealthier, responsible people versus poor and irresponsible people, and men versus women—hide important complexities. Beyond these binaries, we can also see how a Malthusian narrative can oversimplify other things as well. First, Malthus portrayed population dynamics—at least for poorer people—as straightforward and directly determined by inputs of food. Population dynamics are more complex than that! Additionally, it is important to ask how a population is even being defined. If we are referring to the population of a particular country or other clearly bounded political territory (district or county), then identifying the population living there is a straightforward exercise. Grouping people into a territorial population tends to homogenize everyone, which is the work of discourse as embodiment. How are people being labeled, and who is doing the labeling? What effect does the label or grouping have? Grouping together everyone who lives on the same island, for instance, would make sense if we are talking about all residents of the island. However, people living on an island or within the same political boundary do not necessarily share the same political rights or identities, nor is everyone in that place having the same experience.

Similarly, how do we define poor people? Financial indicators of poverty (e.g., living on less than a dollar per day) could be used to define a population quantitatively. Such quantitative indicators of poverty might be relatively easy to measure or estimate, but there are other ways of understanding poverty that are more meaningful. For instance, Gray and Moseley (2005) have looked at how rural wealth and poverty are not always, or even best, reflected in the amount of monetary savings a person holds. Wealth, in some rural communities, may be more appropriately "reflected in cattle holdings, the quality of agricultural implements, housing materials, labour resources, access to land, and the ability of the household to produce food" (11). In other words, poverty or wealth may be more usefully thought of in terms of assets rather than in monetary terms. Poverty and wealth also have temporal dimensions. A person's access to resources may change with the seasons, as they age, or by some other measure of time.

Gray and Moseley go on to consider the importance of entitlement as discussed by Amartya Sen (1981). Entitlement has to do with a person's ability to access resources based largely on social networks and position. Different people within the same population or community group may have very different entitlements. This point highlights a problem in assuming that everyone in the same place, or in what may seem to be a homogenous group of people, has the same access to resources. Women and children, for instance, may have different entitlements than do men, or individuals with particular skills or knowledge may have different entitlements than their neighbors. Gray and Moseley conclude that poverty is most usefully understood as an inability to meet one's needs over time. To understand poverty within a particular context, then, we would need to know more than just the level of monetary holdings and understand more closely the social, cultural, economic, and political situation of the various people under consideration. Without that understanding of context, it is difficult to assess what poverty means in a particular setting and how it is perpetuated. Therefore, referring to "poor people" may actually hide more than it tells us about the actual people in question.

Even if we can identify and define a group of people as a "population," it is also important to understand dynamics of population growth and decline. Although Malthus was concerned about a particular population (poorer laborers) growing through unchecked fertility rates, populations can grow, or decline, for several reasons. Having children is certainly one way to increase a population, but declining death rates keep people around longer and can stabilize the size of a population. Death rates may decline, for instance, when older people live longer or when fewer people are dying from violence or disease. Migration of people, either incoming or outgoing, is another factor of population dynamics, which is in itself complex. People may migrate within or across political or territorial borders, and they may migrate permanently or temporarily for economic, political, or other reasons. Additionally, national governments may encourage or discourage population growth through economic incentives (materiality) or ideological discourses.

A few examples of state-level demographic policy, one antinatalist to curb population growth and another pronatalist to encourage population growth, help to illustrate the point that population dynamics are complex and reflect place-specific political, economic, and social contexts. State-level discourse about population dynamics can take multiple forms, as we see in the examples of China and Russia. China's one-child policy is a well-known example of an antinatalist policy to control that country's population growth. The policy was introduced in 1978 as a way to slow China's growth and generated much controversy through the forcible destruction of extra pregnancies and infants, particularly females. Couples registering more than one child incurred a hefty fine; therefore, many second children were never legally recognized. The one-child policy was successful in slowing growth, but China's population became elder-heavy, short on labor, and heavily skewed in favor of males. Given these population problems, a new policy, introduced on January 1, 2016, encourages Chinese families to have two children.

Russia had the opposite problem. The 1991 collapse of the Soviet Union contributed to emigration, decreased life expectancy, and led to declining birthrates. By 2006, the population of Russia was decreasing by about seven hundred thousand people per year (Charlton 2013). That year, President Vladimir Putin used his televised State of the Nation address to emphasize the demographic crisis. He called for efforts to increase the birthrate and encouraged cash subsidies for couples having more than one child. Some cities, such as Ulyanovsk in the Volga River region east of Moscow, created a Day of Conception. The holiday is in September, carefully timed to be nine months prior to a Russian national holiday in June. Couples whose child is born on Russia's national day on June 12 are eligible to win prizes such as cars and major appliances.

In both the Chinese and Russian examples, we can see how national discourse on population takes multiple forms: narrative form in terms of official statements and policy, material form in financial penalties and rewards, and ultimately in the form of practice in terms of whether or not, or when, couples have children. These two examples reflect cases of state-level discourse on population growth; however, discourse about population growth, decline, and change in terms of cultural composition may happen at other spatial scales (e.g., neighborhoods or cities) and in reference to a variety of processes related to demographics, including fertility rates and immigration. The point here is that, just as poverty is complex, population dynamics are also complex. Population cannot be understood only in relation to food supply. Although that point seems obvious, Malthusian generalizations persist in making determinist statements about direct relationships between resource conditions and population growth. These examples of how poverty is defined and different approaches to encourage or discourage population growth underscore the importance of examining relationships that are portrayed as being simple, direct, and deterministic in which one variable (availability of food) always determines the outcome of another (population growth).

Another point that Malthus oversimplified, or perhaps mispredicted (Smaje 2013), is that food supply can only grow arithmetically. When he was writing, the only way to produce more food was to bring more land into agricultural production and utilize more human and animal labor. As mentioned, although the steam engine was coming into use at the time that Malthus wrote, the advances in agricultural productivity brought about through the large-scale use of pesticides, fertilizers, and genetically modified crops could not have been foreseen. We now know that it is possible to grow more food on less land through the use of these technological advances. We also know that there are negative environmental impacts from the use of fossil fuel–based equipment and chemicals in agricultural production. More than that, crop production is incredibly complex and goes well beyond food supply issues. Technological advances and government subsidies have contributed to a situation of overproduction of food crops in some instances. Now, land is also being used to grow fuel crops in the form of corn-based ethanol and jatropha-based diesel fuel, to name a few examples. Contemporary agriculture reflects a legacy of European colonization in patterns of land use and uneven distribution of economic benefits and environmental costs. Globalized supply chains of mass-produced commodities also shape current agricultural practices and consumption patterns, and both are tied to the altering or even destruction of human and environmental systems. Beyond the production of crops, food supply also raises questions about access and quality of food. Famines have occurred in places where the food supply was ample but poorly distributed. For these reasons, there has been increasing attention to issues of food justice and food sovereignty that emphasize the importance of food access and affordability and the degree to which people are able to make decisions about their own food supply. In short, food production cannot be neatly captured in an arithmetically increasing line on a graph.

The Danger of Determinist Arguments

Just as Malthusian arguments about growing populations overwhelming the food supply are oversimplified and deterministic, more recent uses of Malthusian arguments can also offer a limited understanding of the resource in question. They obscure from view dynamics of power and spatial elements of the very processes they address. We can find examples where deterministic explanations do seem to work, but that does not mean they work in every instance. Deterministic explanations persist, in part, because they can be persuasive and provide a simple explanation. One of the best examples of a determinist argument is Garrett Hardin's classic paper, "The Tragedy of the Commons" (1968). The message that most people remember from this often-cited paper is that if every person sharing a common resource overuses it bit by bit, the whole commons will become degraded. What many people miss in Hardin's work is his message to promote private control of property and to limit population growth—classic Malthus!

Another example of dangerous, deterministic thinking is the bestselling book *Collapse: How Societies Choose to Fail or Succeed* by Jared Diamond (2005). Even though this book is somewhat dated, it reflects a well-known academic stance on these issues. In this book, Diamond writes about a number of past societies that seem to have caused their own demise by overusing their resource base. One example is the population of Easter Island. Diamond describes how this society is thought to have overused the timber supply of the island, thus depleting their fuel supply and leading to collapse. Tim Forsyth (2008, 29) has critiqued Diamond's analysis:

> According to evidence from travellers' [sic] records, and historical ecological pollen counts, Easter Island lost all trees above the height of 10 feet, and 90 per cent of its human population between the years 900 and 1722. . . . Diamond argues that these changes are the result of foolish rates of deforestation on a site that was susceptible to erosion.

Forsyth makes the case that Diamond exhibits Malthusian thinking in his focus on seemingly natural environmental limits rather than on social or economic factors that may have contributed to declines in past and current societies. The fragility of environmental systems is discussed by Diamond as justification for controlling them. Forsyth also discusses how Diamond is selective in his historical cases to support his conclusions, and he does not consider different perspectives on population issues or complexities of population dynamics. Throughout the cases in his book, Diamond draws a line to connect the overstepping of some natural limit to the demise of whole societies, and he extends that line to our current drawdown of the global resource base. He argues that we, too, seem to be following the path of overusing our planetary resources and will suffer the same fate if we do not change our ways. To be fair to Diamond, his work could be interpreted as breaking away from arguments about natural limits to look at how human societies have failed to understand ecological constraints. That is, perhaps we might learn from past societies and avoid their mistakes. Whether or not we will learn these lessons will depend on the kinds of narratives we allow to guide our decision making and actions.

Diamond's work is widely read and popular in part because it provides a simple explanation supported by seemingly clear evidence from the demise of earlier societies. Yet his work has been critiqued for being overly simplistic and deterministic. Although Diamond acknowledges that several factors—political, social, economic, and environmental—may contribute to the failure of a society, he emphasizes the relationship between population growth and too much stress on the resource supply, whether that means agricultural land or forests. In effect, he is returning to a Malthusian argument that portrays *Their* growing population and overuse of resources, particularly in economically developing countries, as a threat to *Us*. He extrapolates the experience of past isolated societies to the whole globe. This problematic move of supersizing geographic scale assumes that local processes and patterns are interchangeable with global processes and patterns. Another critique considers how Diamond's narrative does not examine the significant legacy of colonization or disparities in political and economic power: "Problems of development, including poverty, disease, food shortages and conflict, are not necessarily 'natural,' technological problems or even results of a lack of economic growth, but are complex political problems about distribution, rights and access to resources" (Watson 2010, 103). Instead of exploring that complexity, Diamond's narrative in *Collapse* is popular because it offers a seemingly easy and obvious framework of understanding. That framework is compelling because it offers us straightforward and extreme options. Sweeping narratives of catastrophe and collapse, as we see in Diamond's Malthusian metanarrative, can obscure and distract us from political, economic, and social dimensions of real problems at hand. Situations in which we face either devastation or salvation often serve to shut down meaningful action or agency (Katz 1995).

Finding and Critiquing Malthusian Arguments in the News

It is important to be able to identify Malthusian discourses when we see them. This section demonstrates how we can identify and critique Malthusian arguments in mainstream news media. Here, we consider how it is possible to discern textual or visual narratives and practices, for example, which serve to stabilize the idea that human population growth is a threat to a stable environment. It is important to ask questions such as: How does our attention become focused on certain environmental features? How is the role of humans portrayed, and what kinds of actions are justified? How are particular notions of security emphasized while other concerns about equity or processes of decision making are left out? Which spatial dimensions are emphasized or neglected in mainstream discourses about human population?

To examine the familiar Malthusian discourse that ties human population to environmental scarcity and risk, we can look at a recent article in the *Washington Post*, titled "World Bank: The Way Climate Change Is Really Going to Hurt Us Is through Water" (Mooney 2016). It is worthwhile examining this article because it displays precisely the kinds of assumptions and generalizations of interest in this chapter. This news story illustrates several problematic trends in how environmental issues are linked to risk and security. The article begins with a photograph of a long highway bridge covering an expanse, not of water, but of land, with a caption that reads: "The dried-up riverbank of the Ganges is seen from a bridge in Allahabad, India, on May 3. Much of India is reeling from a heat wave and severe drought conditions that have decimated crops, killed livestock and left at least 330 million Indians without enough water for their daily needs." The article highlights a recent report about the World Bank's concern that climate change will exacerbate water shortages around the world that will then slow economic growth and send entire regions—"much of Africa," India, China, and the Middle East are mentioned—into conditions of economic decline. Climate change in the form of warm temperatures, heightened droughts in some places and flooding in others, and imminent sea level rise pushing salt water into freshwater aquifers are all mentioned to support the argument that "climate change is really in fact about hydrological change." The report observes that billions of people already live in places where water scarcity is a threat. As population grows, so will demand for water, particularly in terms of electricity generation and agriculture. North America and Europe, however, are notably safe from the economic harm that is likely to result from these conditions.

The text of the article continues with a quote from the World Bank report: "Growing populations, rising incomes, and expanding cities will converge upon a world where the demand for water rises exponentially, while supply becomes more erratic and uncertain." The article goes on to reassure us that these dire conditions will not be uniform; some places will "be fine" but other regions will face "looming water scarcity problems" and will have to "address water waste, misallocation, and efficiency in water use." Water-related crises will likely be sudden and extreme and "will hit unstable regions the hardest." An economist at the World Bank and lead author of the report is quoted in the article as saying, "When we have poverty, when we have division, when we have polarization, you add to that a water shock, something like a drought,

Bridge spanning the Ganges riverbed in Allahabad, India.
Source: AP Images

this becomes a threat multiplier." Having heightened our sense of urgency by suggesting the threat of instability and conflict, the article then wraps up on an optimistic note explaining how resiliency in these at-risk places may be fostered through water-saving strategies, such as replacing leaking pipes in cities and arid regions, as a way to bring about greater efficiencies.

This argument is certainly compelling, but it is worth questioning some of its underlying assumptions.

We can look at this news story as a narrative form of a discourse that stabilizes the idea that the world's growing population is putting our water supply at risk. Well, not the whole population, just part of it. The article reinforces several ways of understanding environmental risk and safety that have become so familiar that we do not bother to question them. Fortunately, however, you are reading this book, and you will see how we can question these outdated and potentially dangerous understandings and why such an inquisitive stance is useful. Our focus on environmental geopolitics draws our attention to the ways in which the role and meaning of the environment are vague. How is the environment portrayed? What kinds of processes or measurements count in this discussion? Also, how is the role of humans invisible or selectively portrayed? Finally, how are spatial dimensions or relationships oversimplified, underspecified, or assumed?

Let's go back to that bridge spanning the Ganges. Remember that photographs, graphics, and other visual images are a form of narrative that may serve to support a particular discourse. Much like the image of Earth from outer space discussed in chapter 1, this image of a bridge itself carries no meaning until we bring meaning to it through an interpretation of a discourse. The news story uses this image to support the point that India is experiencing a severe and unusual drought. Why else would there be no river flowing under this huge bridge? The image date is May 3. Just a cursory Internet search confirms that from April through June, the Ganges River is fed mostly by melting snow runoff from the Himalayas. From July through September, however, it is the rainy season when heavy, monsoonal rains can cause flooding. Thus, we are looking at a picture during the low-flow season of the river. The bridge, which appears high and substantial enough to accommodate a significant flow of water from bank to bank, was most likely built in anticipation of the monsoon season. We are not looking at water scarcity; we are looking at water seasonality and reasonable infrastructure planning. Besides, the careful observer would notice that in one area under the bridge there is a plot of rows of what appear to be crops. Again, the temporality of the river's flow appears to be understood and anticipated. Drought conditions may indeed be a problem for people and livestock, but so far, we do not have enough information to know what is causing the drought or why so many people face water scarcity.

The other photo in the article is also worth noting because of its irrelevance to the storyline. There is an aerial photograph of what used to be the Aral Sea in Central Asia. The image is dramatic; it shows the previous extent of the Aral Sea, now reduced to a smattering of small lakes or ponds. The caption reads, "The Aral Sea in 2015. The body of water has shrunken in size dramatically in recent years because of water withdrawals from rivers that feed it." The placement of this image in the midst of a discussion about growing human population and its demand for water suggests that this stark image of declining water supply illustrates just what can happen when a population expands in number and its level of water demand. Although it is not even discussed in the *Washington Post* article, the Aral Sea reflects a different situation entirely. It is an extreme case in which a unique ecosystem and a thriving fishing industry were destroyed over time as rivers were diverted before they could reach the sea. The diversion of the Syr Darya and Amu Darya rivers were part of a centralized, Soviet planning effort to grow cotton in the Central Asian desert. The region is sparsely populated, so the growth of population or the expansion of cities does not explain the destruction of the Aral Sea. The development of a commodity crop in a region not at all suited to growing cotton explains why so much water was diverted to agriculture. Soviet planning had a tendency to disregard environmental systems, with some efforts even attempting to reverse the direction of flow of entire rivers for the benefits of transportation, for example. What is the meaning of including this image in this news story? Central Asia is not mentioned anywhere in the article either as a place at risk of water scarcity or as a place that will be fine. The insertion of this photo suggests that whatever is happening in the other at-risk places (parts of Africa, China, India, and the Middle East) will likely result in the same end state as the Aral Sea. Inserting this stark image without providing context or background suggests that practices leading to the Aral Sea's destruction are the same as the conditions faced in all of the other at-risk places mentioned in the article. If it can happen to the Aral Sea, it can happen anywhere! Yet the comparison is flawed; water use practices and processes vary, as do water systems themselves. These

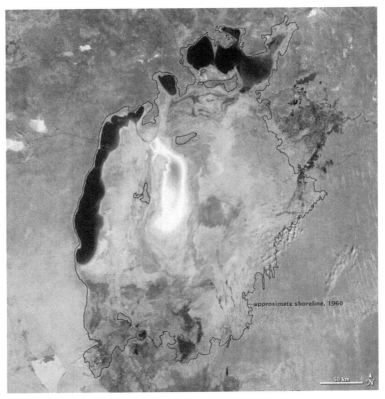

Satellite image of the remaining Aral Sea.
Source: NASA, August 2009

spatial generalizations are unhelpful if we want to understand specific causes and likelihood of water scarcity in a particular place.

The *Washington Post* article establishes a clear geography of water scarcity risk: North America and Europe will be fine, but the areas of concern include parts of Africa (none of which are specified), China, India, and the Middle East (also not clearly defined). Evidently, these places are all in the same boat at risk of water scarcity, and this grouping suggests that patterns of water use and trends in population growth are the same in all of these places. The news story mentions that demand for water will grow exponentially, and it seems that this result is due to increasing populations in these places. Or is it economic growth that is increasing the demand for water? The implication seems to be that increasing demand from a growing population is somehow bad and dangerous, but economic growth is a good reason to use more water. Later, the article adds more information about places that are at risk for water scarcity: they tend to use water inefficiently and wastefully, and there is some kind of inherent instability associated with these places. Under these conditions, the news story suggests, a flood or drought could serve as a "threat multiplier." By this point, it is not exactly clear where we are looking to see such instability, but by generalizing these at-risk places and grouping them together, the instability must somehow be *there* and certainly not *here* where the readers of this newspaper may feel at ease with their secured water supply.

There is a subtle message in the invocation of the term *threat multiplier* in this news story. Perhaps readers of the *Washington Post* are not aware of it, but this term was introduced in 2007 by the Center for Naval Analysis, recognized simply as "CNA Corporation," in a report titled, "National Security and the Threat of Climate Change" (CNA 2007). In their report, a panel of retired US military leaders makes the argument that climate change will exacerbate the likelihood of natural and humanitarian disasters in places where there is political instability and a lack of government capacity to respond. The concept of climate change as a "threat multiplier" brings urgency to the issue and renders it a security issue, a topic that will be addressed in chapter 4 of this book. It is interesting that a World Bank economist is drawing on this idea of water scarcity as a "threat multiplier" to move the topic to the level of national security and greater importance.

Remember, though, that a discourse stabilizes a particular view, and this view of water as an important security issue makes sense when we reflect on what the World Bank does. As an international financial institution, the World Bank loans money to poorer countries, mainly for infrastructure projects intended to foster economic growth. In years past, the World Bank favored large dam projects because they enabled electricity generation and the expansion of the grid for growing cities to attract foreign industry. Many countries that took out World Bank loans, particularly in the 1970s, were not able to pay back even the interest on the loans, and so they diverted funds from other sectors such as education, health, and public safety to make payments. These practices led to a downward spiral in the overall well-being of countries that became more dependent on loans. The World Bank and its large-scale infrastructure projects have long been criticized for making poorer countries more vulnerable to external economic shocks and internal instability. It is particularly interesting, then, that this World Bank economist is suggesting to the *Washington Post* readers that poorer countries face water scarcity problems that will lead to instability and conflict, but the solution offered—replacing leaking pipes and water distribution systems, likely at great expense—is precisely the kind of infrastructure project that the World Bank is renowned for encouraging. As this example demonstrates, examining a discourse can reveal much about which actors or institutions benefit from the promotion and stabilization of particular views.

Before we move on, it is also worth taking a look at the places deemed to "be fine" in the face of increasingly unstable water supplies around the world. North America and Europe appear to be unthreatened by this imminent water scarcity and risk. They are portrayed as secure both in terms of water supply and in terms of economic and political stability. However, it is important to see why not discussing these places in this article is an interesting omission. First, by not discussing patterns of water use in these places, it seems as though there are no problems of "water waste, misallocation, and efficiency in water use." Yet richer parts of the world consume water at a much greater rate per person than poorer countries. For a rough comparison, average water consumption for one person in Mali, Africa, is four cubic meters per year. In China it is thirty-two, and in India it is fifty-two. In France, average annual water consumption per person is 106 cubic meters, and in the United States it is 215 cubic meters per person (World Business Council for Sustainable Development 2009). That is, a person in the United States consumes, on average, fifty times more water per year than a person in Mali, Africa. That consumption includes not only the water that goes into the production of a diet heavy in meat, eggs, and dairy products, but it also includes water for domestic consumption such as watering a lawn and running major appliances such as dishwashers and laundry washing machines. An argument here might be that richer countries can afford to consume more water because they have more water.

A closer look at Kansas tells a different story; Kansas is at risk of running out of water not due to overpopulation and crowded cities but because of what is happening in the sparsely populated western end of the state. Two main activities have led western Kansas to be one of the most agriculturally productive districts in the United States: fattening up beef cattle in feed lots, and growing the corn to feed to these cattle (Philpott 2013). Both of these activities require a tremendous amount of water and are possible in western Kansas thanks to the underground High Plains Aquifer. The production of both corn and beef has increased significantly since 1980. The tripling of the price of corn has encouraged the expansion of farm acreage to increase the production of corn. Additionally, rather than rotating crops of corn, wheat, and sorghum, as done in the past, corn alone has become the dominant crop in the area. The fact that corn requires considerable amounts of irrigation compounds the demand on groundwater. Similarly, Food and Water Watch, a nongovernmental organization focused on government and corporate accountability in food and water issues, considers the intensity of beef production in Kansas to be extreme. More cattle means greater demand for corn. However, the groundwater is being used six times faster than the rate of recharge or replacement, and it has been estimated that 69 percent of the available water will be gone within fifty years (Philpott 2013).

The news story from the *Washington Post* suggests that the United States is not at risk of water-related problems because it is not in the category of countries or regions with political instability, poverty, and "division." It focuses our attention on other places and suggests that economic and political instability are likely results in places where people waste or misallocate water and use it inefficiently. The problem is *there*, not *here*. However, the situation in western Kansas suggests that water inefficiency may take different forms. Inefficiency is not necessarily a reflection of a lack of economic development. It can also emerge in a context of advanced technology that allows the drainage of an underground aquifer to grow a monocrop of a genetically modified organism. What parts of this practice are environmental, and what parts are human generated? The dividing line isn't absolutely clear. Human agency is evident throughout this situation. Agricultural subsidies encourage crop production and agricultural practices that are mismatched to steady water supplies, and policies favor short-term profit over long-term productivity. We can also see human agency in the demand for beef and the common practice of regular meat consumption (look for the front license plates with the simple command, "Eat Beef"). In addition to multiple levels of policies enabling this situation, it is also important to recognize how transportation, processing, and marketing logistics in and well beyond western Kansas make concentrated animal feedlot operations in this area (and elsewhere in the United States) viable.

The example of declining water supplies in western Kansas provides a helpful counterpoint to the discourse that a growing human population threatens the stability of water supplies. It is not just—or only—that there are too many people increasing the demand on a particular resource. It is usually more complicated than that. However, as a society, we seem to be drawn to focusing on human population growth as a major factor in environmental problems. We know that the human population is larger now than it has ever been. According to the United Nations, the world's human population reached seven billion on October 31, 2011 (United Nations, Department of Economic and Social Affairs, Population Division 2015). In response, *National Geographic* published a series called "7 Billion" to consider the many implications of the expansion of the human population on food, water, energy, and even on climate change (Dimick 2014). The world's growing human population seems to threaten our very existence, especially when we look at parts of the world where human population is growing faster than ours and the demand for food, energy, and resources looks like a threat to our own supplies. When we are faced with discourses that emphasize and illustrate these kinds of trends, it is easy to slide into a view of the world that looks at human population itself as a threat to stability.

Baby Bust?

In his critique of Malthusian thinking, Eric Ross (1998, 2000) argues that the predominance of Malthusian views pointing to human overpopulation as the primary problem facing the world today distract from the underlying causes of inequality, poverty, and hunger. He traces the history of the basic tenets of Malthusian thinking that there is a somehow lesser *Them* whose irresponsible behavior threatens *Our* well-being. He makes the case that Malthusian thinking helped to justify and legitimize the Green Revolution. The usual story of the Green Revolution is that it promoted the development of new crops to supply food, particularly in poorer countries with swelling populations. However, this transfer of technology also enriched many companies that benefited from the sale of not just seeds, but also fertilizers, irrigation supplies, farm equipment, and fuel. From this perspective, we can see the Green Revolution as a discourse, in both materiality and practice, that legitimized and prioritized technological solutions to an agricultural problem. A different approach, however, might have focused on addressing economic inequality and uneven benefits of resource use. Indeed, the legacy of Malthus may well be the normalization of the inequalities of capitalism and environmental destruction (Yuen 2012). Even ongoing debates about immigration, welfare, and minimum wage fall into Malthusian assumptions that "provide an enduring argument for the prevention of social and economic change and

... obscure, in both academic and popular thinking, the real roots of poverty, inequality and environmental deterioration" (Ross 2000, 1).

So, it is interesting that the world's population is actually likely to decline.

Earlier in this chapter, UN statistics on global human population indicated that the world's population is larger than it ever has been, yet there is an important, additional detail: the world may be heading for a decline in human population. Although the world's human population, overall, continues to grow, demographic trends suggest that the growth will slow in the next fifty years (United Nations, Department of Economic and Social Affairs, Population Division 2015). Fertility has declined in most places around the world in recent years, and it is possible that the global population could stabilize or even start to decline before 2100. Our attention has been so trained to look for increasing population numbers that we may not grasp that "we're in the middle of a baby bust" (Robbins and Smith 2016, 201). Much mainstream economic and social theory is based on assumptions of growth, but how applicable are these theories and our comfortable perspectives when we may likely be facing population decline? Most twentieth-century theories of political economy, modernization, and economic development were conceived and promoted in a context of human population growth. Many of the theories still popular today were developed with an assumption of continued population growth and surplus labor (more people to work than jobs to be had). The working assumption shaping the way theorists—and then policymakers whose work subsequently affects individuals—was that of a population boom and continued growth in the number of people on the planet and their demand for resources. Now we are seeing trends in lower fertility and the potential for varying patterns of population decline. Above, Russia was given as an example where population is declining for multiple reasons, including emigration. In some places, we see that declining population is contributing to a deintensification of agriculture, deforestation, and other forms of land use. However, just as it is an oversimplification to assume that a growing population will lead to a decline in resource availability or in the health of ecosystems, it would also be an unhelpful oversimplification to assume that a declining population contributes directly to improved ecosystem or resource conditions. It would seem that we need new ways of understanding human-environment interactions.

Resource Scarcity and Management: Water

Malthusian views persist. They have become embedded in discourses about resources other than food, but the theme remains the same: overuse of a resource, mostly by *Them*, is a threat to *Us*. Having established the likely or imminent risk to our well-being, these discourses serve to legitimize taking steps to control the situation. Just as with Malthus, what these narratives tend to overlook is how the initial conditions of disparity and patterns of resource use came to be. Also like Malthus's writing, these discourses perpetuate this disparity by avoiding difficult questions and open debate in favor of promoting managerial responses and other forms of enclosure that limit access to resource use. Let's consider two examples: water and oil.

We have all seen news headlines about water scarcity. Above, we critiqued a mainstream news item focused on climate change, population growth, and overuse of water supplies. Mainstream media coverage of water scarcity tends to be dramatic and centered on the problem of insufficient water supply to meet demand. Although they may not explicitly propose controls on the water supply or on particular populations, they often point to too many of *Them* as the threat to *Our* water supply. Alternatively, the human dimensions of water supply, such as pricing mechanism or dated distribution practices, may be downplayed in favor of an emphasis on technological or managerial solutions.

John Agnew has examined mainstream narratives of water scarcity and how they tend to suggest that there is nothing we can do as a society in the face of growing domestic and industrial demand. In his presidential speech to the Association of American Geographers in 2010, Agnew critiqued deterministic portrayals of water scarcity—in which the presence or absence of water determines our options—as obscuring the potential for meaningful solutions (Agnew 2011). Instead, he suggests that we look at water distribution and access as not so much a geographic problem—where is the water?—but as a social, political, and economic problem: Who has legal access to water? Who can afford it? Whose rights to water supplies are prioritized? Who gets to decide how water supplies are used, channeled, or distributed? Agnew (466) provides a cartographic example of how water, "ironically the most fluid of substances," is effectively granted agency, shaping our future as if there were no way to generate equitable systems of water use and consumption.

Agnew (2011) demonstrates why it is important to question representations of water. He draws two maps on world water from *The Atlas of the Real World* (Dorling, Newman, and Barford 2008). Both maps are cartograms, meaning that countries are increased or decreased in size according to the variable being displayed. The first cartogram (map 2.1) shows "world water resources" in which the size of each country reflects the "annual volume of naturally occurring water for human use" (Agnew 2011, 466). Here, much of North America and Europe are quite small, and the continent of Africa is altogether depleted in size. South American and Southeast Asian countries

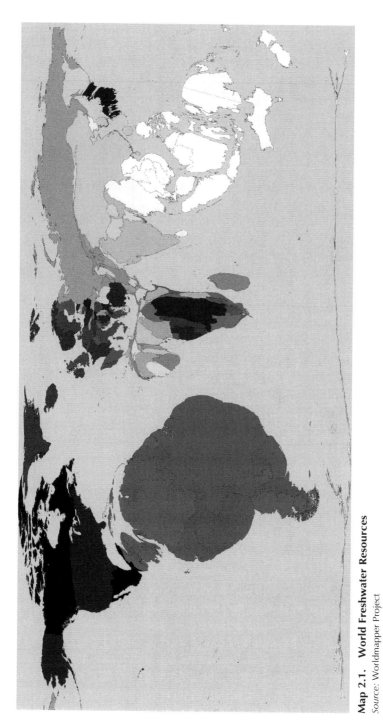

Map 2.1. World Freshwater Resources
Source: Worldmapper Project

Map 2.2. World Water Use
Source: Worldmapper Project

are significantly larger than they would normally appear. From this cartogram, we understand that there are plentiful water supplies in those places. The second cartogram (map 2.2) depicts each country's size in proportion to its total water use each year. Suddenly, India, China, and the United States all balloon in size, leaving South America and Africa decimated. Human population, it would seem, is mismatched to water supplies. Our attention immediately goes to India and China—look how big they are and how much water they are using! That must explain the world's dwindling supplies. We also know that these countries' populations are growing, so it seems to go without saying that those growing populations are threatening the global water supply and, by extension, our well-being.

Here, Agnew steps in to raise an important point: What if the second cartogram showed not total annual water use, but annual use per capita? That is, what if we could see in terms of how much water the average person uses instead of each country as a whole? He points out that the average per capita water use in the United States is three times that of China or India. A cartogram showing this variable would depict the United States as three times as large as those other territorially significant and densely populated countries. His point is that these cartograms lend themselves to support a type of water scarcity fear mongering that points to India and China as using much more than what might be their "fair" share of water.

This selective portrayal of water scarcity echoes Malthus's concerns about the abundance of poor people and the limited supply of food. It suggests that the populations in economically developing countries are threatening the stability of global water supplies and leaves up in the air what, if anything, we can do about it. Such discourses grant water an agency and intentionality that it does not have. More concerning, these discourses obscure the human factor in mediation and decision making. Agnew (2011) uses these cartograms as a visual discourse to discuss ways in which political processes need not be predetermined, wholesale positions on complex issues such as water distribution. It is through a careful examination of political and economic systems, such as subsidies for agricultural water use, the promotion of thirsty ethanol and other energy-related projects, and economic markets for water that a practical approach to politics, one that works through competing views and positions, can serve to generate a more just and fair compromise. Rather than buying into water scarcity narratives that point to inevitable crisis, Agnew reminds us that politics does not have to be a zero-sum game of fixed, oppositional positions. Instead, a thoughtful approach to politics reflects a practical working through of options and courses of action in a particular context at a particular time.

Resource Scarcity and Management: Oil

Another topic fraught with Malthusian narrative—the specter of imminent resource scarcity—is oil. Even though global oil prices dropped sharply in the fall of 2014, largely in response to Saudi Arabia's decision to increase its production, there is still uncertainty about how long the world's oil supplies will be able to support the current (and growing) levels of consumption. The concept of peak oil has become a familiar way to capture an understanding that at some unspecified time, oil production will drop sharply due to basic geology. The concept of peak oil originated with the work of the geologist M. King Hubbert, who was working for a major oil company in the 1950s. Hubbert (1969) generated a graph showing the level of oil production over time (figure 2.2). The graphic, still recognizable and familiar today, was meant to estimate the production of oil in a particular region or from a particular oil field. The line of production follows a bell curve that shows a steep ascent of increasing production, peaks at the point when half of the oil has been extracted, and then sharply decreases to indicate that oil production will fall after peaking. In the mid-1950s, Hubbert predicted that US oil production would peak in the 1970s. Other organizations and scholars continue to estimate when the peak will happen (see Meng and Bentley 2008). At the

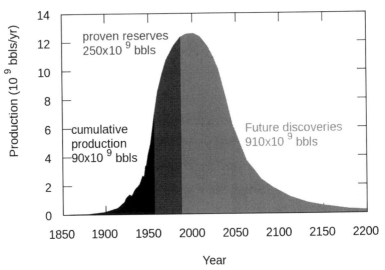

Figure 2.2. Hubbert's Projection. The now-iconic curve of Hubbert's estimation of oil reserves and likely discoveries. What does this graph suggest about geologic calculations and political choice?

Source: Wikimedia/Hankwang at English Wikipedia, CC BY 2.5, https://commons.wikimedia.org/w/index.php?curid=4201781

time when Hubbert was developing and revising his estimation of peak oil, the United States was a major oil-exporting country, and its production outpaced consumption. Hubbert was trying to assess how long US production of oil would continue to grow.

Although it is rarely recognized or discussed, Hubbert was motivated by his understanding that the rapid expansion of fossil fuels was enabling an abnormally high rate of population growth (Hemmingsen 2010). He saw danger in economic pricing systems that allowed unrestricted growth and disregarded the temporary nature of energy availability. He was active in promoting the idea that political and business control should be replaced by technocratic control and a scientific approach to balancing energy availability and consumption. However, "like certain other articulations of resource scarcity, the endurance of Hubbert's Peak has coincided with its uprooting from the geographical and historical context out of which it was formed" (Hemmingsen 2010, 539). Similar to how Malthus's imagery of exponential population growth quickly surpassing food supply shaped popular understanding, so Hubbert's Peak, as the bell curve graphic came to be known, became a touchstone for understanding the world's oil supply. It seemingly explained how oil production would continue to increase until one day, without warning, production would stop growing and then quickly decline. The shift would be sudden, but the timing could not be known for certain ahead of time. Peak oil "refers to an impending, permanent decline in the production of so-called 'conventional' oil as geophysical limits on its availability begin to bite" (Bridge 2010, 523–24). Already, a deterministic tone is evident: crude oil is a physical phenomenon which, like water, is either available or not, and that will dictate either the continuation or the discontinuation of our lifestyles.

The curve of peak oil, however, provides only a model for understanding some aspects of oil production. Not only is there debate and speculation about the timing of the peak, there is also uncertainty about what determines the volume of oil extraction. More than just how much oil is sandwiched in the geologic strata, and how much of those reserves are actually recoverable, there are also questions about what kinds of technology are available (or possible) to extract that oil, how much investment there is (which may be dictated in part by the shifting value of oil), and how extraction is influenced by demand and the availability of other energy sources such as natural gas, tar sands, wind, or solar power. All of these factors change over time as markets and technologies change and more scientific research is done. Yet the graph of peak oil and other, similar assessments of how much oil remains to be extracted appear to offer a grounded calculation of the facts on (or in) the ground. As Gavin Bridge (2010, 526) has commented, "The history of estimating recoverable reserves only confirms the illusory nature of hard numbers; global reserves have been revised dramatically upwards over time as a function of additional exploration and the deployment of new technology." Additionally, geopolitics, such as Saudi Arabia's decision to produce more oil, mentioned above, or the recent change in sanctions that allows Iran to sell its oil internationally, are significant factors in oil supply outside of peak oil calculations. Other factors that are not captured in peak oil calculations but important in determining how oil flows through the global economy are disruptions in pipelines and refineries, development of electric cars, and materials science beyond fossil fuels. Again, Bridge (2010, 526) observes, "By drawing the debate over peak oil into the realm of political choices rather than geophysical constraints, a space has been opened into which questions of need, value and justice may be introduced."

Just as the cartograms of water use and availability discussed above focus on the presence or absence of fresh water, so too does Hubbert's Peak focus on the amount of oil in the ground. The suggestion is that the amount of recoverable oil will determine prices and patterns of consumption in a direct relationship. In both cases, the presence or absence of a particular resource is used as the basis for making suggestions about how that physical resource should be managed so as to avoid some sort of crisis. Volume of the resource is portrayed as a key characteristic for measurement and analysis. However, just as volumes of space are fraught with dimensions of power (Elden 2013), volumes of resources also carry implications for how they came to be valued, who controls them, how they are distributed through space and between places, and who benefits from their categorization, measurement, and use. The physical presence, absence, or volume of a resource such as oil does not tell the whole story. Scholars have also considered the financialization of oil as a significant factor in shaping not only resource use but also our perceptions (and experiences) of scarcity. The price of a commodity resource such as oil is not necessarily directly related to how much of it there is. The price of oil, for example, is shaped by trends in oil company investment in exploration and production (Huber 2011). Indeed, "Speculative trading—and thus perception concerning supply among business agents—is central to shaping global oil prices and thus the social conditions of the oil market" (Zalik 2010, 553). Scarcity, then, is not just a matter of how much oil is left in the ground, but about how prices are determined, how and where markets are shaping demand, and how investment leads to growth or decline in certain economic sectors: "Financialization has permeated and transformed the nature of the production process—at the most fundamental level, the production of nature" (Labban 2010, 550). How we understand scarcity is central to how we represent human-environment relationships. The issues of scarcity and abundance are addressed in greater depth in the next chapter.

These points return us to the different forms of discourse. The graphic discourse narratives captured in Malthus's comparative curves, the cartograms of water, and Hubbert's Peak may serve to legitimize a particular way of seeing the world and interpreting elements of risk or security. Like the image of Earth from space, these visual representations may be used to justify certain policies, actions, or practices. In turn, these practices will be reflected in the material world. Yet not everyone will experience the material world in the same way. How water is allocated or priced, or how and where oil is extracted, refined, and consumed, all have tangible, physical effects that can be understood in reference to the larger, dominant discourse of that resource. Thus, when faced with a representation of a commodity resource, or some other element of the environment and our relationship to it, it is important that we ask questions about how that element is valued and what kinds of institutions (governments, industries, economic systems, etc.) shape our relations with it.

Water and oil, the two examples discussed above, are Malthusian in that they shift our attention to an imminent crisis framed by the threat of resource scarcity. These discourses help to legitimize technological solutions and managerial approaches to solving the resource problem and securing our supply. Population growth is uncontrollable, these discourses suggest, so we must focus on managing the resources "responsibly." This stance overlooks how the resource situation came to be. Just as Malthus's work does not question the impacts of land enclosure and the dispossession of people removed from their land, water scarcity and peak oil discourses shift our attention away from how the current situation was made possible (e.g., government subsidies of industrial, monocrop agriculture, or the political influence of the fossil fuel industry) or that other scenarios might have emerged in different circumstances. By framing the resource issue as a threat to our well-being, all of these narratives, to different degrees, suggest that the irresponsible overuse of resources by some groups of people should be reduced through better management techniques, reliance on market mechanisms, and the development of new and improved technology. These kinds of solutions will, of course, emanate from *Us* who have identified the resource problem despite the fact there may be alternative perspectives about what the problem is. The distribution and justice issues at the heart of each situation are not a focus.

Food Scarcity, Technological Solutions, and Grainwashing

Malthusian arguments are evident in discourses about many types of resource scarcity such as the examples of water and oil discussed above, but they remain central to current understandings of our food supply.

> World agriculture is now facing challenges unlike any before . . . but now the challenge is deepening as new trends—falling water tables, plateauing grain yields, and rising temperature—join soil erosion to make it difficult to expand production fast enough. . . . What happens with the next price surge? Belt tightening has worked for some of the poorest people so far, but this cannot go much further. Spreading food unrest will likely lead to political instability. We could see a breakdown of political systems. Some governments may fall. (Brown 2012, 114)

Again (or still), we are presented with scientific facts about food production and the inevitable crisis that lies ahead because there will not be enough food to go around. Less food means prices will spike, and those who cannot afford it will generate instability for everyone. Just as in Malthus's original arguments, less affluent people are not so much the victims of a system in which they have the least political power, they are instead presented as a threat to stability.

Although it may appear that "a new geopolitics of food has emerged" (Brown 2012, 115) and that every country must now fend for itself in terms of food supply, we would be missing a significant part of what is going on if we are not paying attention to the role of agribusiness. Many of these corporate actors claim to be practicing corporate social responsibility and addressing issues of world hunger. Using the Malthusian argument that hunger and famine result from food scarcity, many agribusiness actors justify the development of technological solutions and ecological modernization toward the production of more food commodities. Yet despite the growing volume of food commodities being produced, there is not only a growing number of hungry people in the world but also a growing percentage of the world's population that is hungry (Scanlan, Jenkins, and Peterson 2010).

A recent study has looked at how large agribusiness companies engage in "grainwashing," a combination of brainwashing and greenwashing (referring to efforts to make something appear to be good for the environment or environmentally sustainable) (Scanlan 2013). Companies such as Archer Daniels Midland (ADM), Cargill, Conagra, and Monsanto promote their practices as environmentally and socially responsible through venues such as corporate environmental reports, mission statements, philanthropy, billboards, print advertisements, television commercials, and Internet content. These are all examples of textual narratives legitimizing a discourse in favor of scientific progress and technological approaches to producing more food commodities. However, they do not consider underlying causes of food insecurity, such as inequality and politics: "Advances like a hybrid corn plan may yield more per acre but do not alter the fact that such innovation is grounded in a capitalist system of profit over people . . . systemic change is needed to correct the injustices associated with hunger and environmental degradation while grainwashing masks needed reform" (Scanlan 2013, 365). From a geographic standpoint, we are reminded that the spatial scale of the state is not the only, or even the most useful, scale at which to understand the processes and implications of grainwashing. Globe-spanning industries operating at many scales, and in many spaces are significant actors shaping not only our food supply but also our perceptions of food supply.

In their efforts to market scientific "solutions" to agriculture, grainwashing distracts attention from "a destructive global food economy laden with harmful inputs and unequal distribution systems and outcomes" (Scanlan 2013, 367). Agribusinesses may claim that globalized food production systems and supply chains, involving transport of agricultural inputs and outputs around the world, make it possible to provide food in many forms to many places. However, these same agribusinesses may actually make matters worse by disrupting local food systems and causing increases in the price of food. Corporate actors find support from a range of other institutional actors including think tanks, research universities, and governments in perpetuating the notion that these practices of production, distribution, and consumption are the best approach to alleviating hunger and necessary in the face of a growing population. Here, we see discourse not only in the form of textual or visual narratives (e.g., advertising or corporate websites) but also in the form of practices and materiality connecting local to global agricultural production, transportation, and processing systems. We can also see discourse in the form of embodiment as the bulk of food supplied to and consumed by most people is developed and arranged by relatively few actors. All of these forms of this discourse about the need for, and benefits of, an industrial, genetically modified food supply work together to stabilize a business, research, and government context in which these industries are dominant and decisive players.

None of this is to say that water, oil, and food supplies are without any problems. The concern here is to examine carefully how each of these and other resource issues are portrayed and addressed, and how particular discourses about resource scarcity, availability, or management are legitimized and stabilized. This kind of critique can help us to identify other, sidelined perspectives about how these situations are made possible and who is benefitting (or suffering) from these arrangements. To what extent are population growth and increasing demand really driving forces of dwindling resource reserves, and to what extent do these claims distract attention away from projects that consolidate power and wealth unevenly or unjustly?

Conclusion

From the viewpoint of environmental geopolitics, it is of particular interest to look at ways in which populations are assumed to have an impact on the environment. Of course, populations have an impact on their environment, and environmental conditions influence human societies. The point is to be thoughtful in how we make observations and statements about these connections. It is important to ask how arguments about human populations and environmental features are stabilized. A recurrent theme through this chapter has been resource scarcity, and we are familiar with this way of thinking. But what about risks in resource abundance? We might usefully turn our attention to increasing volumes in terms of rising sea levels or increasing concentration of CO_2 in the atmosphere as a legitimate concern for our political, economic, and social efforts (Dalby 2013). We might also look at how industrial agriculture and chemically produced fertilizer use has altered the availability of nitrates and the unforeseen consequences of too much available nitrogen in our water systems (Morton 2008, 2015). A Malthusian emphasis on resource scarcity is not necessarily the most helpful discourse in our current context because such a narrow focus can distract from other dimensions such as unequal distribution of benefits and costs of resource use. Similarly, the tendency to focus on human population as shaping our shared experience of risk or security is also problematic. Even a concept as global as the Anthropocene, discussed in the introductory chapter, imparts the idea that humanity's impact on the planet is somehow homogenous. This kind of glossing over of differences and inequities allows us to overlook how industrialization in and colonization by wealthier countries involved a "systematic unequal ecological exchange with dominated/peripheral regions" (Hamilton, Bonneuil, and Gemenne 2015, 7; see also Hornborg 2015).

> The concept of the Anthropocene might produce the false impression of a unified humanity, where all humans are agents of planetary change. Yet the Anthropocene is also rooted in inequalities, where the actions of some cause the suffering of the others. (Gemenne 2015, 173)

It is critical to look at ways in which human-environment relationships are portrayed in terms of posing threats or ensuring security, and we must also ask who or what is being threatened or secured. This chapter has considered ways in which scarcity of resources is discussed as being a challenge for a growing population. We have become used to thinking in these terms, but this chapter has considered how populations are defined and how they can have different dynamics shaped in part by selective discourses. What does a steady or even declining global population mean for our ways of understanding the world? Through discussions of water, oil, and food, this chapter has examined ways in which the environment is often simplified to support particular discourses. All too often, the most dominant discourses promote technological and managerial solutions. We have also considered ways of depicting environmental features that focus on physical absence or presence of a resource without careful consideration of political, social, and economic processes that establish how resources are identified, measured, valued, and distributed. Dynamics of power are evident in almost any conversation about human-environment relationships, but questions of equity, justice, and processes of decision making are not always recognized or emphasized. We have also seen the importance of understanding context and connection among places when we are trying to understand the dynamics of how we relate to and draw from our environmental surroundings.

Throughout this chapter, we have seen how discourses about human-environment relationships take multiple forms in narratives including text and graphics, practices, materiality, and embodiment or lived experience. A recurring theme throughout this chapter, with its focus on the persistence of problematic aspects of Malthusian thinking, is the theme of environmental scarcity. The focus here has been to widen the aperture of our understanding of how scarcity is portrayed and why it is often set next to a concern about too many people or a need for technological or managerial solutions. In the next chapter, we will look at ways in which scarcity—and its seeming opposite, abundance—is utilized in discourses about human-environment relationships. This conversation will turn our attention to related issues of resource conflict and slow violence.

CHAPTER THREE

Resource Conflict and Slow Violence

The topic of resource conflict is interesting because, initially, it seems immediately obvious: people will come into conflict over scarce resources. However, following the discussion of chapter 2, we can recognize that this way of thinking promotes a scarcity narrative that has its roots in a Malthusian perspective. To say that scarcity causes conflict requires many assumptions about what scarcity is and the options people have to deal with it. The very idea of resource conflict is like the images of Earth from space in that meaning is given to it by whatever argument is being made.

Resource conflict is a topic often drawn into discourses about environmental security, and those discourses change over time. From a classic geopolitical perspective, the environment is a security concern in terms of ensuring a state's access to needed or strategic resources either through military means or through trade with allies. In this view, environmental security is often equated with resource security or energy security (Le Billon 2007).

We can see how this understanding of environmental security fits with classic geopolitical approaches discussed in chapter 1. In the early 1900s, Halford Mackinder promoted imperial, territorial control as a way to ensure the supply of desired commodities to Britain from abroad. Mackinder's academic work provided textual, narrative elements of a discourse of imperial expansion and domination. From an environmental geopolitics perspective, we can critique Mackinder's discourse as promoting a limited but persuasive view about how certain environmental features should be shaped to suit a particular political agenda. The maintenance of territorial control of overseas territories and resources allowed Britain to advance its economic interests and to expand its political power and influence. More generally, European imperialism justified the often violent control of distant territories in the pursuit of energy and commodity resources. The European scramble for resources and establishment of colonies throughout the African continent, for instance, is an example of this process of securitization. European practices of empire building reflected a discourse of colonization and appropriation of territory, resources, and even people. Other elements of this discourse, including the materiality—tangible, physical aspects—of altered landscapes as resources, were developed (e.g., plantations of crops such as tea, spices, or silk) and extracted (e.g., gold, timber, fur, etc.). Processes of colonization also took the form of embodiment as groups of people were labeled, assessed, and manipulated by colonizing powers as ethnic groups, subjects, and slaves. Classic geopolitical interpretations of environmental security are also evident in the state-level ambitions shaping the events of World Wars I and II, in that states sought to secure territory, energy, and reliable trade of desired commodities.

The geopolitics of environmental security took on a different form during the Cold War as materials to support nuclear energy became more highly valued and contentious and as both the United States and Soviet Union sought to support countries in their respective spheres of influence through trade in energy and resource commodities. During the Cold War, the idea of security developed in terms of the tense relationship between the United States and the Soviet Union. Much time, effort, and political initiative were devoted to considering how the United States and its allies could maintain security in the face of the looming specter of Soviet communism, weapons development, and political influence in other states. Through the 1980s, the identity of the United States as a world power was in large part shaped by this dominant, bipolar relationship.

The collapse of the Soviet Union in 1991 left the United States without a clear sense of what *security* now meant. Into this vacuum emerged concerns about the environment. Two events in particular that focused international attention on environmental themes were the discovery of the hole in the ozone caused by chlorofluorocarbons and the Chernobyl nuclear disaster in Ukraine. Both events demonstrated Ulrich Beck's point that industrialized society poses a new kind of environmental risk (Beck 2009). Additionally, there were growing concerns about post–Cold War "resource wars" in which countries were expected to come into conflict over dwindling supplies of water, gems, and timber that were concentrated in increasingly unstable states (Klare 2001). Securing petroleum supplies through military means was also a growing concern since the lines of political affiliation evident during the Cold War were no longer clear (Klare 2004). Research in many disciplines over the past few decades has considered ways in which the environment is a security issue and ways in which resources are tied to conflict.

Even this brief, historical snapshot suggests how environmental security and resource conflict have carried different meanings over time. A timeless way of approaching these issues would be to ask: What is being secured, and for whom? (Dalby 2009). When we approach a discourse about environmental security or resource conflict with this question, it clarifies the three key observations that environmental geopolitics makes about dominant discourses related to the environment:

- The role and meaning of the environment are rarely specified.
- Humans' role or agency in these situations tends to be considered selectively. In particular, dynamics of power remain invisible and uninvestigated.
- Insufficient attention is paid to spatial dimensions of human-environment relationships that occur unevenly in different places and are intertwined with local, political, and cultural geographies.

Krabi, Thailand. A haze of smoke from fires set to clear forests in Indonesia for palm oil plantations reaches places hundreds of miles away.
Source: iStock

Palm oil plantation in Sulawesi, Indonesia. Abundance and scarcity tell only part of the story of the expansion of palm oil plantations. Who decides how resources are valued—forest ecosystems, agricultural commodities, indigenous cultures—and how do these decisions shape slow violence?
Source: iStock

In the next section, we will first examine assumptions that make scarcity narratives both possible and problematic. Second, we will look at resource abundance. A focus on abundance reflects a different line of thought that maintains that it is resource abundance and the presence of a resource, rather than its absence, that contributes to conflict. Resource scarcity or resource abundance? We have another binary! To break down this binary and understand what it hides, we explore the question: *What is the "environment" in environmental conflict discourses?* We will take a closer look at resource characteristics and how these matter in disputes over environmental features. Why does it matter what resource we are talking about, and how it is used or valued? This chapter's discussion on resource scarcity, abundance, and characteristics will emphasize shortcomings of resource determinism that assumes that resource features drive conflict. We will then be ready for the final discussion of the chapter that considers the question: *What is being secured and for whom?* This question is directly useful in an environmental geopolitics approach since it helps us to identify particular perspectives about environmental features and how they are associated with security concerns. It allows us to investigate how these perspectives are stabilized through different forms of discourse. The next chapter focuses on environmental security as it relates to climate change. Here, the focus is specifically on nuances and implications of resource conflict discourses.

Resource Scarcity and Abundance

As we saw in chapter 2, Malthusian arguments assume that some form of resource scarcity leads to conflict. This assumption was the foundation for at least two leading research groups that were active in the mid to late 1990s. These research groups shaped the way that resource conflict was understood by academics and by policymakers. Not only did their work influence how people thought about connections between environmental resources and conflict, but also they influenced how prominent these issues became in academic and policy arenas. In other words, the work of these research groups is worth understanding because both of them contributed to a discourse that focused on resource scarcity and violent conflict.

One group, led by Thomas Homer-Dixon, a political scientist at the University of Toronto, studied how changes in the availability of resources were linked to conflict. Specifically, this group studied how different forms of scarcity have negative impacts on people's well-being and thus motivate them toward violence. This research group focused on three forms of scarcity. The first is demand-induced scarcity caused by an increase in the number of people wanting a resource or an increase in the level of resource consumption. This type of scarcity is similar to the scarcity that concerned Malthus. The second form of scarcity of interest to the Toronto Group, as they were known, is supply-induced scarcity in which the stock of a resource was degraded or depleted. Soil erosion, the loss of healthy forests, and overused agricultural land are examples of degraded or depleted resources. The third form of scarcity of concern to the Toronto Group is structural scarcity, in which people have uneven entitlements or levels of access to resource use (Homer-Dixon 1999, 47–52). This type of scarcity is similar to the unequal entitlement structures discussed in chapter 2. The Toronto Group's research focused on how these forms of scarcity influenced other, intervening factors such as economic productivity or the aggravation of existing social tensions. Therefore, this group was looking at different forms of resource scarcity as indirect causes of violence. The researchers considered these processes of scarcity and conflict within a single state, so they focused only on civil violence rather than interstate conflict.

At about the same time, a research group in Zürich, led by Günther Baechler, also a political scientist, was focusing on the negative impacts of environmental transformation. In particular, this Environment and Conflicts Project (ENCOP) looked at how human-caused environmental degradation led to unequal benefits of resource use, or, in their terms, environmental discrimination (Baechler 1999, 111–12). These researchers made the case that environmental discrimination, together with other factors, fostered different types of conflicts at substate and international levels linked to ethnic and identity tensions, regional isolation, and migration.

Both the Zürich- and the Toronto-based research groups considered how different forms of scarcity and political tension or violence were associated with weak states or states with weak civil societies. The work of both groups included case studies within states. An even more fine-grained approach to studying local patterns and processes of resource use and trends related to conflict could include in-depth studies about livelihoods or studies done at the household scale (Deligiannis 2012). Other scholars scaled-up the work of the Toronto Group by applying the findings to interstate conflict (Toset, Wollebaek, Gleditsch, and Hegre 2000; Gleditsch et al. 2006, Koubi et al. 2014). However, it is unclear how the kinds of conflicts studied by the Toronto Group, in particular, might expand over a country's border and become an interstate conflict. This point is important because the framework for understanding resource scarcity and conflict at the substate level might easily be assumed relevant for conflict between two or more states. The misapplication of a framework developed at a particular spatial scale is an example of ecological fallacy that assumes processes that appear to work at one spatial scale would automatically operate the same way at other spatial scales.

These two research groups perpetuated a form of Malthusian discourse that connects scarcity of a particular resource to certain forms of conflict. Since Malthusian ideas about population (*Us* and *Them*) and resource scarcity are so embedded in our way of thinking, other people easily took up ideas from this research on resource conflict. The research produced by these groups was influential and attracted attention from policymakers who saw potential for possible US intervention in foreign resource conflicts. Peter Haas (2002) has discussed the lack of empirical evidence to support the idea that conflict is likely to erupt from conditions of resource scarcity, and he has also pointed out that little research has considered cases where scarcity in some form exists but conflict has not happened (see also Barnett 2000, O'Lear 2005). To that end, Haas (2002, 9) has critiqued this focus on narratives about resource scarcity leading to conflict and observed:

> These discourses persist not because they are accurate, but because they are politically embedded discourses . . . they acquire a taken-for-granted quality as bureaucrats are socialized into accepting the worldview within the administration through standard operating procedures, and because the arguments are often expedient for achieving other goals. In addition, lazy thinkers acquire the ideas in graduate school.

That is, the idea that resource scarcity leads to conflict seems intuitive and correct not because we can find examples everywhere, but because this idea has been repeated so often that it becomes familiar. Examples where some form of scarcity is occurring at the same time and place as some form of conflict may indeed be held up as evidence, but often these examples overlook considerable nuance or other factors that may be at play. The continued promotion of the idea that resource scarcity necessarily leads to conflict is not so much a reflection of empirical reality but a comfortable narrative to form the basis of research questions and policy frameworks. Setting up the question of how resource scarcity in some form will lead to violence or conflict rests on old Malthusian arguments, but it does not necessarily help us to see what is actually happening (or not happening).

Another approach to linking resources and conflict is to look at problems of resource abundance. This approach considers how an abundance of a valuable, commodity resource, such as oil, diamonds, or timber, may contribute to the generation of considerable inequity and instability, depending on how the income from that resource is managed (Olson 1963). Exporting a primary commodity is different than exporting a processed or finished good because a good that has been processed requires inputs of skill, investment, or technology, all of which add expense and value to that product. Exporting timber, for instance, is quicker and cheaper than exporting furniture or paper, just as it takes fewer inputs to export raw cocoa than to make and export Godiva chocolates. Uncut diamonds are not worth as much as cut diamonds, but they are also less traceable and easier to smuggle or sell on illicit markets.

Governments can manage the income from commodity exports in different ways. Some governments manage the income in response to public interests and with some form of oversight to provide benefits for the population of the state. For example, Norway is a significant oil exporting country and has established an oil fund that invests the income to support national well-being through education and a pension fund. However, some governments or leaders are more interested in expanding their own power rather than using export income to benefit the population of their country. Much research on resource abundance has focused on petroleum, oil in particular, and how an abundance of exportable oil may lead to increased centralization of power within a state (Amuzegar 1982; Gelb 1986, 1988; Karl 1997, 2000). Centralized wealth and control over the resource supply may enable corruption and delay government reform (Auty and Mikesell 1998; Auty 2001). Rather than develop skill in statecraft or seek public support, governments of resource-rich countries may just use the income from resource exports to maintain their own power and suppress any opposition. Governments in resource-rich, economically developing countries may actually *waste* resource sectors by overexploiting them in unsustainable ways in order to maintain their power with quickly attained funds (Ascher 1999, 2000). Rather than using resource wealth to strengthen many sectors of its economy and its population (such as Norway's oil fund is intended to do), some states do not cultivate a diversified, balanced economy and simply become dependent on continued export of a single resource (Dunning 2005).

This dependence on a single, primary commodity export has been studied as a driver of civil conflict (Collier 2000; De Soysa 2002), but other research emphasizes that it matters what the particular resource is. Dependency on oil wealth, for instance, appears to be associated with civil war (Fearon 2005), but it operates differently than a reliance on contraband items, such as gems and drugs, which appear to prolong conflicts already underway (Fearon 2004). Additionally, a country's resource wealth may help to fund rebels (Collier and Hoeffler 2004) or motivate a resource-rich region within a state to consider separating from the state (Ross 2006). All of these processes involving commodity resources are captured in the notion of "resource curse" (Lujala, Gleditsch, and Gilmore 2005). These approaches to studying resource-related conflicts draw from political science and political economy in their focus on how state institutions use or misuse resource wealth to stay in power or how these institutions become vulnerable as rebel groups use resource wealth to their own advantage (Le Billon 2007).

We have seen the case made for resource scarcity as a contributing factor to conflict, and we have seen the case for resource abundance as a contributing factor to conflict. What kinds of questions can we ask to break down this binary? It has been observed that renewable resources such as timber, agricultural land, and water may be linked to conflict through their scarcity, and that nonrenewable resources, such as oil or diamonds, may be linked to conflict through their abundance (Koubi et al. 2014). However, these sweeping generalizations are not very useful in helping us to understand unique aspects of resource features and environmental conditions in particular places.

What Is the "Environment" in Environmental Conflict Discourses?

Looking at examples of research on resources and conflict, it quickly becomes clear that studies are difficult to compare because they use different measurements and dimensions of abundance and scarcity. For instance, is an abundance of oil measured by how much oil a country has access to, or the value of oil that a country exports? How is resource scarcity or abundance measured, and what kinds of data are even available? Sometimes data sets of natural resource variables are combined to generate a single, quantitative variable to represent "the environment" or the natural resource conditions of a particular place. For example, one study that set out to analyze several contributing factors to civil conflict generated a single environmental value that could be used in a quantitative analysis of many countries. To generate this variable, the research combined World Bank data sets on multiple environmental and resource features: cropland, pastures, forested areas, protected areas, and mineral wealth. The result was a single variable to be used in calculations to represent "the net worth of the stock of natural resources of any given country in per capita terms" (De Soysa 2002, 407). The meaning of this variable in specific places or for specific groups of people is less than clear.

It may be tempting to take advantage of available data sets without questioning how the data were collected, what was measured, over what time, and with what kinds of sampling techniques, but more data does not mean better knowledge of a feature or process. Using and combining data unquestioningly may actually lead to a misunderstanding of processes or ways in which human systems interact with the environment (for a more detailed look at problems of resource data collection and how environmental features are represented, see O'Lear 2005). Studies on resources and conflict also include different time frames. For instance, some studies cover ten years, some cover twenty years, and others include forty or more years. Studies also consider different geographic areas. Some studies consider specific countries, some consider global regions, and others use "global" data (Koubi et al. 2014).

One consistent point that emerges is that arguments focused either on resource scarcity or resource abundance as an indicator of conflict are both forms of resource determinism. That is, by looking either to resource scarcity or resource abundance as causal factors of conflict, we are putting the resource—oil, timber, agricultural land—into the driver's seat to see how it leads to conflict. In doing so, these research approaches give resources agency in shaping human outcomes. As we saw in the discussion of water in the previous chapter, giving a resource agency, or viewing it as dictating political, social, or economic outcomes, detracts attention from the human systems underlying inequitable access or unjust exposure to environmental harm. Resources and environmental features are not evenly distributed on the planet, that is true, but it is important to look at how environmental features are intertwined with human systems and power. Power can take different forms (e.g., social, economic, political) and can shape how we think about, value, and use environmental features (O'Lear 2010). We can gain insights into relationships between environmental features and power by examining different discourses about those features particularly in the form of narratives (how do we speak about and value an environmental feature?), practices (how do we measure and use particular environmental features?), materialities (how do we transform environmental features and incorporate them into physical systems and structures?), and embodiments (how is the use of, or relationship to, environmental features intertwined with human identities and social systems?). Rather than focus on abundance or scarcity of a resource, we can examine resource characteristics because they reflect both physical, natural aspects of environmental features as well as how a resource is integrated with human systems.

Resource Characteristics

Understanding linkages between environmental features and conflict requires careful consideration of the various characteristics of resources. We need to know more than whether or not a particular resource or environmental feature is present or absent; we need to understand how it is intertwined with social, economic, and political systems. These systems shape the meaning, value, and management of a given resource, and the resource—whether it is diamonds or oil—in turn shapes the kinds of institutions and systems that form around its extraction, management, and consumption. This is what is meant by the social relations of a resource. Philippe Le Billon (2012) has emphasized the importance of examining the social relations of any given resource to understand how a resource may contribute to vulnerability, risk, or opportunity for conflict. Resource wealth can increase a country's or a group's vulnerability to conflict if the resource wealth is not well managed through appropriate institutions and distribution. The risk of conflict is greater around some resource sectors than others depending on the institutions and social relations of that sector (who is managing the resource wealth and making decisions about that resource?), as well as how that resource is valued. Finally, some types of resources offer greater opportunity to armed insurgents through their lootability, or the ease with which they may be smuggled and used to procure weapons or other means of wielding force. For instance, drugs, diamonds, and other gems are lootable and easily smuggled and sold by individuals or small groups of people. They are more likely to support forms of localized warlordism or rebel groups vying for power. Other resources such as natural gas or oil require control by a state government or a group in control of a state since these resources are more complex in their extraction and transport to consumers. These resources require an ability to manage larger operations (Le Billon 2001).

Asking whether or not resource conditions cause conflict is an insufficient question on its own (Barnett 2000; O'Lear and Gray 2006). Resource conditions may provide a useful starting point for an investigation, but there are other important dimensions to consider. We can look at a number of resource characteristics that describe a resource in terms of relations among places and actors (O'Lear and Diehl 2011). That is, we can learn a great deal about whether or not, or how, a resource may be a factor in conflict by considering several questions, such as: Where is this resource located in terms of its distribution? Is it near a political border that might make it difficult to smuggle or otherwise move, associated with a controllable choke point, or close to consumers? What kind of ownership structures does this resource have? What kind of technology is required to extract, harness, process, or refine this resource for consumption? Who controls that technology? The more nuanced kinds of questions suggested here get us closer to understanding how and why a particular resource may be associated with tensions, disputes, or even violence. What these questions also do is move us away from looking at a resource as an isolated thing and instead identify a resource or environmental feature as a starting point for understanding social, economic, and political systems that are what actually generate tensions and conflict among groups of actors.

The important point here is to recognize that resources are intertwined with political, social, and economic systems that give them value and that make their extraction and exchange possible. They are not *just* scarce or abundant, nor are they *just* renewable or nonrenewable. The next section considers a number of ways of understanding how human systems and environmental systems interact to create environmental resources of value to humans. In the words of Michael Watts and Nancy Peluso (2014, 194), "Resources are social processes."

Resources as Social Processes

There are several different ways to think about the interrelatedness of environmental features and human systems. Each approach offers a particular metaphor or ontology—an understanding about the way things are—since it describes a way of understanding the world. Multiple ontologies or ways of interpreting relationships between humans and environmental features exist at one time, and there is no single, correct ontology that will satisfy all people at all times (Demeritt 1994). The distinction of *nature* and *society* into two distinct categories is a result of modernist thinking that pits wild nature against rational, scientifically organized culture, but these categories are maintained through discourses and interpretations more so than a reality *out there* (Latour 1993; Whatmore 2002; Glover 2006). Instead, some would argue, nature and society do not exist separately but are integrated in ways that are specific to particular times and places (Smith 1996). This idea is captured with the concept of *socionature*.

An example of socionature is described by Erik Swyngedouw's (1999) work on the meaning of water and water infrastructure projects in Spain unfolding in particular ways over time in relationship to political agendas, popular demand, and advancements in dam engineering and water use practices in agricultural and urban areas. With this work, he emphasizes that "doing geography then implies the excavation and reconstruction of the contested process of the 'production of nature.' Of course, this perspective also asks a serious question about who controls, who acts, and who has the power to produce what kind of socionature" (461). The introduction of the term *socionature* is an attempt to generate a metaphor to describe a thing or process outside of our familiar ways of thinking and talking about the world.

A similar example, also pertaining to water, is Jamie Linton's historical study of water. He looks at many ways in which water is socially constructed, including, but well beyond, the hydrosphere, the hydrological cycle, or the scientific identification of water as a chemical compound.

> We will be considering water primarily as a process rather than a thing. . . . On this view, things such as H_2O do not constitute the fundamental reality of water but, rather, are fixations that occur at the nexus of the water process and the social process of producing and representing scientific knowledge. . . . Every instance of water that we can think of occurs as a product of the water process and various kinds of social processes and practices. It is in this sense that we discuss the social nature of water—not that society produces water, per se, but that every instance of water that has significance for us is saturated with the ideas, meanings, values, and potentials that we have conferred upon it. (Linton 2010, 4–5)

What he means is that when we look at water as a process, we are interested in the many ways that water is used, valued, intertwined with belief and practice, *and* how it also has measurable, scientific dimensions that we use to refer to particular aspects of water.

H_2O is scientific shorthand for the molecular structure of water, but it cannot tell us, for instance, how farmers in a particular location have a deep understanding of water, soil, crops, and seasons. Similarly, Noel Castree (2003b, 205) has observed that "nature is not simply natural . . . in both discourse and practice it is socially made." In addition to looking at social relations associated with a particular resource or environmental feature discussed above, we can look at ways in which nature is socially made or constructed. More specifically, when we look at resources or even nature as a social construction, we are looking at two different kinds of construction (Demeritt 2002). First, we pay attention to how we construct or develop our concepts about nature or about a particular resource: Why are diamond rings thought to be precious? Why do we care so much about wild polar bears when most of us will probably never encounter one? What is the value of a clean, pristine mountain river? These constructs of resources or nature are evident in discourses about their meaning and value.

A second type of construction is the way that we construct nature in a physical or material sense. How do we extract, harness, or harvest a resource, and what kinds of material infrastructure becomes necessary to process, refine, transport, distribute, consume, or protect a resource or environmental feature? For instance, how do we engineer dams to provide water for consumption and power turbines to generate energy? In both kinds of construction, when we focus on "construct" as a verb rather than on "construction" as a noun and an outcome, we can tune in more precisely to questions such as *who is constructing what and for what ends?* What is the action and the process? This approach is in line with the overall objective of this book to question assumptions about what the environment is and how it is brought into understandings of risk and security.

Other ways to break out of thinking in terms of resource scarcity or abundance include Watts and Peluso's (2014, 196) suggestion to shift our focus from the resource curse to a resource complex: "The resource complex . . . examines both how resources are made regulable objects, how they are governed as parts of particular systems of rule, and what are the political and power relations by which the complex is, or is not, stabilized and rendered self-reproducing." This focus on a resource complex differs greatly from the previous examples of studies of resource conflict that rely on databases of the physical location of particular resources. The resource complex encourages us to see how a particular resource or environmental feature is part of a network of places of production, consumption, and transport as well as how a resource is associated with decision makers, political systems of governance or regulation, economic systems of valuation, and the language and

National Ice Core Lab, Denver, Colorado. Ice sheets and glaciers are part of the planet's hydrosphere, but ice cores stored for scientific research on past climates become a different kind of resource.
Source: Atlas Obscura (public domain)

processes of securitization (Floyd 2010). Again, this kind of approach views environmental resources not as stand-alone variables in conflict situations but as integrated with a variety of institutions, actors, and processes.

Other scholars have offered the term *resource environments* to capture not merely a feature of the physical landscape but the ways in which a particular environmental feature is shaped by (and in turn, shapes) human systems. The term *resource environments*

> directs analytical attention away from resources as substances with essential qualities that are assumed to exist "in nature" to the complex arrangements of physical stuff, extractive infrastructures, calculative devices, discourses of the market and development, the nation and the corporation, everyday practices, and so on, that allow those substances to exist as resources. (Richardson and Weszkalnys 2014, 7)

Just as the introductory chapter presented the idea of the Anthropocene and the blurring of distinct categories of humans and nature, here we are also encouraged to think about ways in which different systems interact to create value in particular environmental features that come to be regarded as environmental resources. Those resources are understood within a resource environment in which they are measured, valued, extracted, and consumed.

As an example, we can look at the resource environment of petroleum. Chapter 2 discussed the representation of peak oil as incomplete or even misleading since it neglects processes of valuation, financialization, extractive technologies, the development of other energy systems, and patterns of demand. Similarly, when we look at the resource environment of petroleum, it is not just the amount of oil or gas still in the ground or currently in refineries and pipelines. The resource environment also includes the physical infrastructure to extract and transport oil as well as the accounting and financialization practices that determine the value of oil and how and where it will be consumed. It includes the role oil plays in the promotion of national interests (e.g., our freedom to consume or the deployment of troops to secure supplies and transport routes), the influence of corporations (including automobile manufacturers and airline industries that profit from continued reliance on these modes of transport), and everyday practices that shape consumption and our beliefs about oil.

Thinking through these linkages of a resource environment or a resource complex allows us to see the working of power as it relates to a particular resource or environmental feature. Timothy Mitchell (2009, 2011) has examined these connections with fossil fuels more broadly in his work on carbon democracy. He looks at how physical characteristics of first coal and then liquid petroleum shaped or shut down the possibilities of democratic management of these fuels. Concentrated energy in the form of coal enabled the development of densely populated, urban areas in Europe in which people were no longer reliant on dispersed wood fuel. Cities, large populations, and a concentrated energy source made industrialization possible and created the demand for increased agricultural land in order to feed and clothe the working population. This concentration of power, growth of industrial output, and increased need for agricultural land, in turn, motivated larger-scale agriculture as well as overseas colonization and the acquisition of colonial territories and the creation of slave populations. Through these coal-enabled processes, the balance of power shifted toward Europe.

Differences in the physical characteristics of coal and petroleum also influenced different relationships of power as petroleum came into use. For instance, coal miners working deep underground and out of sight of managers had the responsibility of determining how much coal to excavate from particular chambers depending on their structural integrity and extraction potential. When they coordinated their efforts, coal miners developed significant political power exercised in coal miner strikes first in Europe and later in the United States. Energy networks, including coal mines, railways, and docks, were critical to the movement of coal and reflected the concentrated power and political influence of laborers working in these sectors.

After World War II, a shift toward liquid petroleum brought about new forms of power. Although oil workers also exercised political influence through labor strikes, their work above ground kept them under constant supervision and in a less authoritative role than coal workers. The transport of oil through pipelines or by overseas routes rather than by rail made it more difficult to have significant impact through a labor strike. Yet this relative ease of oil transportation brought new concerns to owners and managers of oilfields. It was no longer sufficient to control production in a particular region, as with coal, because less expensive oil could arrive from many destinations. In this way, the expansion of the petroleum industry generated new forms of management and control that were more centralized and less democratic than the previous patterns of coalfield ownership, management, and labor (Mitchell 2009). In tracing these relations over time, Mitchell (2009, 422) shows connections between "energy and politics, materials and ideas, humans and non-humans, calculations and the objects of calculation, representations and forms of violence, and the present and the future."

This example demonstrates several dimensions of resources discussed so far. It demonstrates the different social relations associated with coal and liquid petroleum since these materials are extracted and transported in different ways. This example also illustrates different resource characteristics beyond the mere physical location of the point of extraction. Both coal and liquid petroleum generated different geographies tying together source, consumers, refinement processes, consumption, labor and management relations, and power dynamics among different groups of people. Coal and liquid petroleum both demonstrate different socionatures and ways in which physical and human systems are intertwined. In each case, an understanding of coal and of liquid petroleum was constructed: *What is it? Who controls it? How can its value be leveraged for power?* Also in each case, physical and human systems were constructed: extraction, transport, management systems, labor relations, ownership rights, calculations of value and exchange, institutions of expertise, consumption practices and associated technologies, and so forth.

Other work has considered specific forms of violence associated with liquid petroleum. Matt Huber's (2011) research has focused on the importance of ensuring that a particular resource is sufficiently scarce to keep its value high. He looks at the example of oil extraction in east Texas and Oklahoma in the 1930s and the expansion of small-scale, "mom and pop" oil rigs. The rapid increase in production of oil raised government concerns about overproduction and the risk of a drop in the value of oil. To stave off such a crisis, martial law was implemented to control oil drilling and limit the production of oil. The presence of military troops stopped people from extracting however much oil they wanted. This control over extraction can also be seen as the taking (or blocking) of private property through the threat of violence. Huber discusses how this "production of scarcity" was critical for the post–World War I economic plans of the United States and the central role that oil—not cheap oil, "but cheap *enough* oil" (823)—would have. Beyond this historical example, Huber considers how similar intentions and practices may have motivated the US invasion of Iraq. Could it be that the United States wanted to prevent Saddam Hussein from increasing oil production and opted to interfere through violent disruption of those plans?

Conflict Is Not Always the Only or First Response

Much of the academic scholarship and policy attention on resource conflict focuses on armed, violent conflict associated with environmental resources. Armed conflict is indeed an important process to take seriously. The focus on armed conflict, however, is also partly because armed conflicts are quantifiable. That is, they can be counted and measured. Conflict databases are generated to enable large, statistical studies of conflicts aimed at identifying trends in conflict over time. Such databases suggest that conflict can be measured, studied, and examined so that conflict is better understood. However, producing a lot of data on conflict (or any other process) is not the same as producing knowledge about that process. Any time we are presented with data, we should ask questions about the data that were collected. How were they collected? Who collected them? How were the metrics or parameters determined; that is, how were the important variables identified? It is also critically important to ask about what kinds of data were *not* collected. Which features of the process were *not* measured? What kinds of information are missing from the data set?

Aspects such as the time of the onset of a conflict or its duration are relatively straightforward to quantify and indicate. What about the intensity of a conflict? Conflict intensity is often measured in battle deaths (e.g., some data sets only consider conflicts with at least one thousand battle deaths, whereas other databases include conflicts that resulted in twenty-five battle deaths). How else might we measure intensity? For instance, battle deaths may be one, obvious, and immediate indicator of the intensity of violent conflict, but what about long-term injuries or indirect deaths (e.g., people in displaced persons camps who die of disease or lack of food or water)? How can those features be measured in a comprehensive and systematic way? What about other aspects of conflict that are not easy to measure or even observe as an outsider? Le Billon (2007, 172) has noted that "historical context, identities and power relations" are the kinds of factors of a conflict that reflect the chronic, ongoing, and multiscalar aspects that are overlooked by many quantitative assessments of conflict. In addition, when we are interested in how environmental features are related to conflict, there are important questions to ask about how those features are indicated in any data set on conflict.

An earlier section of this chapter considered the issue of how to include environmental features in conflict databases. Often, if they are represented at all, environmental features are captured in conflict data sets in narrow measures of presence/absence, area, or dollar value. Such measures may allow a researcher to fill a database box with a number, but they do not necessarily help us to understand different meanings of a particular feature or resource. Although researchers use conflict databases to compare conflicts, these data can hide the fact that much of what *counts* in the databases is oversimplified. This observation leads us to question how comparable measures of different conflicts actually are (Koubi et al. 2014).

Linking environmental features and armed, violent conflict can also make several assumptions that hinder a better understanding of human-environment relationships. A focus on such conflict ignores the fact that conflict happens for several reasons, that it is not necessarily irrational, and it is not necessarily the first or only response to a challenging situation. We will look at these issues in turn. First, conflict is much more complex than simply having a shortage of a resource (as a Malthusian argument might assume). Whether or not armed conflict erupts has to do not only with a particular resource or environmental feature but also how it is valued, distributed, and controlled in a given location and how that resource and location are tied to users and values in other places. Conflict is a social process, so armed conflict is shaped by perceptions and realities of relative poverty and changes in well-being (or expectations of well-being). Armed conflict depends greatly on how people are motivated to engage in conflict or in peaceful activities. Barnett and Adger (2009) have examined multiple dimensions of violent conflict as it relates to environmental change, and they remind us that individuals must often be recruited to engage in violent conflict. People's participation cannot be assumed. Indeed, "the role of individuals in initiating, sustaining, resisting, or solving violent conflicts is a major lacuna in the literature on development and violent conflict, and on environmental change and violent conflict" (125). These researchers also emphasize that armed conflict can serve the interests of people who seek to challenge the status quo; "wars are not irrational, but rather are the product of a set of rational decisions that lead to a violent reordering of economic and political systems and social relations" (127). Focusing on violent, armed conflict related to environmental or resource conditions can be headline grabbing, but it can also draw attention away from the fact that there are alternative responses to challenging situations. In that more encompassing light, we can revise the question about how resources or environmental features are associated with violent, armed conflict to a question that invites a more thoughtful and insightful examination: *What is being secured and for whom?*

Objectification of Nature and Discourses of Security and Risk

The discussion above has demonstrated why it is important to go beyond thinking about resources in terms of being scarce or being abundant and why it is unhelpful to assume that resource or environmental conditions drive conflict. Environmental features such as timber, diamonds, oil, or water have multiple geographic dimensions beyond merely being located in a particular place, and they do not have intentional agency. Environmental features have also been discussed as being integrated with human systems such that each side of the human-environment dynamic is produced or shaped by the other. This point raises the question, though, of how we understand the starting point of this mutual production. If we take seriously the argument that there is no distinct, pure "nature" outside of human existence, then it seems problematic to say that human and environmental systems produce and shape each other. If they are not separate to start with, where do we begin to understand this relationship or process? Scholars have explored this theoretical discussion at length (Lefebvre 1991; Smith 1984, 1996; Latour 1993; for a discussion see Swyngedouw 1999). For the purposes of this book, the important aspect of this discussion is to disrupt the idea of natural resources as standing completely apart from human systems that value, extract, alter, refine, commodify, transport, trade, consume, or waste them.

Let's return to the question of *what is being secured and for whom?* This question helps us to think about how discourses form to influence our thinking about why it is important to control environmental features and who benefits from that control. There is a tendency to interpret environmental or resource conflict as having to do with controlling territory (e.g., forests, diamond mines, and illicit drug crops) or flows of resources (e.g., water, oil pipelines, and trade and transportation routes). Such an approach to conflict is like a tabletop exercise that may be understood in two dimensions (much like the game of Risk), but it is important to question the assumptions and abstractions on which this understanding of control is built. That means backing up to the European Enlightenment of the eighteenth century.

What we find is that common ways of understanding environmental features today—our discourses about the environment—have roots in Enlightenment thinking. During the Enlightenment, there was an emphasis on the importance of *securing* the natural world "to develop reliable, replicable scientific knowledge of nature, rendering it available for human exploitation" (Philo 2015, 322). *Nature* was portrayed in these discourses as excessive (Yusoff 2009) and in need of human control. Capitalism, as an economic system, was emerging around the same time as this scientific mode of thinking. Commodities to move capitalism forward needed to be carved out of nature. Methods of calculation were developed to meet capitalism's rigid forms of value and accounting, and "nature was no longer allowed its own enchantment . . . It was instead nature *secured*, buttoned down, bracketed, boxed; a bundle of resources, a giant necropolis of dead matter for utilization rather than a vital, living landscape for co-dwelling" (Philo 2015, 323). The territorial state was also emerging as a way to organize and exercise power. James Scott, in his book *Seeing Like a State* (1998), considers the many practices that state powers—people in charge of defining and defending particular states—use to make their state and their control over territory legible. One of the key practices was a shift from thinking in terms of nature to thinking in terms of *natural resources* that could then be categorized, studied, isolated, measured, valued, and made useful for human systems. That is, nature became an object to be taken apart and manipulated for purposes of capitalist development for the benefit of territorial states.

In this process of objectification, nature is valued only in terms of human systems rather than seen as having any inherent value. Practices of abstraction are key to the objectification of nature. Nature becomes reduced to (or expressed as) a single, quantifiable dimension. For instance, a forest might be measured in terms of board feet of timber or a river measured in terms of annual volume of flow. Both of these measures may be helpful for certain purposes, such as planning a timber harvest or assessing potential for building a dam. However, neither measure can stand in for all of the meanings and ecosystem functions of either a forest or a river. Such quantified measures reduce a complex, nonhuman system or feature to a single indicator reflected in standardized practices of calculation (Linton 2010). The particular feature, then, becomes objectified and understood as distinct from being human (Loftus 2015). These renderings of nature or the environment standardize its value into something exchangeable for something else thought to be of the same value. The domination over reducing and producing this limited meaning of value—this abstraction—has been described as a form of violence (Sayer 1997; Smith 1984; Loftus 2015). Continued use of these abstractions, such as putting a price tag on elements of nature, legitimizes particular arrangements of power and forms of knowledge. We could also refer to this quantified interpretation of nature as postpolitical (Swyngedouw 2010a) since it serves to promote one method or view and shuts down discussion of alternatives. This valuing of environmental features may also be interpreted as an *apolitical ecology* because it fails to look at how this narrow assessment of a particular feature fits within broader systems of influence and how it fails to consider other points of view (Robbins 2004).

This legacy of Enlightenment thinking—the practices of abstraction that make nature something separate from humans and something to be measured and managed—provides a foundation for *securing* resources and other environmental features. The securing of environmental features is well suited to the ambitions of territorial states, but we can also see how abstractions that separate the environment from human systems are also suited to other forms of territoriality (Sack 1986) or ways of controlling access to, and benefits from, environmental features. In a recent forum on insecure environments in the *Geographical Journal*, geographers look at how different environmental features—water, energy, and food—are often at the center of "efforts to 'territorialise,' to containerise" (Philo 2015, 325) and exemplify the persistence of Enlightenment-era thinking. However, when we examine these abstractions more closely, we see that more than state-level interests are at work here.

Water Security

Water security is most often reflected in one of two main discourses. The first frames water security as a problem of providing a population with enough water, avoiding too much water in the form of floods, or too little water in the form of drought. These kinds of discourses usually center on states and nationalistic concerns over water shortages and the risk of interstate conflict. We saw an example of this discourse in the story from the *Washington Post* in the previous chapter. A second dominant discourse on water security, prevalent in policy discussions, steps outside of the state-centered view and emphasizes the need to provide access to safe supplies of water (or to help a population avoid the risk of floods). This discourse goes something like this: "'We' struggle to ensure safe secure access for 'other' vulnerable populations, rather than securing 'our' boundaries and fueling conflict over a limited resource" (Loftus 2015, 367). However, both of these discourses about water security—one focused on securing water within state boundaries and the other focused on securing water for populations of vulnerable "others"—are founded on a perspective that

> quickly slips into a form of determinism: water insecurity is the result of insufficient rain rather than the unjust distribution of supplies of potable water. The surprising ability of the rich to be able to access water supplies when the poor are unable is portrayed as a technical issue, to be solved through engineering solutions rather than through a transformation of the choreographies of power out of which such unjust distributions emerge. (367)

This critique of the dominant discourses on water security is similar to the critique by John Agnew (2011) offered in chapter 2: water provision and access shouldn't be about uneven power relationships and dictating technomanagerial solutions to the most poor (Loftus 2014). Notice how both of these dominant discourses on water security rely on the notion that *we* need to manage water supplies because *they* do not have the ability or ingenuity to do so. This division into *Us* and *Them* is an example of embodiment or identity in discourse because it labels people into groups without taking into account varieties of experience and different types of knowledge and water use practices.

Both of these dominant water security discourses also serve to support material outcomes such as dam building, water diversion projects, and other infrastructural aspects that reinforce the perspective about who should be controlling water and benefitting from its use. Both of these water security discourses also support practices that maintain or rely on water allocation arrangements. One example is the practice of maintaining a suburban lawn through efforts of fertilizing the grass, mowing it, and keeping it well watered even in climates where a green lawn can only be sustained through phenomenal effort (Robbins 2007). The priority of maintaining a green lawn as a sign of status ("keeping up with the Joneses") rests on the assumption that water is plentiful enough to be used in this way without questioning bigger-picture issues of justice and equity in water use and allocation arrangements. Green suburban lawns reflect discourse as practice and the prioritization of certain values: it is important to demonstrate status and fitting in with society by using abundant water supplies to grow (essentially) a crop that we do not even need.

Energy Security

Another topic addressed in the forum on insecure environments is energy security. In his analysis of energy security, Gavin Bridge (2015) recognizes that popular and policy interpretations of energy security tend to focus on the importance to states of ensuring steady flows of energy resources (most notably oil) to maintain economic activities and quality of life for its population. We see versions of this kind of energy security thinking in the news when there is talk about US demand for oil or gas and actions taken here or in other places to ensure that we have the energy sources that we need. The concept of energy security often motivates scenario planning for energy infrastructure and shapes technical and operational decisions for managing energy flows. The notion of energy security is also often a guide for thinking through and promoting the reliability and safety of critical energy systems, not just the stability of states and the safety of their populations. However, in his examination, Bridge (2015, 336) argues that "energy security is a term whose meaning is unsettled." Although the meaning of energy security (similar to the meaning of water security) seems immediately important, there is no single, clear definition. That lack of specification allows the couplet to be used in any number of ways to justify or support particular agendas. Both parts of the couplet are sufficiently vague as to make the concept exceptionally malleable. "Energy" does not distinguish among foreign oil reserves, solar power, wind energy, or energy conserved rather than used. What kind of energy are we talking about? What kinds of places are implicated by different forms of energy, and who controls how sources are used and made valuable to human systems? Similarly, how is "security" being measured and assessed? Who is enjoying it or paying for it?

Just as importantly, we can look at the flip side of any claim to security. What kinds of *in*security are being created or normalized in these discourses? What kinds of *in*security are generated through practices of energy extraction and use? Hildyard, Lohmann, and Sexton (2012) have considered how *securing* energy may, in fact, mean ensuring benefits for private corporations and wealthy people through dispossession and enclosure. In Malthus's time, land tenure systems in England were changing and placing more control over land into the hands of the elite. These practices of enclosure and dispossession forced many people to move off the land and into cities. Processes of enclosing previously open or public lands left people outside of the enclosure, dispossessing them of the benefits of the land. Similarly, the management of energy systems may lead to uneven benefits. Oil refineries and hydraulic fracturing pads are toxic hot spots that expose nearby populations to untold levels of air and water pollution that can result in irreversibly degraded health. Additionally, the process of hydraulic fracturing, or fracking, can involve the subsurface injection of fluids, either the ancient brine trapped in the rock and brought to the surface with oil and gas (produced water) or hydraulic fracturing fluid. These injection processes have been linked to increased seismic activity referred to as injection-induced earthquakes (Ellsworth 2013). These human-caused earthquakes may be induced up to ten kilometers away and are much deeper than the injection point (Rubenstein and Mahani 2015). As map 3.1 illustrates, the number of induced earthquakes increased sharply after 2009 with clusters of activity particularly evident near hydraulic fracturing operations such as in central Oklahoma. As with other forms of energy resource expansion, calls to enhance national-level energy security by extracting shale gas reserves can contribute to localized, negative impacts on the environment (Jones, Comfort, and Hillier 2017). We can also consider environmental insecurity inflicted on people living in communities near massive strip-mining activity. Although the coal extracted at these massively altered sites may be used to generate electricity for people living in distant towns and cities, peo-

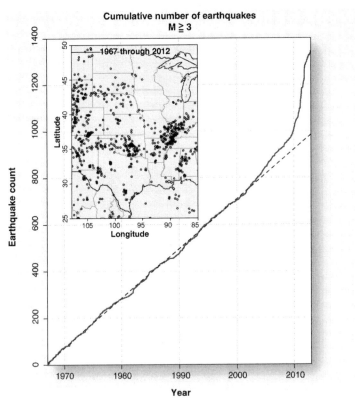

Map 3.1. U.S. Continental Earthquakes

Note: The solid line depicts a higher than predicted rate of earthquakes per year, particularly in the middle of the continent where hydraulic fracturing activity has increased since 2009.

Source: Ellsworth (2013, 1225942-2).

ple living just downstream from the removal of mountain tops are at a greater risk of exposure to polluted and unmanaged flows of water, silicate dust from explosions of geologic strata, drinking water contaminated with heavy metals and other toxins, and excessive levels of dust in the air they breathe. That is, mining companies and coal-burning power plants in this instance are enclosing not just the coal, but all of the other affected environmental features (air, water, ecosystems, topography, etc.) and dispossessing nearby citizens of a safe, livable environment while granting them no say in how their surroundings are being managed.

Food Security
Industrialized food production generates other forms of insecure environments (Nally 2015). In the interest of food security, there has been a significant increase in the phenomenon of land acquisitions in the last decade. Countries with insufficient arable land to grow their own food crops have turned to utilizing land in other countries mostly for industrial-scale production of commodity crops used for food and sometimes energy production. For instance, jatropha is one crop used for biofuel production and grown on an industrial scale. Land acquisitions for this purpose are motivated by an interest in energy security, and the discourse operates in a similar way to those supporting food security. There has also been an increase in land acquisitions motivated by green agendas linked to biological conservation, biodiversity preservation, and biocarbon sequestration, and these forms of appropriation of nature also raise questions about who is making these decisions and who is benefitting or losing out from them (Fairhead et al. 2012).

Land acquisitions, sometimes referred to as land grabs, would seem impossible in our current global context of established territorial states. What kind of state would willingly surrender control over significant segments of valuable, arable land? Saskia Sassen (2013) has examined the interworking of governments, international institutions, corporations, and legal norms that make the acquisition of land in foreign countries an increasingly common practice. Unlike past forms of imperial expansion when one political entity forcibly took control of "new" land, current practices of land acquisition involve multiple types of actors and subject "national, sovereign territory . . . to non-national systems of authority" (25). She considers how institutions such as the International Monetary Fund (IMF) and the World Trade Organization (WTO) exert a formative influence by laying the groundwork of political and economic infrastructure that makes these transfers of control possible. Global-reaching interests like corporations and agribusiness sectors have an easier time, then, embedding themselves through this infrastructure in these weakened states and are able to *reorient* the utility and purpose of land.

> The vast foreign land acquisitions illustrate a range of such reorientations, including: growing food for a foreign country's vastly expanded middle classes, access to abundant water supplies for manufacturers of mass-consumption sodas, developing palm plantations for making biofuels, and the constructing of large ports and roads to access minerals. What was once part of national sovereign territory is increasingly repurposed for a foreign firm or government. (29)

These are examples of the discourse of food security as practice, and they have tangible, material effects in places where land use is reoriented, water supplies are tapped for distant consumers, ports are built to facilitate interaction with the global transport system, and roads are constructed so that mines can extract and export mineral wealth. These activities are outwardly focused and produce "a partial denationalization deep inside nation-states, a structural hole in the tissue of national sovereign territory" (43). Someone in the state is benefitting from these arrangements through some form of payment or increased political control, and certainly other actors in the global system are benefitting in the form of profit and influence.

Looking at these dynamic networks and collaborations—these assemblages—of actors, policies, and legal systems, helps us to see that entire states are not the victims of these processes. The "structural holes in the sovereign

Christopher Columbus and the International Monetary Fund. What, exactly, is being secured for whom in land acquisitions then and now?
Source: polyp.org.uk

tissue of national sovereign territory" can point to uneven patterns of injustice and insecurity. As David Nally (2015, 347) has argued:

> Land grabs are the outcome of complex, and in many cases novel, political processes involving policy assumptions and incentive structures that lock communities into violent trajectories of historical change and render silent or irrelevant alternative pathways to develop. Land grabs are *made* . . . and so it stands that they can be *unmade*.

Returning then to the question of *what is being secured and for whom?*, we can see how these three examples of *securing* particular environmental features—water, energy, and food—each involve Enlightenment-era thinking in terms of calculating and separating elements of nature so that they may be commodified and managed for the expansion of power. No longer is sovereign, state power the only or even the most obvious form of power. We see how other actors such as international organizations and profit-seeking corporations may have a significant influence in shaping physical, material environments. They also encourage certain practices and forms of consumption. These efforts also lead to distinctions between *Us* who get to enjoy the benefits of secured environmental features, and *Them* who are rendered insecure in any number of ways by our efforts to secure resources. Additionally, we can see from these examples why the conflict label is problematic. Conflict tends to evoke images of armed, violent conflict, but not all conflicts take this form. In the examples discussed here, we can see layers of political maneuvering, economic finesse, and the obstruction of deep, cultural understanding in favor of the prioritization of science and technology. Conflict is indeed embedded in these processes, but it may not be readily visible. It may take the form of state-to-state or corporation-to-state negotiation and pressure, and it may involve different values among involved actors or groups or different priorities between state and local agents. Conflict is not the most helpful label or frame for understanding causes, effects, and disparities when it comes to how a broad sweep of challenging environmental conditions is resolved or quelled.

Collaboration and Common-Pool Resources

Alternatively, we can broaden our perspective beyond a focus on conflict to consider ways in which people collaborate or otherwise work to build peaceful conditions. An excellent area to look for examples is the work on common-pool resource management. Before we consider how common-pool resources may be managed justly and sustainably, it is important to clarify some terms. Common-pool resources are those that are large enough that multiple users may draw from them, but it is possible "to define recognized users and exclude others altogether" (Ostrom 2008, 11; see also Ostrom, Gardner, and Walker 1994) from using the resource. Additionally, anyone's use of a common-pool resource subtracts from the available benefits of that resource. Forests and fisheries may be examples of common-pool resources when there is limited access and finite benefit to gain. In contrast, a commons is a type of system to which "it is difficult to limit access, but one person's use does not subtract a finite quantity from another's use" (Ostrom 2008, 11). An example of a commons system is knowledge. Enabling or blocking access to knowledge may be a challenge, but one person's use of knowledge does not diminish the amount of knowledge left for others to use. The distinction among types of commons is important.

In the environmental realm, the concept of commons often brings to mind the work of Garrett Hardin and his significant paper, "Tragedy of the Commons," published in *Science* in 1968 and still widely referenced today. In that paper, Hardin warned of the unavoidable tragedy that would follow unmanaged use of public commons. He uses the metaphor of a pasture on which several herdsmen graze their cattle. Hardin assumes that each individual will selfishly maximize his own benefit from the commons by placing additional animals to graze in the pasture, thus leading to a declined pasture that can no longer be used for grazing by anyone. He argues that "freedom in a commons brings ruin to all" (1968, 1244). He uses this metaphor to argue that responsible people (*We*) need to ensure that irresponsible people (*They*) neither breed freely nor assume that they have a right to global commons such as food supply or other resources. Yet this violently Malthusian stance (see chapter 2 and the discussion there on Malthusian arguments) assumes that all commons resources are open-access rather than communally held, joint property (Ostrom 2008). The use of such commonly held resources is often guided by agreed-upon rules. Additionally, Hardin assumes that only state-established, centralized control of a commons can avoid the tragedy of overuse, overharvesting, and the decline of a resource (Dietz, Ostrom, and Stern 2003; see also Ostrom et al. 1999). However, it is important to see that "tragedies of the commons are real, but not inevitable" (Ostrom et al. 1999, 281).

Common-pool resources can be managed if appropriate rules and institutions (the means of implementing those rules) are established. Common-pool resources such as forests and fisheries are at the same time depletable and renewable, and each case of a common-pool resource is unique. There is no one-size-fits-most blueprint for a set of rules or governance institutions to manage a common-pool resource, but design principles may guide sustainable use. To be appropriately managed, a common-pool resource must have clearly defined boundaries. Governance systems should recognize multiple user groups and account for the monitoring of the resource. A common-pool resource governance system should not be wholly external to the resource, such as a centralized government. Instead, there should be "multiple layers of nested enterprises" (Ostrom 2008, 18), and institutional diversity should be a protected aspect of common-pool resource management (Ostrom et al. 1999). Conflict, or rather dispute, will be inevitable in a common-pool resource context, so governance systems must enable the identification of conflict as well as the means for resolution of differences.

Collaborative management of common-pool resources provides a helpful counter example to a more familiar (and Malthusian) way of thinking that scarcity will inevitably lead to conflict. Although not all resources may be managed as common-pool resources, this example allows us to think differently about who benefits from resource use and how that is determined. When we consider the question, *What is being secured and for whom?* common-pool resources remind us to look behind the discourses explaining, justifying, and enabling particular kinds of resource extraction and use. It helps us to see who indeed is benefitting and how those arrangements are reinforced by text or narrative, by material realities of infrastructure and altered environments, by the ways in which groups of people are identified, labeled, empowered or disempowered, and by practices touted as *needed* or *unacceptable*.

From Resource Conflict to Slow Violence

A shortcoming of a focus on conflict is that it tends to emphasize *hot conflict* that is visibly violent and immediate. Sabotaged oil rigs, maliciously destroyed dams, armed disputes over access to environmental features, military troop deployments to secure energy or water infrastructure—these are the kinds of events that capture media attention. There tends to be a focus on quantifiable events: When did it occur? How many people were hurt or killed? How much land or territory was lost or gained? Again, we see familiar, Enlightenment-era thinking in that only that which may be counted actually counts.

In stark contrast to this way of thinking about conflict is slow violence. Unlike camera-ready, violent conflict in which danger and destruction are immediately evident, slow violence is a form of danger and destruction that unfolds more slowly over time. It is a form of conflict that operates at spatial and temporal scales that do not grab headlines. Johan Galtung, a scholar and a founder of the field of peace studies, identified this kind of violence in a publication in 1969. He recognized direct violence as a physically manifested incapacitation happening at the hands of an actor who intends the outcome. Direct violence occurs as a discernable event by a perpetrator who has a purpose. Asher Kaufman (2014, 441) has commented on this kind of violence: "To be sure, it is tempting and perhaps natural to study direct, physical violence. It is easy to see it, to collect data on it, to know who the perpetrator is, and to discern cause and effect. Undoubtedly, it is necessary to study this form of violence because of its devastating outcomes." Galtung (1969, 168), however, took an alternative approach and defined violence as "the cause of the difference between the potential and the actual, between what could have been and what is. Violence is that which increases the distance between the potential and the actual." With this understanding of violence, Galtung recognized that violent incapacitation is not necessarily direct or intentional. Instead, he looked at structural or indirect violence that is built into the structures of society. It is evident as unequal power and, as a result, unequal life chances. He noted that "structural violence is silent, it does not show—it is essentially static, it *is* the tranquil waters" (173). A similar concept of "creeping environmental change" was put forward by Michael Glantz (1998) to describe ecological degradation that happens imperceptibly over time.

More recently, Rob Nixon has expanded upon Galtung's approach with his work on slow violence. In his book, *Slow Violence and the Environmentalism of the Poor* (2011), Nixon offers a closer examination of slow violence as exposing destructive elements of dominant narratives about human-environment relationships. Nixon looks at several cases in which people have worked to challenge a dominant discourse about human-environment relationships. Nixon tells the story of people in Nigeria struggling for environmental justice in the face of powerful actors controlling the country's oil supply. He writes about the grassroots Green Belt Movement in Kenya that sought to promote a different understanding of security following years of authoritarian rule and environmental destruction. He describes cases where resource development, such as the construction of large dams, has led not only to ecological destruction but also to the displacement of supposedly surplus people. These are examples of slow violence not only because they are destructive over time but also because the violence they involve has to do with who gets to decide the course of human-environment relationships in a particular place. In each case, dominant discourses take the form of narrative and policy, practice, materiality, and certainly identity in that the people most negatively affected by these decisions were also the most powerless and usually rendered invisible by the dominant discourse. Part of the violence in each of Nixon's cases is the very invisibility of alternative perspectives and approaches to valuing both humans and environmental systems.

In this work, Nixon (2011, 11) focuses on "the representational challenges and imaginative dilemmas posed not just by imperceptible violence but by imperceptible change whereby violence is decoupled from its original causes by the workings of time." Consider the "representational challenges" Nixon refers to here. If we are talking about violence that is not immediately evident and that, over time, emerges without a clear perpetrator or intentionality, how do we represent slow violence? How can we measure this process and outcome in numbers or in images? Given society's penchant for Enlightenment-era abstraction through quantification, slow violence poses a challenge. How do we know slow violence when we see it?

Slow violence may emerge from specific decisions about known or unknown risks. For instance, long-term health impacts can result from decisions such as what kinds of additives are allowed in food, what levels of contaminants are acceptable in water supplies or construction materials, and what kinds of waste management practices are enforced across a range of industrial activities from mining to manufacturing. Slow violence can result from a lack of understanding of processes, interactions, and effects. After the explosion at the Chernobyl nuclear facility in Soviet Ukraine in 1986, the diffusion, stability, and health effects of radioactive fallout were not fully understood. Since radioactive material is largely invisible, our understanding of radioactive contamination requires construction to make it *visible* as a known hazard (Kuchinskaya 2014). The Soviet government attempted to control what was known about the effects of Chernobyl, the spatial extent of the danger, and how people should respond to the event, such as whether or not to stay in the area or eat food grown in areas near ground zero of the explosion. The Soviet government delayed communicating critical information about the radioactive cloud, and this may have been due to disputes among experts regarding radioactive risk. Due largely to poor communication about risks to humans and ecosystems, thousands of people living in affected areas of Ukraine, Belarus, and Russia and emergency workers at the site were affected by the radiation. Yet it is impossible to know definitively how many deaths, incidences of cancer and radiation sickness, fetal deaths, and other long-term and fatal health effects are directly attributable to the Chernobyl accident. There is no accurate way to quantify specific and direct effects on human well-being that this incidence had immediately after the explosion, in the time since then, or into future generations. It could be argued that the Soviet government's poor management of the Chernobyl disaster contributed to a weakening of public trust and an enabling of political opposition that contributed to the collapse of the Soviet Union (Pickett 2016). The accident at Chernobyl and how information and uncertainty about it were managed illustrate the insidious nature of slow violence as it unfolds over space and time.

University and college students reading this book may not recall the *Exxon Valdez* oil spill of 1989. The *Exxon Valdez* oil tanker ran into a reef causing over eleven million gallons of crude oil to spill into the waters of Prince William Sound in Alaska. In addition to the marine ecosystems, over 1,300 miles of wild shoreline were damaged (see map 3.2). That was nearly thirty years ago. As of 2010, fewer than half of the wildlife populations and habitats that are being monitored have recovered, but many have not. Government sources have concluded that "there appears to be no hope for recovery" (Holleman 2014). The *Exxon Valdez* was not the first, or anywhere near, the largest oil spill (see map 3.2), but it is an example of the tremendous and enduring damage that oil spills inflict on ecosystems and on human health and well-being.

It is not always clear what is known or unknown about a hazard or risk, and uncertainty can also play into slow violence. Naomi Oreskes and Erik Conway look at examples of the power of doubt in their book *Merchants of Doubt: How a Handful of Scientists Obscured the Truth on Issues from Tobacco Smoke to Global Warming* (2010). They tell the story of how the tobacco industry was

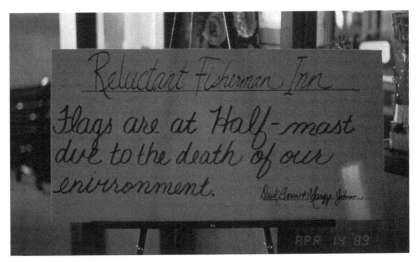

Sign at the Reluctant Fisherman Inn in Cordova, Alaska. Local residents lamenting the damage to Cordova's fisheries in the wake of the Exxon Valdez oil spill, April 14, 1989.
Source: Wikimedia Commons

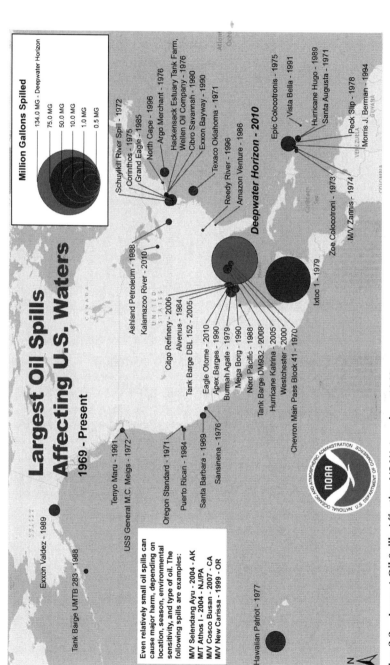

Map 3.2. **Largest Oil Spills Affecting US Waters since 1969**
Source: National Oceanic and Atmospheric Administration (NOAA), Office of Response and Restoration

under increasing pressure as scientific evidence linking cigarette smoking and lung cancer was mounting. Instead of trying to combat that evidence directly by supplying counter evidence, the tobacco industry worked to create doubt about whether or not cigarette smoking is a direct cause of cancer. That is, people in the tobacco industry did not have to disprove the science linking cigarette smoking to cancer, they just had to generate doubt in people's minds and weaken the perception of risk. In the same way, the authors argue, people who are benefitting from the status quo, such as leaders in the fossil fuel industry, are trying to create doubt about the causes or the likely impacts of climate change. In both instances, generating doubt about how our lifestyles contribute to risk may be seen as perpetuating conditions that undermine our well-being and keep us from considering alternatives.

Slow violence is clearly relevant for human suffering, resulting from decisions made and actions taken, but it can also be relevant for environmental features such as wildlife, ecosystems, and ecosystem services, such as clean air, water, and soil. Throughout this chapter, there has been repeated mention of how resources are valued. That point becomes particularly important when discussing slow violence because economic pricing of nature does not necessarily take into account the full cost of those uses. Environmental externalities are impacts, usually negative, which are not reflected in the price or other valuation of resources. For instance, earlier in this chapter there was a description of strip mining for coal. The price of a ton of coal, its dollar value, does not take into account the downgraded water and air quality resulting from strip mining, the destruction of ecosystems and landscapes, or the health of people affected by strip mining operations. Those are all externalities. Those are all, too, aspects of slow violence.

It is also important to recognize spatial aspects of slow violence: "What appears to be equitable or sensible at one level of environmental decision-making may, in fact, have significant implications for slow violence in particular places where impacts of higher-level decisions play out over time" (O'Lear 2016, 5). This point reiterates a theme throughout this chapter; namely, that connections between and among places and processes merit attention if we are to analyze discourses—as text or narrative, practice, materiality, embodiment, and identity—about human-environment relationships. These discourses, such as those that explain how resource scarcity leads to conflict, tend to narrow our thinking to focus only on a certain place, a particular process, and a given time. However, when we think in terms of slow violence with its longer time horizons, spatial inequities, and uneven distributions of power, we are better equipped to examine familiar, persuasive, but narrow discourses.

Conclusion

This chapter has discussed several aspects of resource conflict to demonstrate how this label is not very useful in helping us to understand the many different ways that environmental features and resources become tied up in different forms of dispute, tension, and violence. The chapter began by looking at resource scarcity and resource abundance as limiting our thinking to the confines of environmental determinism. Treating environmental features as though they have intentional agency hides the fact that economic, social, or political arrangements are most often to blame for the skewed distribution of environmental benefits and costs. This point demonstrates directly a key theme of environmental geopolitics: humans' role or agency is often obscured from view rather than openly examined. In particular, dynamics of power often remain invisible and uninvestigated even though they may have considerable influence over outcomes. Focusing on the role of resource scarcity or abundance diverts attention from human systems—political, economic, and social—that shape the way we use and value environmental features such as timber, metals, gems, arable land, or energy resources. Taking a closer look at resource characteristics is helpful in understanding how particular resources and features are associated with these human systems. Is a resource lootable and easily smuggled? What kind of refinement or processing does it require to be useful? What kinds of transportation networks move this feature to consumers, and how do consumers know that this feature is useful or valuable? These kinds of questions get us closer to thinking about the *socionature* of environmental features and how resources are social processes. Resources and the human systems that utilize or value them shape each other. Thinking in terms of a resource complex also helps us to think spatially about environmental features. How are their source locations, transportation networks, refining processes, consumption, and associated waste connected across different places, and what kinds of effects do these interactions have on specific places, peoples, and environments?

Security and risk do not emerge directly from the presence or absence of a particular resource. Rather than looking at resources as a stand-alone stockpile, examining how a resource or environmental feature is integrated into societal systems as a constructed commodity allows us to see how security and risk are also constructed. How a given resource or environmental feature is used, valued, controlled, who benefits from its use, and the spatial patterns of positive and negative impacts of resource use may all contribute to the kinds of risk or security—possibly even both—associated with that resource or feature. Ultimately, resources are constructed as they are integrated into human systems, and human systems also respond dynamically to these resource uses. Think of the example of different power dynamics associated with coal versus liquid petroleum. This chapter has discussed examples of how various aspects of resources are reflected in discourse in the form of text and narrative, practice, materiality, and embodiment or the identification and labeling of groups of people.

Similar to these complexities of resources, conflict has also been discussed in this chapter as an oversimplified and malleable term that does not adequately capture multiple forms of disagreement or tension related to environmental features. Conflict is most often understood as armed, violent conflict, and there are unfortunately many instances of this kind of conflict. However, this understanding of conflict draws our attention away from other forms of violence and injustice. Conflict databases can be useful for investigating some aspects of armed conflict. However, it could be argued that the tendency to focus on quantifiable aspects of conflict reflects Enlightenment-era thinking that established now familiar practices of abstraction and objectification of resources. (How much is a diamond worth? How are "safe" levels of pollution of air or water determined?) However, asking *what is being secured and for whom?* allows a more nuanced examination into processes of dispute or disagreement through which the status quo is challenged or altered. This question also brings to our attention the fact that some groups of people benefit from engagement with environmental features, while for other people the same activities may generate insecurities. What this means is that risk emerges differently for different groups of people and in different places. Although it is of course important to study, understand, and address armed conflict in its many variations, focusing solely on armed conflict and other forms of hot and quantifiable violence obscures other ways that some people may be particularly vulnerable to violence that is less obvious or immediately evident. Finally, a focus on conflict overlooks alternative approaches to problem-solving and dispute resolution that may be collaborative and equitable.

The critique of the concept of resource conflict throughout this chapter has emphasized the importance of looking beyond the physical aspects of a particular resource (e.g., diamonds, oil, food supply) and a fixed location to recognize entanglements of human and environmental systems. They shape and change each other. Between asking the question of *what is being secured and for whom?* and an appreciation of slow violence, our ability to analyze discourses related to environmental features expands. We are able to see how power dynamics and priorities are exercised and justified. Beyond text and narratives—how these processes are discussed, promoted, or silenced—

material realities are more evident, practices are revealed as perpetuating or challenging certain views, and lived experience of environmental benefits or injustice may be better understood. With this comprehensive and nuanced understanding, we find ourselves in a better position to develop policies and practices that are more just and that are context appropriate rather than one-size-fits-all. To that end, this chapter closes with an example from a researcher who interviewed subsistence farmers in India about their experiences of increasing temperatures and unpredictable weather patterns associated with climate change (Wapner 2014). He recounts his conversations with these farmers who grow only enough food for their families, not for sale, and their anticipation of having less food available as well as fewer seeds. He talks about their "climate suffering":

> Climate suffering, like much hardship, is not simply a fact of life but a consequence of politics. It emerges from configurations of power that grant privilege and, like many structures, operate through the "soft knife of routine processes" [Arthur Kleinman, Veena Das, and Margaret Lock, eds., *Social Suffering* (Berkeley, CA: University of California Press, 1997), x]. These processes are themselves hard to see. They stretch from the coal mines of China, tar sands of Canada, falling rainforests of Brazil, and oil deposits of Saudi Arabia to tailpipes, kerosene lamps, iPhones, rice paddies, and thermostats throughout the world . . . climate suffering is the epitome of what Rob Nixon calls "slow violence." . . . Scorching drought and torrential rains may originate from everywhere and thus nowhere, but still arrive like a stiletto. (2014, 4)

The farmers were not stricken by sudden plight that might generate international media attention and humanitarian aid efforts. Their situation was a slow, if somewhat fitful, decline in the quality of their livelihoods and future prospects. Who is to blame? There is no direct perpetrator who set out to target their well-being. They were not fighting among themselves as Malthusian scarcity narratives might anticipate. Their way ahead is uncertain, and arguably, it is our way ahead, too. We turn, then, to the topic of the next chapter, which examines climate change specifically and why it is important to understand efforts to *secure* the climate.

CHAPTER FOUR

Climate Change and Security

Most readers of this book will be familiar with issues surrounding climate change. No longer confined to the shrouded halls of scientific institutions, climate change is a topic that appears frequently in the popular press. For instance, *Rolling Stone* magazine's October 2015 front cover was devoted to "Obama's Climate Crusade." Just over a year later, after Donald Trump was elected as US president, *Rolling Stone* headlined climate change again with a new battle plan that began: "Calling the Trump energy and environment squad 'climate deniers' is like pointing out that your local crew of meth heads has bad teeth. It's true, and it also confusing the symptom with disease" (McKibben 2017). Most Americans' understanding about climate change is based on exposure to media and news coverage, the Internet, and videos of distant places rather than on personal experience. That may be, at least in part, why polls in the United States indicate increased polarization in public understanding of climate change despite the fact that scientific consensus is becoming more aligned (Weber and Stern 2011). Concern about climate change by the US public competes with other issues, such as the economy and political events (Capstick et al. 2015). Meanwhile, the US government—and the military in particular—has been paying increasing attention to climate change and implications for national security. How has climate change become a security issue, and what does that mean?

This chapter examines how climate change is linked to security and risk and examines how themes of territorial geopolitics play into these discussions. Following the theme of environmental geopolitics that is the foundation of this book, this chapter focuses on climate change and security discourses with a focus on US climate security discourse to consider how:

- The role and meaning of the environment are rarely specified.
- Humans' role or agency in these situations tends to be considered selectively. In particular, dynamics of power remain invisible and uninvestigated.
- Insufficient attention is paid to spatial dimensions of human-environment relationships that occur unevenly in different places and are intertwined with local, political, and cultural geographies.

As we look at the official climate security discourse in the United States, we will consider how elements of this discourse are stabilized. Specifically, we will consider how and why climate change became a military and security issue for the United States and how this climate security discourse has been both stabilized and critiqued. The field of critical security studies offers a helpful approach to interpreting discourses of climate security. Finally, we will reconsider how we think about risk in our efforts to build security.

Chapter 3 considered environmental security in terms of debates about resource conflict. A key idea in that discussion was to ask the question, *What is being secured, and for whom?* (see Dalby 2009). Here, we can apply the same question to political, economic, and social responses to climate change. As discussed in chapter 3, one critique of discussing environmental issues in terms of security is that it sets up the wrong kinds of problem-solving approaches (Deudney 1991). That is, military organizations, established to use physical force as needed to maintain the territorial integrity of a particular state, are unlikely to be the appropriate sort of organization to deal with boundary-transcending, environmental issues that are better addressed through collaborative efforts (for more discussion on this point, see Gilbert 2012). Another critique was that the United States and other Western or rich world governments were building up environmental concerns as a security threat as a way to boost the legitimacy of military institutions (and budgets) after the end of the Cold War (Barnett 2001). With the end of the Cold War, this argument goes, Western military organizations no longer had a clear enemy, so they positioned environmental issues as new threats to justify the maintenance of military power. This move by richer parts of the world to securitize the environment—to portray environmental threats as a risk to human well-being—was also critiqued as a reinforcement of the priorities and consumption patterns of wealthier parts of the world over the needs of people in less economically developed places (Dalby 1999). Yet others saw in environmental security a way to broaden and deepen a traditionally rigid understanding of security to new objects and referents such as the biosphere (Myers 1993; see also Buzan, Waever, and de Wilde 1998).

Climate impacts are increasingly tied to security. Washington, D.C.–based Center for Climate & Security released a report on June 9, 2017, titled *Epicenters of Climate and Security: The New Geostrategic Landscape of the Anthropocene* (Werrell and Femia 2017). In that multiauthored report, chapters address concerns about state sovereignty, strategically important waterways, island states at risk of sea level rise, the potential of using scarce water resources as a weapon, implications for nuclear power, melting Arctic ice, food security, human migration and displacement in response to a changing climate, and other concerns tying climate dynamics to security. Indeed, warmer temperatures and more frequent droughts and floods are linked to unstable food and water supplies and may contribute to increased tension in vulnerable places where backup options are not readily available (Schwartz and Randall 2003; Parenti 2011; DoD 2010). Climate security would seem difficult to address on the basis of individual states since impacts of climate change do not adhere to territorial state boundaries. Yet what we see in the US government statements, discussed in the following section, is an emphasis on national security against the threat of climate change impacts. Official US discourse on climate security reinforces the idea of security within the sovereign territory of the United States. From an environmental geopolitics perspective, this stance raises questions about what climate security might actually look like. Does *climate security* somehow render some states stable and protected in the face of unprecedented shifts in severe weather patterns, floods, droughts, melting glaciers and polar ice, increasing acidity of the oceans, and altered atmospheric composition, while other states remain somehow at risk? What is being secured and for whom—and where—in discourses about climate security?

It is useful to consider a range of actors and interests beyond the state so that we can more easily see the workings of geopolitical discourse. Recall from chapter 1 that a geopolitical discourse serves to stabilize a particular view of the world that sets a spatial agenda: some places or processes are to be secured from other processes that pose some sort of threat. Discourse may be in the form of narrative, text, image, practice, materiality, or embodiment. With critical geopolitics, we can question the positionality of a discourse to ask whose interests it serves. With this kind of approach, we can get beyond simplified arguments that *we*, here, need to act in some way to secure ourselves (or our space or way of life) from some threat *there*. Environmental geopolitics also helps us to see how environmental themes may be selectively portrayed to highlight or obscure elements of security or risk.

Stabilizing a US Climate Security Discourse

Toward the end of President Obama's term in office, there was a great deal of activity and attention paid to climate change and security. Within months of President Trump's swearing-in ceremony in 2017, however, he announced that the United States would withdraw from the Paris Climate Accord that was negotiated by 196 parties at the twenty-first Conference of the Parties of the United Nations Framework Convention on Climate Change (UNFCCC) in December 2015. The only UNFCCC member states that did not sign the agreement were Nicaragua and Syria; the Holy See could not sign the agreement because it was not yet a full member. In September 2017, Nicaraguan president Daniel Ortega reversed his country's stance and agreed to sign the accord. Nicaraguan leaders had thought the agreement did not go far enough in requiring wealthier countries to pay more to mitigate the damage disproportionately incurred by them. However, as Nicaragua is ranked as the fourth most vulnerable country to the effects of climate change according to the *Global Climate Risk Index 2017* (Kreft, Eckstein, and Melchior 2016), President Ortega decided to stand in solidarity with other countries likely to be early victims of climate change (Grandoni and Firozi 2017). As for President Trump, several of his own advisors tried to discourage him from withdrawing from the Paris Climate Accord. Additionally, Article 28 of the agreement allows a member to withdraw only if that country gives notice three years after the agreement is in force in that country. That means the United States could not officially withdraw from the Paris agreement until 2019, and even then, international law could prevent acceptance of the withdrawal if correct steps for withdrawal from either the UNFCCC or from the Paris agreement are not taken. As of this writing, it remains unclear how the Trump administration will follow up or follow through on its announced plans to withdraw from the agreement, and it also remains unclear if efforts will persist in linking climate to security.

This section of the chapter focuses on recent US government documents and statements about the role of climate change in security matters. Our consideration of these documents that predate the Trump administration follows Lene Hansen's (2006) approach to discourse analysis introduced in chapter 1. Regardless of whether or not this examination proves to be entirely historical or insightful for future military practice, it allows us to examine how these texts, as examples of US climate security discourse, stabilize a certain understanding of climate security.

From an environmental geopolitics perspective, we are interested in how this discourse specifies the role and meaning of the environment, how the

Climate Change and Security 107

Activist artists of the Brandalism project created posters to challenge corporate sponsorship of the UN COP 21 Climate Conference in Paris. The aim of this project was to satirize corporate messaging, question consumerism, and highlight planetary effects of fossil fuel consumption.
Source: http://www.brandalism.ch

role of human agency and power dynamics are presented, and how spatial relationships among places and processes are considered. Of particular concern in this section is how US climate security is spatialized. That is, how do these documents present climate change as linked to places and spatial processes that are secure or that pose a threat? What kinds of places or spatial processes are prioritized for security, and what kinds of places or spatial processes are described as a risk that justifies some action? As we look at these discourses linking climate change to risk and security, we want to know, *What is being secured where and for whom?* Adding *where* to this question helps us to focus on the identification of spaces of security and risk in this discourse. In the next section, we will shift our attention to security as practice and the extent to which these texts establish climate security as a practice, not *just* as a textual discourse.

In 2006, Margaret Beckett, then UK Foreign Secretary, used the term *climate security* to move the topic of climate change into a place of priority on the international agenda (Beckett 2006, cited in Trombetta 2008, 595). She was one of the first to use the term *climate security*, and it has come to mean different things. One study on how media in different countries represent climate security found that in some countries, like the United States, the United Kingdom, and Australia, climate change is increasingly tied to security concerns, but in other countries, such as India and South Africa, the media are using less security language in their coverage of climate change (Schäfer, Scheffran, and Penniket 2015). There are also differences in the scale and dimensions of security linked with climate change. Some countries focus more on national security, and others emphasize human security considerations. Media coverage in richer, Western countries focuses more on national and energy security, whereas food and water security tend to get more attention in the media of less economically developed states (Schäfer, Scheffran, and Penniket 2015). The point is that, just as there are multiple, simultaneous geopolitical discourses explaining the world in different ways, so there are also multiple, simultaneous discourses about security related to climate change.

National security has traditionally been associated with military endeavors, and climate change has received increasing attention from the US military and defense establishment. In 2006, the Center for Naval Analysis (CNA), a nonprofit research organization, convened a military advisory board of retired US military leaders to assess implications of global climate change on national security concerns. Their first report, in 2007, identified climate change as a *threat multiplier* that could contribute to instability not only in already volatile areas of the world but in relatively stable places as well (CNA 2007). The report recommended the integration of climate change issues into national security and defense planning. This report was not an official government document, but it drew considerable attention since high-ranking, former military leaders wrote the report, leaders who, in retirement, could more freely make policy recommendations. What we see in official government documents, which are forms of discourse, is that official documents that establish the priorities of the US government and, predominantly, the US Department of Defense (DoD), increasingly reflect the stance of the CNA report. Climate change is portrayed as a threat multiplier. For our environmental geopolitics perspective, we are particularly interested in the spatial and geopolitical dimensions of those threats.

Shortly after the release of the CNA 2007 report, the National Defense Authorization Act of 2008 required that the *National Security Strategy*, the *National Defense Strategy*, and the *Quadrennial Defense Review* (QDR) all include guidance regarding projected risks of climate change and strategies for mitigation, capacity building, and response preparedness to disasters influenced by impacts of climate change. To that end, the QDR of 2010 (DoD 2010) recognized that climate change, while not a direct cause of conflict, may contribute to instability and poses risks to US military installations. By 2014, the QDR (DoD 2014b) recognized that the impacts of climate change, together with other global dynamics such as urbanization and increasing population and consumption levels, "will influence resource competition while placing additional burdens on economies, societies, and governance institutions around the world" (8), thus requiring enhanced preparedness, risk mitigation, and "operational resiliency" (25).

Although these official defense-related documents recognized risks associated with climate change, the CNA produced a second report to communicate its concern that not enough was being done to address the threats posed by climate change. The second CNA Military Advisory Report (2014) articulated heightened concern regarding climate change. The authors note that climate change has the potential to be a catalyst for cooperation, but that climate change impacts may also be "catalysts for conflict" (2). The report recognized that climate change was rapidly becoming a more significant concern, and that stalling to act would foreclose options to address climate change risks.

The fall of 2014 saw the release of the *Department of Defense 2014 Climate Change Adaptation Roadmap* (DoD 2014a). While not a policy issuance per se, this document utilizes the concept of climate change as threat multiplier to consider how climate change impacts might influence any number of security threats from the diffusion of infectious disease to terrorism. It also outlines how climate change impacts could reduce the capacity and operations of the US military. For instance, melting Arctic ice and new conditions of seasonally open waters for navigation and resource exploitation may require greater US military capacity in that region. Sea level rise will negatively impact many coastal US military installations in the domestic United States. Quoting military strategist Carl von Clausewitz's famous dictum that "all action must, to a certain extent, be planned in a mere twilight" (DoD 2014a, forward), the *Roadmap* urges military planners to take action now, in a context of imperfect knowledge, to build joint capacities despite uncertainty, politics, or ideology.

Let's pause to note some trends in these documents so far. Each of these documents contributes to the stabilization of a discourse that positions climate change as a threat that should be dealt with as a security issue. The texts stabilize a particular framing of climate change impacts as something that can and should be addressed by military means or seen as threats to US military capacity. In positioning climate change impacts this way, this overall discourse sets parameters for the conversation. First, the discourse presents anticipated climate change impacts themselves as the threat, not the human systems that have contributed to climate change in the first place. Second, with that move, the discourse draws a line between human and environmental systems. This distinction is important because it renders the environment as something that is separate from humans and something that we can study, analyze, and manage as a distinct entity. This point returns us to the discussion from chapter 1 about the Anthropocene and humans' irreversible alteration of environmental systems. We can argue that viewing humans as separate from the environment allowed for destructive practices to be carried out with incredible global reach and unprecedented rate of change in the first place. The concept of the Anthropocene encourages us to see our fate as intertwined with that of our planetary life support system. A discourse that positions climate change as an environmental feature that threatens human well-being overlooks how human activity has contributed to the many systemic alterations that are grouped together under the label *climate change*.

These trends in isolating climate change impacts from human causes persist in more recent documents that further establish climate change as a security issue. The US government discourse on climate security gained considerable authority with a recent policy initiative. The first official US policy issuance regarding climate change as a security issue occurred on January 14, 2016, with the release of the Department of Defense Directive 4715.21: Climate Change Adaptation and Resilience. Unlike the *Climate Change Adaptation Roadmap*, this Directive is a policy issuance and, as such, "establishes policy and assigns responsibilities" to all components of the DoD and instructs the DoD to "manage risks associated with the impacts of climate change" (DoD 2016, 1). The policy aims to help the DoD achieve three main objectives:

- facilitate federal, state, local, tribal, private sector, and nonprofit sector efforts to improve climate preparedness and resilience, and to implement the *DoD 2014 Climate Change Adaptation Roadmap*
- help safeguard the US economy, infrastructure, environment, and natural resources
- provide for the continuity of DoD operations, services, and programs. (DoD 2016, 1)

No longer merely recognizing climate change as an urgent problem that should be addressed, somehow, at some point, this Directive operationalizes climate security for the US Department of Defense. It is a surprisingly short document of only twelve pages, and the policy statement itself is quite succinct:

> 1.2. POLICY. The DoD must be able to adapt current and future operations to address the impacts of climate change in order to maintain an effective and efficient US military. Mission planning and execution must include:
>
> a. Identification and assessment of the effects of climate change on the DoD mission.
> b. Taking those effects into consideration when developing plans and implementing procedures.
> c. Anticipating and managing any risks that develop as a result of climate change to build resilience. (DoD 2016, 3)

We might not expect a lot of detail in either of these brief passages—the statement of purpose and the policy priorities—but the brevity of these passages suggests that the components are mostly straightforward. The wording in the policy statement, for instance, suggests that identifying and assessing climate change effects is a straightforward process. It suggests that established methods already exist for taking effects of climate change into consideration and that planning efforts can smoothly fold in these considerations. Anticipating and managing risks also appears to be a clear process.

In truth, these steps are far from straightforward or clear. Approaching a complex task, such as identifying and assessing climate change effects on a defense mission, would seem to raise a nearly insurmountable number of questions and would require expert determinations at several points: How do we distinguish climate change effects from other kinds of impacts on a mission? How do we measure, understand, and anticipate those effects, and how they might play out in relation to other factors? What appear to be simple and straightforward policy priorities and guidelines are actually more likely to make for a complicated decision-making process fraught with options and opinions. From our environmental geopolitical perspective, we might look at these policy objectives and ask what the "environment" and "natural resources" in the statement of purpose refers to since safeguarding those things could mean any number of required actions. In the policy guidelines, "effects of climate change" could stand for a wide array of issues as discussed in the *Climate Change Adaptation Roadmap*—sea level rise, food shortages, diffusion of disease—and could be interpreted in many ways. Policy statements indeed tend to be vague. How they are interpreted and acted upon makes all the difference. Both of these statements, from the

Climate Change Adaptation Roadmap (DoD 2014a) and the DoD Directive (2016), could be used to support a variety of actions.

Let's look at two more recent documents before we step back to assess the US climate security discourse overall. On September 21, 2016, two important climate security documents were released: a memorandum by the National Intelligence Council titled "Implications for US National Security of Anticipated Climate Change," and a Presidential Memorandum titled "Climate Change and National Security."

The National Intelligence Council Report (NIC 2016) is informational and does not offer policy directives or even policy guidance. Instead, it uses the Intergovernmental Panel on Climate Change (IPCC) reports to analyze "possible impacts of climate change on national security" (3). The report identifies six possible pathways through which climate change is likely to challenge national security in the United States and other countries:

- threats to the stability of countries
- heightened social and political tensions
- adverse effects on food prices and availability
- increased risks to human health
- negative impacts on investments and economic competitiveness
- potential climate discontinuities and secondary surprises

The report provides examples of these pathways and considers different kinds of risk that may be likely now, over the next five years, and over the next twenty years. It includes a graph of projected average surface temperature change from the IPCC Fifth Assessment Report, and a map showing extreme weather events around the world from 2014 to 2015. The report acknowledges that "specific extreme weather events remain difficult to attribute entirely to climate change" (5), but notes that the IPCC anticipates irregular patterns of extreme weather events as becoming more frequent. It recognizes that climate scientists consider the risk of abrupt climate change to be low right now, but that the risk of abrupt changes is likely to increase over time. The report also recognizes that even gradual changes could lead to significant and unforeseen impacts. Again, there is no policy guidance or even judgment about conclusions made by the IPCC. The purpose of this report is to communicate how the intelligence community interprets the science reflected in IPCC reports as having implications for national security.

In a very different move, the stated purpose of the Presidential Memo (Obama 2016) on climate change and national security is to establish a framework that "directs Federal departments and agencies . . . to perform certain functions to ensure that climate change–related impacts are fully considered in the development of national security doctrine, policies, and plans" (Section 1). It recognizes that "climate change poses a significant and growing threat to national security, both at home and abroad" (Section 2). The Presidential Memo directs action at the highest level of government. The memo designates high-level leadership—the National Security Advisor and the director of the Office of Science and Technology Policy or people whom they designate—to oversee a new working group of members from a wide range of government agencies. The broad representation from across the branches and agencies of government provides a "whole of government" approach to climate security. The task of this working group is to identify and consider risks of climate change impacts and recommend data collection and intelligence analyses. The working group has a deadline by which it must produce an Action Plan to inform policy implementation. The memo elevates the issue of climate change impacts by requiring the consideration of these impacts in the "development and implementation of relevant national security doctrine, policies, and plans." Elevating an issue and prioritizing it, however, are two different things. Two important points to note about the Presidential Memo are as follows: it does not require the prioritization of climate change impacts over other factors, nor that climate change considerations should alter the established operations of the government.

Now that we have taken a cursory look at these government documents that stabilize a discourse of climate security, let's return to the three key observations that motivate an environmental geopolitics approach to examining discourses about human-environment relationships: the role and meaning of the environment; humans' role or agency considered selectively; and insufficient attention paid to spatial dimensions of human-environment relationships.

The Role and Meaning of the Environment in Climate Security Discourse

First, how do these documents specify the role and meaning of the environment? All of the documents considered here address climate change impacts, and they provide varying levels of detail as to what those impacts might be. Collectively, the documents describe the scope of climate change as including more frequent extreme weather events, unprecedented Arctic ice melt, negative impacts on food and water supplies, diffusion of disease and human health concerns, vulnerable energy infrastructure, disruption of transportation services, increased vulnerability of coastal locations, growing cities, and regions that are already experiencing water insufficiencies. The environment seems to include everything from natural systems, such as weather and ecosystems, to human-built structures, such as energy, food, and water supply systems that enable societies to process, move, and utilize these resources. As noted above, when such a varied list of items, processes, and systems is labeled as *climate change impacts*, it becomes difficult to ascertain which parts of these things are natural and which parts are human made or caused by humans. It certainly does not help us to see the intertwining of human and environmental systems and the effects they have on each other. They are all grouped as climate change impacts. Presented this way, it seems as though something outside of, or beyond, human activity is generating a threat. Using the term *climate change impacts*, as noted above, seems to separate what is natural from what is human so that climate change impacts become many forms of environmental threat. This separation does not facilitate an understanding of how human activity has altered many of the systems on which human life depends. The environment, in all the many forms that could count as climate change im-

The Svalbard Global Seed Vault, Norway. One of over a thousand seed banks around the world, the Doomsday Vault was established in 2008 as a global repository to preserve seeds and ensure crop diversity. A counterargument to this approach, however, is that encouraging indigenous agriculture might be a better means of enabling crops and other plants to adjust to a changing environment.
Source: Atlas Obscura (public domain)

pacts, is positioned as a threat to our way of life; therefore, according to this discourse, we must address these impacts as a security concern.

Second, what is humans' role or agency in climate security? In the Presidential Memo, President Obama mentions increasing global-scale efforts to "curb greenhouse gas pollution," but he does not directly state that greenhouse gases are understood to be the main contributing factor, chemically speaking, that is altering the planet's atmosphere. The other documents are also silent on the causes of climate change. Therefore, the discourse stabilized by these documents portrays humans as threatened by climate change, but not as contributing to climate change. The global fossil fuel–powered economy and human alteration of environmental systems are not addressed, so they are rendered invisible in this discourse. It is an important omission because without that recognition, there is no impetus for us to think about changing the activities that have brought us to this point. The focus on *impacts* positions climate change (the environment) as the threat, not our own extractive, economic activity. This omission allows the discourse and policy guidelines to focus on adapting to climate change rather than changing the activities that have caused it.

The solutions to climate change that tend to be put forward are mostly different forms of the same, problematic activity bound by the structures of neoliberal capitalism and modernity. Even though humans have not faced a situation as vast in its implications as climate change, we have tended to approach climate change as a problem that we can solve with traditional approaches such as economic calculations, governance solutions, and international treaty making (O'Lear and Dalby 2015, 3). So far, there has not been any sweeping, fundamental shift in thinking to recognize that ecological change is altering the very conditions for our political, economic, and societal systems (Hommel and Murphy 2013). Despite the bestselling book by Naomi Klein that boldly demonstrates how capitalism is the cause of our climate change predicament (Klein 2014), or Joel Kovel's (2007) discussion of capitalism as the enemy of nature, the idea of stepping back from our current operating system seems incomprehensible.

More broadly, the roots of climate change may be seen to lie in modernity and the way that modernity shaped humans' relationship with the environment. Modernity, a topic that can and has filled volumes of scholarly work, is the way of thinking that sets nature apart from culture. It is reflected in the notion that there are universal truths of knowledge and science, and that to wield this knowledge is to wield power. It is the mindset that enabled European colonization of the "New World" because peoples and places that were foreign or different were seen as merely another resource that could be used to expand the home economy. Modernity is also the mindset that views capitalism and its inherent competition as the rational way to organize human-environment relationships. There is much that could be said about modernity, but for our purposes, Leigh Glover (2015, 17; see also Glover 2006) has nicely summarized how the framework of modernity has shaped our response to climate change thus far:

> Modernity's response to climate change has three defining features: global management of the climate system largely through the knowledge systems of science and technology; the application of liberal-democratic governance through suitable institutions at national and international scales; and the management of the natural world for human purposes.

Glover discusses how each of these three defining features is fraught with contradictions that render the entire framework of modernity ill suited and inappropriate for addressing the issue of climate change in a meaningful way. Two particular shortcomings of current global management of the climate system—and Glover points out the hubris of thinking that humans can and should understand and intentionally manipulate the entire planetary system—are that we emphasize the role of states and that we simplify climate change to the measure of temperature. States, he argues, tend to focus on their own interests and on the relative short term, neither of which is conducive to addressing an issue as vast and far reaching as climate change. Then there is the issue of using planetary temperature as shorthand for climate change. Identifying a certain average temperature for the planet as preferable, and then working backward to calculate how many parts per million of carbon dioxide are allowable in the atmosphere to generate this temperature, lends an air of mathematical precision to a process that is complex, multifaceted, and dynamic. This approach also establishes an understanding that it is still possible to bring the numbers into a *safe* range and that humans can actually achieve that level of coordination and precision around the planet.

This reliance on the efficacy of science (more is better) reflects modernity in its faith in observation and measurement of physical, linear process. Hand in hand with prioritizing science, this view also prioritizes technology. It promotes the idea that more science will lead to better technologies that will somehow solve the problem. The emphasis is on developing cleaner fuels or greater efficiencies in energy consumption, but this focus does not help us to think about reducing consumption. That would be uncomfortable! New and better technologies will save us so that we do not have to change our habits or go without. We return to this discussion in the next chapter.

Returning to Glover's critique of modernity as our current approach to addressing climate change, he argues that environmental systems and natural resources cannot be protected in free market systems that rely on competition and perpetual growth. The economic system only protects environmental features to the extent that doing so does not disrupt the economic system. The relationship, in fact, is contradictory: "Modernity's relationship to ecology, as demonstrated in the climate change crisis, is marked by contradictions. Globalized models of industrialization have come to undermine the ecological systems on which the model is based" (Glover 2015, 28). Although economic incentives can help to reduce the production of greenhouse gases, these incentives will likely have the more significant effect of perpetuating current practices and delaying more fundamental changes. Glover suggests that we view climate change as a symptom of inequalities in well-being caused by a collection of current practices in policymaking, corporate activity, accounting methods, and marketing and points out that "our collective success in addressing climate change may well depend on the extent to which these forms of oppression can be rejected or overturned" (28).

Glover's discussion highlights how dynamics of power remain invisible and uninvestigated in many of our conversations and discourses about climate change. The tendency in our modern capitalist systems is to start unquestioningly with the assumption that there can be no other way to value resources, that there must be constant economic growth, and that science and technology will solve our problems. We do not tend to question the idea that resources or entire ecosystems are valued as though there is an objective, underlying truth to economics. Our society not only expects constant growth and upward mobility but also these improvements are expected to happen at an increasingly rapid rate. We want to have what we want, and we want it now. Similarly, it would seem that our scientific understanding of the world is quite advanced, yet the threat of climate change impacts seems to be moving in on all sides. Is it really as simple as doing more science and somehow applying that science to policy? The US discourse of climate security tends to point outward to threats imposed on us by an array of climate change impacts, but the discourse does not encourage much reflection on the systems that humans have established and prioritized that have shaped our current situation. Unless we look more closely at human agency underlying climate change, it is unlikely that our efforts, limited within problematic ways of operating, will lead toward meaningful change. Perhaps that is the key point: the current system favors some groups of people; changing the system would ultimately threaten that arrangement. Until we investigate or challenge the ways in which entrenched power dynamics perpetuate the situation of climate change, we will be unable to alter our course.

Returning to the US government documents on climate security, we can see how they stabilize the importance of certain forms of scientific knowledge and how they spatialize climate security. These are two useful aspects of climate security to examine from an environmental geopolitics perspective. One way in which the government documents we are considering here reflect modernity is in their predominant focus on addressing climate change by emphasizing science. The Presidential Memo creates the Climate and National Security Working Group and directs it to "develop recommendations for requirements for climate and social science data and intelligence analyses, as appropriate, that support national security interests" (Section 4.c.i). It also directs the identification and cataloging of climate science data, modeling, simulation, and social science data, as well as the identification of data gaps. It directs the production of "science-informed intelligence assessments" (Section 4.c.vi) and the sharing of climate-related data. The memo also calls for increasing the capacity for climate modeling, which represents components of the climate system mathematically, and for the development of "quantitative models, predictive mapping products, and forecasts to anticipate the various pathways through which climate change may affect public health as an issue of national security" (Section 4.c.xvii). The NIC Report (2016, 3) states up front that it "takes as a scientific baseline the reports produced by the Intergovernmental Panel on Climate Change" without evaluating or questioning the science of the IPCC reports. The persistent emphasis on science, and physical, mathematical science in particular, in these documents promotes these forms of knowledge as the only, or best, way to understand climate change. The reports do mention social science, but physical science is predominant. The message in these documents is that through measurements and modeling, an objective truth about climate change can guide policy responses and other actions both here and abroad. Again, the focus is not on trying to understand activities and contributing factors that have brought about the measurable symptoms of climate change, but about studying the symptoms (e.g., temperature, characterization of greenhouse gas sinks, etc.) to anticipate and address national security concerns related to climate change. The view being stabilized in these documents is that more science leads to better policy and practice.

There are those who are skeptical of claims drawn from climate science. There are also those who view climate change as a hoax and deny altogether that changes are happening. However, climate skeptics, for the most part, accept that the planet's climate is changing and that humans have contributed to those changes. Where skeptics tend to diverge from mainstream thinking about climate change is that they are less convinced of the amount or degree of human contribution to the changing climate. They tend to oppose what they view as drastic policy responses to climate change. A concern for climate skeptics is the difference between causation science and effect science. Causation science is able to connect human activity directly to changes in the atmosphere and ocean, and for many climate skeptics, that kind of science is persuasive. However, climate skeptics see science that cannot show direct human influence and that makes assumptions or extrapolations about effects of human activity on, for instance, coral reef die-off, sea level rise, the demise of polar bears, and so forth, as irrelevant. Climate skeptics also question how the sensitivity of physical systems is reflected in climate science. Many studies about atmospheric and oceanic change produce a wide range of values and possible future scenarios. Climate skeptics are wary of what they see as alarmist interpretations of these studies that gravitate toward the extreme findings rather than more middle-of-the-road, median values. For instance, a key question of climate science is: If atmospheric CO_2 is doubled, what happens to temperature? There is not a linear relationship due to feedback mechanisms such as clouds and aerosols. Will they absorb more heat, or will they reflect more heat? Climate skeptics emphasize that we do not have a full understanding of how these processes will interact, and so climate science should not serve as the basis for policy. Climate skeptics tend to oppose climate-related policy responses that would slow or obstruct international trade, involve significant transfers of wealth from richer to poorer countries, or transfer political power to supranational organizations such as the United Nations. Climate skeptics argue that these policy responses would likely have near-zero impact on climate but would have steeply negative impact on economic well-being. For climate skeptics, there is insufficiently clear evidence that human contributions to climate change should alter familiar practices of modernity and capitalism.

This discussion of modernity, capitalism, and science all point to our environmental geopolitics observation that, in discourses related to environmental issues, humans' role or agency in these situations is often considered selectively, and dynamics of power remain invisible and uninvestigated. We have come to understand these intertwined ways of thinking as the only possible option. They are not the only way to make sense of the world, but they are dominant in our society. Examining discourses of climate security means questioning the modes of thinking underlying our current circumstances. Without questioning how capitalism operates in relation to environmental systems or how our standard modes of science are innovative in some ways

Climate change graffiti. Public commentary allegedly by the anonymous graffiti artist known as Banksy.
Source: Matt Brown/Wikimedia

but blind in other ways, we will not be able to see as clearly how dominant discourses shape our thinking and our action (see O'Lear 2016). Who benefits from these foundational ways of thinking? What are the power dynamics that maintain these ways of operating? When we set prices, values, and quantitative measures on things, we are utilizing human-generated systems of understanding. What other options are available, and what alternative perspectives might those other options help us to understand? Once again, returning to our environmental geopolitical perspective, human agency tends to be considered selectively in these situations, and dynamics of power tend to remain invisible and underinvestigated.

Spatializing Climate Security

Our third observation from an environmental geopolitics view is that, in environment-related discourses, we do not pay sufficient attention to spatial dimensions of human-environment relationships that occur unevenly in different places. From an environmental geopolitics perspective, it is interesting to look at how these government documents spatialize climate security. That is, how do these documents describe where the threat or risk is, and where is security being ensured? These documents, including the *DoD 2014 Climate Change Adaptation Roadmap*, the DoD Directive, the NIC Report, and the Presidential Memorandum, are all understandably focused on US national security since they are produced by organizations established to prioritize the interests of the United States. Yet they offer different ways of understanding spaces of risk and security. The *Climate Change Adaptation Roadmap*, for instance, considers how climate change impacts could increase the demand for US military in disaster relief and humanitarian efforts abroad. It also considers how climate change impacts could alter or impair training and operations in various locations involving increased fire hazard, amphibious landings, and "climate-aggravated flashpoints" (DoD 2014a, 9). Negative impacts on the built environment, such as US military bases at risk of sea level rise, and on the natural environment, such as impacts of thawing permafrost in Arctic regions, are also associated with climate change impacts. In short, the *Climate Change Adaptation Roadmap* considers the risk of climate change to be anywhere that the US military is currently operating or in places where new operations may be needed. Security is also located with the US military and its activities whenever capacity is maintained. In this instance, the *where* of climate change risk and security is wherever the US military and security agencies can maintain the status quo or pursue US national interests without too much trouble and through "refinements of existing processes" (9).

The Presidential Memo takes a different approach to spatializing climate security. Near the beginning of the document is the statement:

Sec. 2. Background. Climate change poses a significant and growing threat to national security, both at home and abroad.

National security, by this view, does not end with the territorial borders of the United States. Part of being secure *here* requires addressing risks in other places. At home (here), climate change could negatively impact the readiness of the US military or other security organizations and limit the capacity of these organizations to respond elsewhere to support international stability. International stability is a concern here because it is in the interest of the United States to have a predictable setting for the supply of commodities, transportation, and political engagement. Other ways in which the Presidential Memo links US national security to risk or threats *abroad* include human migration and displacement due to the impacts of climate change; global water and food security issues; and global-scale health issues involving humans, plants, and animals, and including possible pathways for such climate change impacts to have a national security–level impact on public health. In other words, there would appear to be many ways in which climate change could have negative impacts in other places that have connections back to the United States either through the movement of people, commodities, or environmental features. The Presidential Memo does not identify any places in particular or even the process by which threats elsewhere could have an impact on the United States. Indeed, it is even possible that these climate change–related risks could unfold within the US territory.

Let's look at a few examples to illustrate the kinds of concerns mentioned in the Presidential Memo. First, the memo points to the potential impacts of climate change–related human migration on US national security. An often-cited example of this concern is the conflict in Syria that has been associated with climate change–induced drought and a massive outmigration of people to Europe and elsewhere. Although an ongoing and unusual drought certainly contributed to the disruption of farming and food supply, the situation in Syria also involves a nonresponsive government, upstream control of river flow by dam building in Turkey (Gleick 2014), and complicated political relationships at the international level. This case of massive human migration illustrates the concern of climate change as a threat multiplier. Conditions were already difficult in Syria, and a climate change–induced drought seems to have made the situation much worse.

This linkage between climate change and the situation in Syria appears to be widely accepted, but one group of scholars has raised the question: "Is there clear and reliable evidence that climate change–related drought in Syria was a contributory factor in the onset of the country's civil war?" (Selby et al. 2017a, 240) They look to academic literature, government and nongovernment reports, rainfall data, climate model simulations, and personal interviews with Syrian refugees in Jordan. Following these investigations, they determine that there is "no good evidence to conclude that global climate-related drought in Syria was a contributory causal factor in the country's civil war" (241). They do recognize that impacts of anthropogenic climate change may have contributed to the onset of the conflict in Syria, but they caution against making unsupported or unprovable claims (Selby et al. 2017b; see the complete Forum on Climate Change and the Syrian Civil War in *Political Geography*, vol. 60, 232–55). There are many ways in which a changing climate could feasibly contribute to increased economic, social, and political tensions—and it likely already is. Scholarly work using statistical models to make claims about climate change and conflict has been challenged, however, for treating climate change as a variable that can merely be added to existing conflict analysis models rather than treated as an altogether different influence on human-environment relationships (Meierding 2013). Quantitative studies on climate change and conflict, although useful in many ways to assess trends and patterns, should be carefully interpreted. Not only are there a variety of methods that might be used, certain forms of evidence that can or cannot be included, and a variety of conditions and contexts that might be considered, but quantitative studies linking climate change and conflict should also be cross evaluated with qualitative and other forms of data and expertise (Detges 2017).

Returning to the Presidential Memo and how it links climate change to national security; it also identifies global-scale health issues involving humans, plants, and animals and the movement or diffusion of a particular health issue as a concern for national security. Here, we can think of the Zika virus, which has been shown to cause severe birth defects. At the time of writing, there is no vaccine or cure for Zika. Mosquitoes carry the Zika virus and are vectors of other pathogens, too, such as malaria and dengue. Mosquitoes are of particular concern in the context of climate change since warmer temperatures speed up their life cycle and allow them to mature and reproduce more quickly. Warmer temperatures also allow mosquito populations, as well as the populations of other disease vectors, to thrive in places that were previously too cold. Outbreaks of Zika are more likely in densely populated areas with poor sanitation, open water sources, and few window screens, so there are important human factors involved, too (Gillis 2016). Several factors contribute to disease epidemics, not just the presence or absence of a pathogen, yet climate change is thought to amplify the risk of vector-borne diseases and concerns for public health.

The Presidential Memo also states that global water and food security issues pertain to US national security both in terms of ensuring adequate supplies for the US population but also in terms of shortages elsewhere that could potentially lead to social unrest, political instability, and an increased need for disaster relief. Chapter 3 examined discourses on food security and water security, and, like other forms of security discourse, they are more complex and multifaceted than traditional security connotations suggest.

In each of these examples, there is a process *abroad* (although any of these processes could also reasonably unfold here in US territory) that is seen as something to be addressed, managed, or otherwise contained in order to limit the threat it poses to US national security in terms of economic strength, political stability, or public well-being. Any action taken on these kinds of issues would be usefully examined by asking, *What is being secured where and for whom?* It is helpful to look at how these examples of climate change–related threats abroad are linked to US national security, and how these human-environment relationships lead to uneven outcomes in different places.

Climate security discourse is somewhat contradictory. On one hand, climate change is understood as a global phenomenon and is analyzed by means of global data assembled from local data sets and global circulation models. A global view of climate change relies on an international network of scientific institutions and researchers using advanced techno-scientific methods. References are also made to global climate security as the international community tries to identify governance structures that will encourage cooperation in addressing climate change. We might ask what global-level security might actually mean in a world where economic disparity has become the norm (Litfin 1997). On the other hand, the concept of security is still often attached to traditional associations with the territorial state. The US climate security discourse is an example. What is the meaning of climate security in a world of many states? To what extent can we reasonably focus on *our* security as if one area of the planet's surface may be rendered secure even while entire planetary life support systems are shifting? These kinds of questions lead us to question what *security* means, and this point brings us to critical security studies.

Critiquing US Climate Security Discourse

Chapter 1 introduced the academic field of critical security studies as looking beyond a state-centered focus on military threats to study security more broadly. Security issues, in contrast to other political issues, tend to be understood as urgent and justify "responses that go beyond normal political processes" (Peoples and Vaughan-Williams 2015, 94). Why are some issues considered to be security concerns while others are not? Some of the early work in critical security studies, emerging from what is known as the Copenhagen School, examined how some issues are securitized and promoted to the level of high politics. This school of thought argued that the successful securitization of an issue takes it out of the realm of normal politics into a state of exception. From there, democratic procedures no longer dictate decision making, and the law itself may be suspended in order to deal with the urgency of the issue (Waever 1995; Buzan, Waever, and de Wilde 1998). From this view, securitizing any issue involves two steps. First, a speech move must frame the issue as a security concern. A speech move might be in the form of statements by a political representative or another narrative or document issued by a recognized authority. The second step of securitization, according to the Copenhagen School, is that the intended audience accepts that notion of security. It is relatively straightforward to identify the first step of securitization. Speech moves to securitize an object or issue are necessarily easy to identify since they intend to draw immediate attention. The US climate security documents examined in the previous section of this chapter exemplify this kind of securitizing speech move. It is more difficult, though, to find evidence that the intended audience accepts the construction of an object or issue as a security concern. How would we know if an audience accepts a particular presentation of an issue as a security concern?

One way to assess how securitization is understood is to look at securitization as practice. Practice, as discussed in chapter 1, is a form of discourse that serves to stabilize a particular understanding of the world. Practices may serve to implement a spatial discourse, resist a spatial discourse, or construct an alternative space to reflect a different understanding. Maria Trombetta (2008) has considered how efforts to legitimize climate change as a security priority have resulted in two main types of practice. The first practice is shaped by an understanding that we cannot prepare for all possible threats, therefore, we focus on emergencies only. This stance reflects Ulrich Beck's work on risk society (1992) also introduced in chapter 1. Although modern technologies enable advances in, say, transportation or energy and food production, these technologies also carry new forms of uncertainty and risk. Beck observed that, in a risk society, the aim is to study, measure, and model risk so that we may better prepare for emergencies when they do happen and be prepared to take calculated losses. Citing Giorgio Agamben, Trombetta emphasizes this point: "Today, there are plans for all kinds of emergencies (ecological, medical, military), but there is no politics to prevent them" (Agamben 2002, 24, cited in Trombetta 2008, 590). This kind of practice-by-response would likely fall back on a territorial understanding of the world and aim to keep threats out or contained elsewhere while securing well-being within certain borders.

This is where the second practice of climate security comes in: prevention. Trombetta, again citing Beck (2006), argues that "having a security logic based on evoking and governing through emergencies" (Trombetta 2008, 590) makes considerably less sense than trying to prevent catastrophes in the first place. It is not possible to remove oneself or one's society from the globalized web of risk, and this point is particularly true for climate change even though the impacts will certainly differ from place to place. Trombetta argues that securitization is about moving from the first practice of emergency response to the second practice of prevention. What is more, she argues that one of the problems with the Copenhagen School's two-step approach to securitization—a speech move and acceptance by the audience—is that it does not allow enough flexibility into our understanding of security. It imposes a rigid view of security as something to be identified by and achieved within territorial states. However, that understanding of security does not necessarily encompass climate security and instead requires new ways of thinking and practice (Trombetta 2008).

Another challenge to the Copenhagen School's two-step process of securitization comes from Rita Floyd (2010). She argues that a securitization move or justification of a threat is successful *not* when an audience accepts the discourse, but when there is a change in the relevant behavior of the relevant agent: "What matters are the consequences of securitisation alone" (7). In other words, in this view, climate security becomes *real* when there are actual changes in behavior to address climate change. That would (possibly) mean that we phase out our reliance on fossil fuel–based industrialization and economic growth based on income disparities in favor of sustainable and equitable ways of living.

Is there evidence of behavior change in response to the urgency of climate change? Can we identify new practices in acknowledgment that climate change poses an existential threat? The discussion earlier in this chapter of Glover's (2006, 2015) work on postmodern climate change suggests that the kinds of practices emerging in response to climate change—carbon offsets, green consumerism, and more—are simply more of the same valuation system that created climate change in the first place. He argues that these are not new practices. Naomi Klein makes the point even more boldly: capitalism, she argues, is *the cause*, not the solution to climate change. Other evidence we might point to as examples of practice as prevention might involve institutional changes such as government activity or different economic accounting practices that reflect the value of environmental features beyond an economic price tag. Here, we can look at the Presidential Memo and its creation of a whole-of-government working group as setting a pathway to new practices. The recognition of climate change as an important issue, and the formation of this working group are necessary first steps, to be sure. However, the Presidential Memo directs the working group to consider risks of climate change impacts alongside other concerns; it does not direct the group to prioritize climate change–related risks in its decision making and planning. President Obama's administration put climate change officially on the agenda, but there is no clear indication that the practice and process of decision making have been significantly altered.

One argument is that what *has* shifted is how climate change impacts are understood as a risk (Oels 2013). Since the 1990s, climate change has been addressed predominantly through a traditional risk management approach. This approach relies on a scientific assessment of acceptable levels of risk and views risk as manageable. The reliance on scientific interpretation of climate change reinforces the notion that risk is measurable, knowable, and controllable through appropriate calculation. We see this approach when, for instance, IPCC Reports about global temperatures and greenhouse gas concentrations in the atmosphere are used to shape international agreements aiming to reduce global greenhouse gas emissions. However, since the early 2000s, a different approach to understanding risk associated with climate change has emerged. This approach is risk management through contingency (Dillon 2008). Instead of viewing risk as scientifically calculable, risk management through contingency embraces the idea that risk or threats are possible, but not predictable. Tolerable risk is not identified because scientific knowledge is viewed as uncertain. Climate change, in this view, is not a future possibility; it is already happening. The emphasis turns to building capacity to cope with variability and shocks, and scientific questions become less about global forecasts and more about regional and local impacts of climate change.

In order to foster adaptation and build capacity for resilience to climate change impacts, risk management through contingency focuses on identifying vulnerable groups of people and vulnerable places (O'Brien et al. 2007, 79). Policy responses within this approach focus on government interventions to enhance the most vulnerable peoples' capacity to cope in uncertain environments. These policy responses, unlike traditional, science-based risk management approaches, tend to be social in nature, such as "poverty reduction, diversification of livelihoods, protection of common property resources, and strengthening of collective action" (O'Brien et al. 2007, 80, cited in Oels 2013, 24). Another way to view this approach to climate change risk is that "sustainable development is redefined as resilience of communities to [climate] change" (Oels 2013, 24). That is, established sustainable development projects are redefined as responses to climate change impacts. This approach also involves the *climatization* of security in which established practices of military and defense organizations are applied to climate change impacts as a problem to be addressed by military and defense-oriented means (Oels 2012). In the interest of conflict prevention, strategies focus on preparing for disasters, preventing the need for migration related to climate change impacts, and encouraging stability and resilience to environmental variability through development assistance. In either case, we do not see new and different practices that recognize climate change as an existential threat requiring aggressive efforts at prevention. We see established approaches and practices renamed with a climate change label.

Flooding in Bangkok, Thailand, October 2008. US Naval officer viewing unusual monsoon flooding that affected 8.2 million people across sixty-one provinces. How are military organizations likely to be called upon—and prepared for—climate impacts?
Source: US Department of Defense

Other authors have arrived at a similar conclusion that the dominant climate security discourse in the United States repeats established practices by framing climate change as territorial danger that should be addressed through military and defense approaches (Diez, von Lucke, and Wellmann 2016). That study compared the dominant climate security discourses in four countries to see how different discourses lead to different policy initiatives. The researchers observed that different places portray security aspects of climate change differently. They observed a continuum of threat from an immediate, existential danger to a more diffuse and less easily identifiable risk. They note that different discourses identified different referent objects to be secured in the face of climate change: the individual (much like human security), the state, and the planetary environment or ecosystem. For instance, climate security discourse in Germany tends to focus on danger at the individual level and emphasizes the role of scientific and civil society actors over the military. Germany has been relatively successful in advancing climate change mitigation measures, while Mexico, on the other hand, has not been as successful in securitizing climate change. Climate security must compete with other security concerns, such as organized crime and violence aimed at citizens. In part because there are other immediate security concerns in Mexico, climate security tends to be portrayed as a more diffuse risk to individuals. Despite projections of severe effects of climate change that are likely to occur in Mexico, scientific articulation there about climate change is cautious rather than urgent. For these reasons, links between climate and security in Mexico appear to be weaker than in Germany or the United States. In Turkey, however, attempts to securitize climate change are more difficult to find and have mostly been unsuccessful. In the United States, different administrations, such as Clinton's and Obama's, promoted efforts to mitigate climate change, but political and economic actors who stood to gain from the status quo have resisted these efforts. Linking climate security with danger at the territorial level and focusing on military approaches to containing spillover effects of climate change impacts elsewhere has given the federal government a way to act on climate change without prioritizing mitigation efforts.

According to another study, the military and defense approach to climate security in the United States is not new. Instead, it represents yet another phase of an ongoing militarization of the environment in the name of national security. Robert Marzec describes how the intelligence community introduced the concept (now turned academic field) of *natural security*, which understands adaptation to a shifting environment as a central feature of national security. This focus brings scientists and scholars together with intelligence and military experts to think through "adaptive techniques of natural security" (Marzec 2015, 3). Here, Marzec (2015, 4) suggests a different meaning of environmentality:

> The ecosystem . . . has now entered the national and global security imaginary . . . and its protection and development—its governance—has become a central military concern. Natural security and the rallying cry of adaptation are symptoms of a generalized phenomenon—what I refer to . . . as environmentality. Environmentality is, in part, the name for a militarized mentality, one that commandeers a consciousness to wholly rethink and replace a rich, complex, multinarrative environmental history with a single ecosecurity imaginary . . . environmentality is essentially environmentalism turned into a policing action.

There are two key practices associated with this view that couples nature with security: enclosure and adaptation. We discussed enclosure in chapter 2 as a practice to gain control of previously publicly used land for the benefit or interests of a small number of people. Here, enclosure is much the same in terms of intention to control space for the benefit of a few. Military technologies of enclosure include practices such as mapping, surveillance, and information-gathering techniques that expanded significantly in scope and reach during World Wars I and II. These practices or technologies *enclose* land by making selected aspects of it known, measured, and visible for certain purposes. They make it possible to secure places through privileged forms of knowledge of the land and a sense of control over resources or systems.

A second key practice that ties nature to security is adaptation. Marzec observes that adaptation is a necessary guiding concept in the face of inevitable climate change. The idea of adaptation is important for guiding scientific efforts that will help humanity to adjust to the unprecedented changes we face in our planetary life support system. However, Marzec urges caution when we see the concept of adaptation tied to the promotion of security. Security has tended to be associated with territorial politics and *Us* versus *Them* thinking, which is not necessarily the most useful way to think about our current, collective situation. Notions and labels of security tend to limit the way we think about problems and solutions. Worse, Marzec argues, security thinking closes down other possible ways of thinking. Thinking within the familiar box of security "supplants the hard work of thinking alternative futures to a neoliberal paradigm" (2015, 2). He reminds us that there have historically been options for alternative ways to think about our entangled relationship with nature and points to

> such diverse traditions as the wilderness sublime of Wordsworth and Thoreau, the ecstatic environmentalism of John Muir, the romantic primitivism of Jean-Jacques Rousseau, the land ethic of Aldo Leopold, the embittered inhumanism of Robert Jeffers, and the scientific environmentalism of Rachel Carson and Barry Commoner—to name only a few. (2)

Yet instead of seriously considering other ways of understanding our engagement with nature or the environment, there is a tendency to limit ourselves and our societies to thinking in terms of security. The problem with shaping environmental politics to fit the confines of security is that our options become limited toward "restrictive measures of homeland security" (3). In Marzec's words, "Adaptation provides perfect camouflage for military institutions bent on governing environmental anxieties from the standpoint of national security" (3). Security is the new war and the primary motivation for military activity. War, however, requires political approval and a clearly identifiable adversary. Security, "more insidious and ubiquitous" (225) than war, is promoted as a necessity for daily existence to maintain our way of life.

To be clear, though, military organizations do not necessarily define their own missions. It is more likely the case that government agencies or even economic actors identify military organizations as the appropriate institutions to address a problem even though military skills and might are not the best or only means of response. Indeed, utilizing military-based adaptation techniques is promoted as clear-headed and obvious:

> The common-sense solution of adaptation is found to be desirable not only by the state but by its citizens . . . adapting to the impending event of sea level rise, for instance, appears in all obviousness to be the clear-headed answer that cuts through not only the muddle of the "debatable" status of global warming but also the red tape of "big government" that keeps individual subjects from realizing their own freedoms and desires. (Marzec 2015, 25)

Security discourses stabilize the importance of militarized adaptation measures, and military and security organizations present seemingly apolitical decision making and action as "slicing through politics as usual" (215). It may be that a government is promoting a security discourse to make it appear as though something is being done beyond the gridlock of bureaucracy.

In a similar effort, the Transnational Institute is an organization based in Amsterdam and opposed to corporate efforts blocking meaningful action on climate change. This group asks the question, "What are the implications of institutions such as the Pentagon or corporations such as Shell re-framing climate change from an environmental and social justice issue to a security one?" (Buxton and Hayes 2016, 4). This group examines political and corporate power plays that favor militarized and corporatized responses to climate change that lead to "acquisition through dispossession" (14). They point to the example of carbon trading as a false solution that perpetuates the status quo and diverts attention away from just solutions. In order to amplify alternative responses and nondominant perspectives, this organization seeks to lift the veil of security narratives to show underlying workings of authoritarianism and profiteering.

They also question the incremental normalization and acceptance of military and corporate-minded responses to climate change that promote concepts of adaptation and resilience. These concepts, the group argues, serve mostly to push the burden of responsibility onto people who have not benefitted so much from advanced economies and who are the most vulnerable to risks associated with a changing climate. Instead, they argue, the focus should remain on the best responses for "people, not profit," and their work aims to show

> how concepts like "security," "adaptation" and "resilience" have joined the ranks of modern-day weasel-words: hollowed-out, appropriated and twisted to the point that they can mean anything and nothing at the same time. This requires critical thinkers to keep their spin-detector finely tuned toward corporate

and security elites promising to tackle the problems posed by climate change. More than that, we must simultaneously support the systems, structures, ideas and capacities that will genuinely contribute to a just adaptation while resisting those designed to entrench profiteering and authoritarianism. (239).

These challenges to an unquestioning acceptance of security narratives are well in line with an objective of environmental geopolitics. It is valuable to question and unpack terms and concepts that can serve as Trojan horses carrying unseen political agendas forward. It is also important, however, to be thoughtful about assumptions we might make about any particular group of people or organization. It is possible for corporations to support meaningful change that has a positive impact on people's lives. For instance, companies in India are working to bring electricity into rural homes by way of small-scale solar grids, and larger companies can influence positive change such as promoting large-scale organic farming or better distribution of basic health care to people in need. It is also likely that military units will be the frontline of response to humanitarian disasters, so to dismiss them as necessarily violent or destructive may not be conducive to generating options for responding to climate change.

Risk versus Not Knowing

These discussions on climate security (and securitizing climate and climatizing security) reinforce the idea that security is the opposite of the threat of danger or risk. The way in which we understand, study, measure, and promote climate change impacts as risks directly shapes how we respond to those risks. The previous section focused on the US security response as a dominant discourse, but other possible responses have also been mentioned in terms of how other countries have developed ideas about climate security and in terms of theorists who have thought outside of the security paradigm. Just as it is important to consider how security is stabilized as an idea and an acceptable category of action, it is also important to consider how risk is conceptualized and portrayed.

Chapter 1 introduced Ulrich Beck's work on risk and his observation that scientific progress and technological advances have brought about a new form of modern society that faces unprecedented kinds of unintended and uncontrollable risk. He labeled this situation as *risk society*. In recent re-readings of Beck's work, scholars have reconsidered Beck's contribution to our understanding of risk. One argument is that in identifying risk society, Beck recognized that we live in a social reality that is different from what had come before. Therefore, implicit in Beck's work is a call for a radical shift in how we understand our social reality: "to bring Beck into security studies, then, means to study 'security' *from within* his 'new world'" (Selchow 2016, 382). If we take seriously Beck's observations about the conditions in which we are living as a new kind of society, then we need to find new ways to think about and interpret it. One way to do this is to reconsider the very concept of risk.

Beck described risks in modern society as being difficult if not impossible to measure, as noncompensable (undesirable loss or suffering cannot be reasonably paid off or balanced by an opposing force), and as delocalized (the effects of, for instance, pollution, in one place are most likely tied to causes in other places). Another way to think about these conditions is *not knowing*: not knowing how to reasonably measure impacts, not knowing how to articulate the nature or form of loss, and not knowing how processes in different places are connected. There is considerable not knowing associated with the unintended side effects and the unpredictability of modern hazards. For Beck, things that were not known were inevitably a form of risk. Perhaps, though, a more useful way of thinking about these unknowns is to think of them in terms of not knowing or ignorance: "Non-knowledge should not generally be understood as unawareness or as the mere absence of knowledge, but rather as a specific kind of knowledge about what is not known" (Gross 2016, 388). Nonknowledge is not an empty space. Instead, it is information that makes possible new perspectives on security.

A shortcoming of focusing on risk is that it blurs what we know and what we do not know about a situation. For instance, the practice of risk assessment, which is a form of identifying and measuring potential threats, does not always reflect "clear knowledge about probabilities and outcomes" (Gross 2016, 394) since that information may not actually be available. In this case, "Risk then is merely a ritually used concept designed to smooth over conflict-laden issues for involved stakeholders" (394). A more responsible approach would acknowledge what is not known so that we might use that information to ask more meaningful questions about the implications of decision making. Reconceptualizing risk as nonknowledge allows more specific information to be brought to bear on security studies:

> Translated into issues of security studies, one could say this exemplifies a shift from conceptualizing security on the basis of knowing to a conceptualization of security in terms of not knowing. Put differently, to give people security and protection means that not knowing becomes a crucial aspect of a sense of security or safety. (394)

Increased knowledge and innovation open up areas of nonknowledge that may be useful in asking more creative questions.

This point about knowledge and nonknowledge, or ignorance, makes it all the more important to pay attention to knowledge production: Who is generating new knowledge, and what are the advantages and limits of that knowledge? How are new scientific understandings or innovations influencing decision-making options and outcomes? What about these new innovations or understandings are less clear or not known, and what might we learn from those areas of ignorance? For the purposes of our consideration of environmental geopolitics, we could usefully examine how new forms of knowledge and forms of not knowing are brought into textual and narrative discourses as well as discourses in the form of practice, materiality, and embodiment. How do different discourses of knowing stabilize our understanding of our relationship with environmental features, and how much attention are we paying to what we do not know about these relationships?

Conclusion

Throughout this chapter we have asked the question *What is being secured where and for whom?* In the case of climate security, we have seen that, in the US discourse, security *here* can imply action on many fronts elsewhere. We also see an identification of nature as posing a variety of threats in the form of climate change impacts, but there is little recognition of humans' role in generating the situation. Security, then, is outward looking rather than reflective about ways in which human systems might have—or may yet—develop differently. Military and defense-based conceptions of climate security persist but do not clearly demonstrate a meaningful change in practice that might indicate recognition of the unprecedented context we face in climate change. How might we utilize our nonknowledge or ignorance of our situation to generate meaningful responses in terms of practice? How might we examine what we do not know about climate change to bring about material discourses that reflect a creative and more flexible response to our dynamic reality?

The next chapter follows this line of thought by looking at science and imagery as ways of understanding and responding to environmental issues. Although there is a tendency to think that scientific understanding directly informs environmental policy, we will see that the relationship is not so clear. Just as this chapter has considered ways in which climate change science both informs and limits political responses to climate change, we will see in the following chapter how the production and selective promotion of knowledge is reflected in discourses about human-environment relations.

CHAPTER FIVE

Science, Imagery, and Understanding the Environment

We understand environmental features through direct experience in many ways. We change our outdoor activity plans according to the day's weather. We have the option to buy out-of-season produce because it has been shipped to our grocery store from a distant place. We notice that air feels fresher to breathe in a mountain setting or more unpleasant in a city at rush hour. However, much of what we (think we) know about the environment is influenced by information and data that other people have generated or interpreted. Often, our ideas and understanding about environmental features are shaped by scientific work and through the selective calculation and representation of information. Is the global atmosphere actually changing in composition? Are forests really being cut or burned down to make way for other land uses? Do our food crops actually require more water than might be available in the long run? How do we truly know about these processes, and what do we know about them?

There are many approaches to studying environmental features, and there is a wide range of scientific approaches, methodologies, and practices that have been established to examine and forecast environmental patterns and trends. Just as there are many scientific disciplines, there are many ways of studying and understanding the environment. In our society, there is a tendency to assume that the *right* science, and enough of it, will lead to the best policy. Science is thought to bring objective certainty and clarity to our understanding of environmental features and to decisions about how to manage resources.

This chapter challenges that view by investigating ways in which the three observations of an environmental geopolitical analysis—the unspecified role of environmental features, obscured power dynamics, and limited spatial clarification—come into play as science is used to inform policy and public understanding of key environmental issues. We will see why it is important to examine how science and scientific information stabilize discourses about the environment, particularly when these discourses say something about security or risk. This chapter looks at examples of the selective use of scientific information to construct and promote ideas about how we can maintain a secure environment or about how environmental features pose risk. It is important to think critically about how scientific information is used to support arguments about security and risk if we are to see a bigger picture of human-environment relationships. Asking questions about the selective use of science may, in fact, lead us to clarifying questions about human agency, power dynamics, and spatial connections that we might otherwise overlook.

The first chapter of this book discussed risk as a future event or concern. Risk is often discussed in terms of a threat that we can work to minimize. This understanding implies that risk can be somehow measured, calculated, modeled, and assessed. Security is often portrayed as the opposite of risk, so if we can measure, assess, and otherwise control the risk, it follows that we can achieve security. In either case, we can see how scientific approaches are invoked to aid in the observation, calculation, and prediction of risk and security. Yet no form of science can fully capture all dimensions of any particular issue or circumstance. Additionally, no form of science can adequately integrate complex human dimensions of a given situation. Often, our studies of human-environment relationships must simplify the human and environmental dimensions out of sheer necessity. Atmospheric circulation models represent data in grids or pixels rather than at all possible location points so that calculations are manageable. Biological studies focus on particular systems, processes, diseases, or interactions to look for cause-and-effect relationships. Even social science studies can only look at some variables of any social phenomenon: demographic measures, type of government, linguistic dynamics, and more. Simplification is necessary because otherwise it would be nearly impossible to generate clear observations about how things work. What is important for a meaningful critique of discourses about human-environment relationships is that we understand both the advantages and the limits of different scientific approaches. Scientific disciplines are not *wrong* or *right*, but each has its own constraints about what it can say about the world. Since scientific arguments can serve to stabilize discourses, we should give careful thought to the advantages and limits of the type of science being used to support an argument and about other approaches we might look to for additional perspectives.

To help us develop a curious stance toward the uses of science in discourses about the environment, the next part of this chapter discusses science and technology studies, or STS. An STS view helps us to understand science not as a kind of objective reality or truth, but as a view of the world that is socially constructed. Science is socially constructed in that it does not reveal truths about nature so much as it reveals trends in human values, our understanding about the world, and how we use scientific methods and technologies to observe the world. Scientific knowledge offers to explain "the way it is," but it is helpful to see that there may be other, simultaneous alternatives to understanding and portraying human-environment interactions. STS allows us to look at how the use of knowledge and information is selective. This perspective is useful when taking an environmental geopolitics approach because it provides tools and questions that help us to see how any particular scientific approach is both selective and necessarily incomplete. That is not to say that science is not useful; it certainly can be. Yet we must maintain a critical stance toward scientific claims so that we allow ourselves room to see what is missing from these claims. Often what we find is that what is missing is precisely what is at the heart of an environmental geopolitics approach: unspecified roles or functions of environmental features; human agency and obscured power dynamics; and a limited view of spatial processes and connectivity.

Science, Technology, and Society

Chapter 1 discussed the images of Earth from space to make a point about the interplay between information and understanding. Different groups of people imposed their own meanings on those first images of our planet as a way to illustrate their particular political agendas (Jasanoff 2012). The images served as scientific evidence to stabilize different discourses about human-environment relationships. Some people used the images to portray Earth as isolated and limited. Other people used the images to show that the state system is invisible except through actions that assert state boundaries and interests. From an STS perspective, the images themselves mean nothing. They are a product of scientific endeavor in the form of space exploration and image capture. It is only when the images are incorporated into preexisting narratives that they carry any meaning. So, instead of taking science and scientific findings, such as images of Earth from space, as the objective truth about the world, STS considers how different forms of science become accepted and how different scientific interpretations, or particular ways of understanding the world, are explained, promoted, and used to stabilize particular discourses or narratives about the world. In essence, an STS approach helps us to understand how we generate, value, and use science and scientific information. In our focus on discourses about human-environment relationships, this kind of approach helps us to clarify and comment on ways in which scientific information is used to stabilize particular ways of seeing the world.

A brief overview of science and technology studies is helpful here. STS is an interdisciplinary field that examines how science itself is composed and how it intertwines with trends in society. STS allows us to take apart science methods so that we can "understand how science works, both internally and within society at large" (Howe 2011, 361). Scholarship in STS considers how knowledge is produced not so much by individual scientists but through widely accepted practices among scientific and policy communities (Latour and Woolgar 1979; Sarewitz 2004). That is, STS asks questions such as: How are scientific practices established? What kinds of knowledge do those practices produce? How is that knowledge utilized by society more broadly? STS is also a way to study how society shapes science by asking how societal trends shape the kind of science that is valued or not valued.

The first chapter of this book made the argument that there is no single, *correct* geopolitical interpretation of events. Instead, there are many, simultaneous discourses, perspectives, and ways to understand and describe the way the world works. The same may be said about science from an STS perspective. Since science offers many different ways to study the world, there are multiple, simultaneous ways of understanding the world scientifically. Indeed, "science offers to tell us how nature is" (Yearley 2008, 921). To that end, scientists in different fields use agreed-upon practices to speak as proxies for plants, animals, and environmental systems. Different scientific disciplines focus on different aspects and processes of the world. For example, a plant geneticist studying genetically modified organisms, such as hybrid wheat crops, will look for results of intended manipulation of the plant's genetic structure. However, an ecologist might look at the same crop of hybrid wheat and see unintended outcomes that occur when a hybrid plant is introduced into an ecosystem (Sarewitz 2004). Which perspective is correct? Both are correct within the parameters of their own scientific community. STS allows us to examine origins and consequences of science and technology with a focus on the interplay of science and technology with places, practices, and things (Hackett et al. 2008). Researchers working with an STS approach have looked at ways in which scientific inquiry differs across place and time and produces different forms of knowledge in different historical, political, technological, and cultural contexts (Hackett et al. 2008; Jasanoff et al. 1995; Spiegel-Rösing and Price 1977).

There are multiple subfields and approaches within the broad field of STS. For this chapter, a useful focus is a co-constructivist approach. This kind of inquiry examines how society and technology coproduce, or co-construct, and shape each other. Understanding society and science as interwoven and influencing each other allows room to examine ways in which human values, intentions, and political conflict shape what society accepts as meaningful science. At the same time, a co-constructivist view sees science as constructed by social, political, and cultural influences, and society must also be constructed to accept and use the facts and artifacts being produced by certain forms of science (Sismondo 2008). This kind of approach understands science and technology as actively social: "They do not provide a direct route from nature to ideas about nature; the products of science and technology are not themselves natural" (14). Rather than assuming scientific objectivity, a co-constructivist approach, instead, looks at science as a practice in composition (Goeminne 2010; see also Rappert and Balmer 2007). Sciences are methods and languages that serve to construct or compose a particular view of environmental features. Any given scientific discipline can only stabilize a particular—and necessarily incomplete—understanding of environmental features.

The very practice of separating nature or the environment as distinct from humans and as things that are objectively knowable is a feature of modernity (Latour 2004). Such separation limits an ability to understand iterative or back-and-forth processes. However, if we think in terms of the Anthropocene, discussed in chapter 1, we can identify many ways in which humans and environmental features shape each other: the extraction and burning of fossil fuels to support transportation, construction, and mechanized exploitation of a range of resources; the alteration of ecosystems and commodity consumption through industrial, monocrop agriculture; diversion and containment of flowing water for energy generation; research on biological interactions and the expansion and promotion of the pharmaceuticals industry; and so forth. The modernist view forces us to separate ourselves from the environment to enable a stance of management and control of what is not *us*. Yet when we look we can see that human-environment relationships are intertwined and mutually influential. Humans have altered environmental forms and processes, and in turn, our bodies, societies, economies, and politics are all shaped by what we think of as outside environmental influences.

Just as there is a tendency to separate human systems from environmental systems in the way we think about the world, there is also a tendency to separate science from politics. Society often turns to science as a form of objective, value-neutral *truth* with the expectation that such scientific insight can and should guide an otherwise value-laden policy process (Jasanoff and Wynne 1998). We tend to think of science as providing objective and clear insights to guide our decision making. This understanding of science has been called the "god trick" (Haraway 1988) of objective, scientific authority. The god trick of scientific knowledge portrays it as unquestionable and universal rather than a selective way of sorting different kinds of information. When science is viewed as unflawed and objective *truth*, people often turn to it to make *unbiased* policy decisions. Yet both scientific and policy processes are fraught with values and imperfect information. Carl Sagan (1994), renowned for his scientific contributions and commentary, observed: "Science is far from a perfect instrument of knowledge. It's just the best one we have. In this respect, as in many others, it's like democracy." STS offers a means to question assumptions underlying the idea that objective truths of science lead us directly to good policy and the appropriate use of power. This is the idea of *speaking truth to power*, and it sanitizes complex processes involving the selective use of scientific information.

The modernist view of science as pure truth that is uncontaminated by power and violence demonstrates that "objectivity becomes objectification" (Nandy 1988, 20). Claims to objective truth can actually marginalize some views or sources of information. For instance, claims about global warming might point to scientific evidence about trends in the planetary atmosphere, but this perspective obscures the fact that richer people in the world have contributed far more to this situation and will likely be more resilient than poorer people who are vulnerable to the impacts of a dynamic climate. Indeed, *facts* are constructed within a context of practice, and even technology is malleable (MacKenzie 1990). We can usefully ask how a technology, such as nuclear power or electric cars, might have developed differently within society. We can also ask how a technology, such as coal-fired energy production or personal cell phones, becomes socially rigid or fixed rather than challenged or replaced (Bijker 2001). A co-constructivist STS approach repoliticizes science and technology by examining the construction of knowledge as integral to political processes rather than distinct from them. It allows an investigation into how science and societal institutions are intertwined with power dynamics. In other words, science and society are understood as co-constructive through iterative, back-and-forth processes that shape not only what kinds of science are conducted or valued but also how the resulting forms of knowledge influence how people understand and engage with the world.

Environmental geopolitics can make use of this way of thinking about science in order to take apart discourses about human-environment relationships. An objective of this book is to advance environmental geopolitics as a way to examine how human-environment relations are securitized or portrayed as risks with particular spatial associations. Places, spatial processes, and patterns are often drawn into dominant narratives about environmental risk and security. So far, the chapters have considered ways in which discourses about risk and security are stabilized. Next, we will look at examples of the selective use of scientific information. We will see how scientific evidence, and sometimes even the black box of *science* in general terms, can support particular discourses about humans and environmental systems. This selective use of scientific knowledge imparts a particular sense of where environmental security and risk are happening. As with the other chapters in this book, this chapter will emphasize ways in which the environment is oversimplified toward a particular view of security or risk. It will also highlight ways in which we overlook human agency while nature is blamed as posing threats to human well-being. Additionally, the discussion here will consider spatial dimensions of environmental risk and security as they are promoted with certain kinds of scientific information.

Good News Is in the Eye of the Beholder

Media coverage on environmental issues can often be doom and gloom. News stories grab our attention with coverage of extreme disasters, sobering forecasts, and bleak prospects for sustaining our interaction with environmental systems. We should read such stories carefully and critically. A central theme of this book is that we should pay attention to how any argument about environmental security or risk is stabilized. That stance is also good practice for how to read positive stories about the environment since those, too, build a case based on selective information. Regardless of the tone of the news story, we can draw examples from media coverage to examine how scientific information is used to support discourses about human-environment relationships. This kind of inquiry is the cornerstone of environmental geopolitical analysis.

In late December 2016, *The Washington Post* ran an article titled "It Wasn't Entirely Bad News. Here Are Five Positive Environmental Stories from 2016" (Dennis and Mooney 2016). The focus on positive aspects of human-environment relationships is certainly refreshing and commendable. Yet we can look at the brief coverage of these stories to illustrate why we should be cautious to accept arguments—positive, negative, or otherwise—about how our relationship with environmental features is risky or secure. A comprehensive examination of news media through an STS lens is not achievable in a single book chapter. Here, the focus on a single news story serves as a small window into a broad and dynamic informational landscape that we interact with every day. This sample of news items demonstrates an environmental geopolitics approach. We can use this single news story to consider how scientific information is used selectively to portray a particular issue, but also how we can look for other types of scientific knowledge to generate a more complete understanding of human-environment relationships.

"Global Carbon Emissions Appear to Have Stopped Increasing"
Pointing to data from the Global Carbon Project, the story states that emissions of carbon dioxide, a key greenhouse gas, are plateauing. Global economic growth has continued, so this trend is taken to suggest that economic growth is decoupling from carbon emissions. Economic growth continues without the carbon emissions, so we must be moving in the right direction. What this exclusive focus on carbon dioxide misses, however, is the fact that other heat-trapping greenhouse gases are an increasing concern because they are becoming more, not less, prevalent. Methane, for instance, or natural gas, are significant concerns. Although it is cleaner than coal because it releases less greenhouse gases when burned, methane itself is a potent greenhouse gas when it is released unburned into the atmosphere. Methane does not stay in the atmosphere as long as carbon dioxide does, but it is thousands of times more powerful at trapping heat than is carbon dioxide (Howarth, Ingraffea, and Engelder 2011; Karion et al. 2013). How often, though, is methane just released into the atmosphere? A lot! Methane leaks into the atmosphere at nearly every point in the natural gas production and consumption chain from the hydraulic fracturing site, in transit to storage facilities, at the storage facility, en route to consumers, and often at every gas stove, fireplace, grill, clothes dryer, furnace, or other end-use appliance. These are material realities of our reliance on and acceptance of natural gas as a widespread source of energy. The production and promotion of these appliances, the ease with which they are connected to the natural gas supply line, and the pricing of natural gas that makes it relatively inexpensive to use in so many ways reflect materialities and practices that mutually reinforce our demand for natural gas.

Another group of substances that are gaining attention for their impact on the atmosphere is hydrofluorocarbons (HFCs). When scientists discovered the hole in the ozone layer in the 1980s, they traced its cause to the release of common refrigerants known as chlorofluorocarbons (CFCs). The

Science, Imagery, and Understanding the Environment   143

international community banned these substances, and industry turned to hydrofluorocarbons as a replacement for use as refrigerants and for insulation and air conditioning. Now, though, scientists and policymakers acknowledge that what seemed like a good idea for the ozone layer is actually doing excessive harm to the atmosphere in terms of trapping heat. HFCs stay in the atmosphere only for about fifteen years as compared to carbon dioxide, which remains in the atmosphere for centuries, but HFCs are hundreds to thousands of times more potent at trapping heat (*Economist* 2016). World leaders have spent the last decade discussing how to address this issue, and recently, considerable progress has been made. Following a meeting of international leaders in Kigali, Rwanda, an amendment to the Montreal Protocol, which bans the uses of ozone-damaging CFCs, was agreed upon that aims to reduce the use of HFCs starting in 2019 with many economically developing countries joining the effort in 2024 or later (Johnston, Milman, and Vidal 2016).

It is indeed good news that carbon dioxide emissions are flattening and that HFC use will be tapering off, but there remains much work to address the overall heat-trapping profile of the atmosphere due to human-generated

Air-conditioning units on a backstreet in Little India, Singapore. Hydrofluorocarbons are greenhouse gases that are getting more attention due to their impact on atmospheric warming.
Source: iStock

substances. If people have heard of any greenhouse gases, it is probably carbon dioxide. Emphasizing the progress made in terms of carbon dioxide is certainly persuasive: we are doing better with our greenhouse gas emissions . . . as long as we look at this particular greenhouse gas. However, it is important that the potency of less known gases is also included in news about the changing composition of the atmosphere. Otherwise, we might end up repeating the unintended outcome of the Montreal Protocol that helped to replenish the ozone layer at the expense of increasing the heat-trapping potential of the atmosphere. This example highlights how a selective use of science—information on trends in different greenhouse gas emissions—can lead to very different perceptions of what is actually happening with trends in the atmosphere. How these trends are presented and portrayed (or ignored) ties into how we understand planetary risk or the stability of environmental and human systems.

Carbon dioxide emissions have been the center of attention in many policy efforts in part because there are available data on carbon dioxide emissions and levels in the atmosphere over time. This focus is a result of the dominance of techno-scientific approaches to measuring, visualizing, calculating, and forecasting certain aspects of a dynamic climate (O'Lear 2016). Focusing on carbon dioxide has generated entire fields of specialization and practice. The very notion that carbon dioxide is something that may be bought, sold, and traded is made possible through the creation of certain techniques of measuring and accounting as well as through technologies that enable these practices (Oels 2005). We now have ways of measuring and accounting for things such as "the national carbon sink," "carbon credit," and even our "personal carbon budget" (Lövbrand and Stripple 2011). Each of these measures has been constructed as an identifiable problem that may be managed and governed by authorities deemed to have the appropriate expertise. The measure known as the tonne of carbon dioxide equivalent, or tCO2e, is an accepted unit of measure that allows for calculations of emissions, cuts, trades, and negotiations within established systems of governance and authority (Paterson and Stripple 2012). Carbon dioxide has become the standard by which to compare greenhouse gases through carbon dioxide equivalences, but allowing for carbon dioxide emissions or cuts to represent other gases is an oversimplification (MacKenzie 2009). It is like comparing apples to skyscrapers.

Yet despite all of these technical definitions and calculations, carbon dioxide is not actually traded directly. Instead, the right to emit carbon dioxide becomes something that is discussed and debated by certain actors—governments or industries—who are considered legitimate participants in carbon markets and negotiations. That is, these scientific measures are intertwined and mutually reinforcing with systems of power. Expanding the discussion to include other compounds, such as methane and HFCs, that operate very differently in the atmosphere, opens up a conversation about what kinds of scientific knowledge *count* when we are talking about atmospheric composition and warming. It also points to ways in which current practices, such as emissions trading schemes and other policy approaches, may have limited effect. We might not know the implications of continued reliance on some chemicals, so broadening our scope of what kinds of scientific knowledge we look at helps us to formulate a more complete picture. Unless we understand the insecurities involved in our heavy use of natural gas and some refrigerants, we would not know to look for alternatives or ways to lower our consumption. The kind of science we accept and rely on influences—and is influenced by—our practices and how we interact with environmental features. That is why it is useful—arguably, even critical—that we expand the kinds of scientific information that we are using to guide our policies, our day-to-day behavior, and the material structures and infrastructures on which we rely.

"Worldwide, Wind and Solar Are Booming"

"Not only has the U.S. solar industry added 4,143 megawatts of solar-generating capacity in the final quarter of 2016, but thousands of wind energy turbines have been installed around the world" (Dennis and Mooney 2016). These statements about the growth of solar and wind power are certainly positive. It is helpful, though, to put these numbers into perspective. According to the US Energy Information Administration, wind-generated electricity capacity increased by 100 percent between 2009 and 2015. Solar electricity capacity, both at the large, utility scale and in the form of distributed photovoltaics (PV) (i.e., rooftop solar panels), has increased by 900 percent in the same time. These numbers sound impressive, but let's look at wind and solar compared to all forms of electricity generation. In the United States, wind and solar shares of total electricity capacity were 6.7 and 2 percent, respectively. Capacity refers to how much electricity each of these sources could theoretically generate in ideal conditions. In reality, wind and solar actually generated only 4.7 and 0.9 percent of the total electricity "as a result of the intermittent availability of these resources" (US Department of Energy 2016, 1). Therefore, a 100 percent, or even a 900 percent, increase in wind and solar capacity, while a positive trend, translates into very little actual wind- and solar-generated electricity.

The Washington Post presents this growth in wind and solar energy as a significant increase. Once we put the amount of actual electricity-generating capacity into perspective, however, we might ask why wind and solar energy systems are not expanding more quickly, especially in the United States. For instance, Western Europe is leading the world in terms of offshore wind energy development. The United Kingdom alone has twenty-nine wind farms with more under construction (Crown Estate, 2017). The United States has considerably more coastline than the United Kingdom, so there would seem to be great potential for offshore wind energy development. Both onshore and offshore wind turbines, however, depend on geographic factors, such as the strength and consistency of wind, investment, and human population both in terms of energy demand as well as public resistance to landscapes altered by enormous wind turbines. In the United States, there is only one offshore wind farm in operation comprised of five wind turbines. It is located off Block Island, an island of Rhode Island (US Energy Information Administration 2015). Offshore wind turbines are challenging to build and maintain. Transporting equipment to the site, anchoring turbines, and conducting maintenance in difficult environments are all expensive aspects of offshore wind energy generation. Although the United States has a great deal of coastline, there have been investment setbacks preventing the expansion of offshore wind power. Having coastline, clearly, is only one element in

Wind turbine foundations. How do we measure renewable energy capacity vs. actual electricity generated by wind and solar infrastructure?
Source: iStock

increasing offshore wind energy capacity. Onshore wind energy potential in the United States, however, is abundant particularly in areas of low population density. This example of offshore wind energy capacity illustrates why it is important to understand spatial dimensions and uneven geographic factors—the third observation of environmental geopolitics—shaping things like renewable energy.

Wind and solar power, more generally, are also a challenge for electricity markets made for the era of fossil fuel (*Economist* 2017). It is not just a matter of generating more wind and solar energy, but the entire business model of electricity generation and delivery will need reconsideration in light of renewable energy. It will require substantial investment to redesign and build electricity grids that can accommodate renewable energy, connect the sources and the consumers, and offer sufficient storage capacity for intermittent times when the sun isn't shining or the wind isn't blowing. Wind and solar energy have low marginal costs since they do not have to buy fuel. That means that the more renewable generators there are in a power supply system, the more they push the wholesale price of energy down. Add to this the growing reliance on distributed photovoltaics or rooftop solar panel systems. Increasing numbers of businesses and industrial users as well as household consumers are supplying their own electricity rather than relying on the grid. That means there are fewer customers to cover the costs of the grid, thus presenting a challenge if the grid needs to be overhauled to support renewable energy. Although moving away from the traditional grid may be the goal eventually, fossil fuel–based electricity and electricity generated by nuclear and hydroelectric power are still necessary during peak demand times and during intermittent wind and solar times. Expanding the electricity grid toward renewables and maintaining the existing public systems will require considerable investment. If prices for electricity continue downward, then there is less incentive for profit-seeking investors to invest in these systems. Reconfiguring energy grids toward renewable sources will take investment, subsidies, or both, and it will require a reconsideration of how electricity is used, priced, and valued—all of which will be shaped by politics. The electricity grid is an excellent example of how material infrastructure is intertwined with scientific knowledge, consumer practice, economic incentives, and challenges to maintain or disrupt how decisions are made.

This discussion about renewable energy illustrates the second observation of environmental geopolitics: humans' role or agency tends to be considered selectively, and often, dynamics of power remain invisible and uninvestigated. The topic of renewable energy requires that we consider current political and economic structures associated with electricity generation and use. How do the current systems of electricity generation benefit some people or groups over others? How is the price of electricity set, and what might alternative approaches to the buying and selling of electricity look like? What exactly does the price of electricity in any given location cover, and how are other costs—such as pollution from burning coal—external to the price of electricity? How might both producers and consumers be motivated to use more renewable energy sources? Additionally, we can look at how the physical infrastructure of electricity generation—the production, storage, transfer, and consumption of electricity—are material discourses about human-environment relationships. How were these physical systems, such as power plants and electricity grids, established, how are they maintained, and how do they enable or challenge the expansion of nonrenewable energy? Thinking about the expansion of renewable energy sources requires that we ask questions about the current discourses of electricity provision—in the form of policy, pricing, production, and infrastructure—and how those discourses are stabilized by the reliance on certain forms of information or scientific evidence.

"World Leaders Seem Determined to Combat Global Warming (Well, Most World Leaders)"

> In late 2015, leaders from nearly 200 countries joined a landmark climate accord negotiated in Paris. Each country pledged to help slash greenhouse-gas emissions, with the goal of avoiding the most drastic effects of global warming in the decades ahead. In 2016, countries began the first steps of backing up those promises. In October, the accord officially entered into force when more than 55 countries, representing more than 55 percent of global emissions, ratified the deal. The following month in Morocco, representatives took initial steps toward implementing the deal's ambitious goals. That said, the fate of the Paris accord is uncertain. (Dennis and Mooney 2016)

Making pledges is one thing, but reaching the intended goal is quite another. Most countries whose leadership promised to reduce emissions face obstacles in meeting their initial agreements. During his presidential campaign, Donald Trump repeatedly threatened to pull the United States out of the Paris climate agreement. As of this writing, it is unclear which of his advisors Trump may listen to on the issue of whether or not to pull the United States out of the Paris agreement. If the United States does step back from its commitments, there is speculation that other countries may not follow through on meeting their emission reduction pledges.

The Paris Climate Conference (COP 21) in December 2015 was indeed groundbreaking in that it led to the first ever, legally binding, global climate agreement involving 195 countries (European Commission Climate Action 2017). The governments agreed to a plan aimed at limiting the increase in global average temperature to below two degrees Celsius above preindustrial levels. The plan also calls for countries to "undertake rapid reductions . . . in accordance with the best available science" (1). Additionally, governments agreed to meet every five years "to set more ambitious targets as required by science." It would seem that science is driving international efforts to rein in climate change, but is that the appropriate role for science? This chapter has introduced science and technology studies as an interdisciplinary approach to looking at how we use and interpret science. *Science* is often treated like a black box: mysterious in its inner workings, but thought to produce the *right* answers. But are we asking the *right* questions?

As the section on STS points out, there are many different scientific specializations, each with particular methods and focus. So, when policymakers say they will rely on the best available science to guide them in the complex process of reducing greenhouse gas emissions, which type of science will they be using, exactly? More science does not necessarily mean greater certainty or clear policy guidance. Uncertainty is an inherent part not only of scientific practice but also of nature. The parameters of uncertainty in any given field are familiar to specialists in that field, but characterizing and communicating nuances of uncertainty to nonspecialists can be difficult. Policymakers, for instance, tend to see uncertainty as something that should be reduced or eliminated altogether. Environment-related controversies seem to get stuck in scientific uncertainty, but this focus on scientific uncertainty obscures differences in values and political agendas. Calls for more science can actually be an effective strategy to stall decision making and action. Daniel Sarewitz (2004) has written about why some scientific issues become politicized, and why some political issues tend to become scientized.

> When political controversy exists, the whole idea of "reducing uncertainty" through more research is incoherent because there will never be a single problem for which a single, optimizable research strategy or solution path can be identified let alone characterized through a single approach to determining uncertainty. Instead, there will be many different problems defined in terms of many competing value frameworks and studied via many disciplinary approaches. (396)

Sarewitz argues that instead of relying on science to set policy, a more constructive approach would be to identify values and objectives first, and then identify the most appropriate scientific information that can bring about those outcomes. He notes that "progress in addressing environmental controversies will need to come primarily from advances in political process, rather than scientific research" (399). That is, world leaders should first specify the outcomes they are seeking. For instance, addressing specific impacts of climate change through appropriate change in human behavior or adjustments to economic or social practices could be prioritized. Then, it would be more clear what kinds of scientific information can help to move us toward those desired results. As it is, combating global warming by making pledges to reduce greenhouse gas emissions is such a broad effort that the desired outcomes—and the scientific means to achieve them—are not at all clear. It is a positive sign that shared concerns about our dynamic habitat are bringing world leaders together to think through the options for response. Ideally, these conversations will advance shared objectives first, and then identify the type of science and scientific approach that can guide forward progress toward those goals.

"Technology Is Providing a Glimmer of Hope"

Accompanying a photo of a rugged, snowy landscape in Iceland is the text:

> Officials at Reykjavik Energy took carbon emissions from a geothermal plant (along with emissions of hydrogen sulfide, a dangerous gas) and stowed them away in the rocky ground 400 to 800 meters (1,300 to 2,600 feet) deep. Once injected into basalt rock, the carbon dioxide rapidly was mineralized, or turned into rock. (Dennis and Mooney 2016)

The article describes carbon dioxide injection as an advanced way to store carbon dioxide underground rather than release it into the atmosphere. Once injected approximately two thousand feet below the surface, the mineralized carbon dioxide cannot be released back into the atmosphere. This method of deep injection of carbon dioxide is under study for use in industrial-scale carbon dioxide storage. If this technique proves to be successful and cost effective, it would seem to have the potential to replace our inadvertent storing of carbon dioxide in the atmosphere, with the effect of warming the planet, with intentional storage of carbon dioxide within the planet's surface. Carbon dioxide storage technology would appear to offer a promising way to reverse at least part of a problematic situation.

Indeed, research in many directions may lead to real-world improvements and solutions to problems we have created in our relationships with the environment. Well-known examples of technological advancements include fuel-efficient vehicles and high-speed public transportation; food that can be grown in suboptimal conditions with less water or poor-quality soil; low-energy, LED lighting (which also supports vertical, hydroponic farms); wind- and solar-energy-harnessing technology as discussed above; batteries for storing solar and other forms of energy; and more efficient use of raw material inputs across a wide range of production and packaging. One of the seductive aspects of technology is that it makes it seem possible to buy or consume our way out of a problem. In our society, and others like it, neoliberal values have been deeply ingrained in most of us, and we have been trained to think more in terms of our options as consumers rather than our options (and obligations) as citizens. Green consumerism is the widespread prioritization of choosing products that are in some way environmentally responsible because they are made with sustainable materials, have less packaging, were transported a shorter distance, or in some way reflect an effort to be kinder to our planet. This effort to consume responsibly may well reflect thoughtfulness on the part of the consumer and a genuine interest to do less harm to the environmental system.

The message that we do not hear as often, though, is to consume less. Instead of buying green, we might usefully ask ourselves, Do I need to buy this item at all? Granted, we all require food, shelter, clothing, and some basic goods. Planned obsolescence and the failing of things we have can also

Paper or plastic? The question we are not asking is how much energy does the frozen-food aisle require? Contemporary food systems have a huge carbon footprint considering the amount and diversity of energy required from the field and factory to transportation, packaging and storage, preparation, and waste management.
Source: iStock

necessitate replacing those things. The clever, triangular logo "Reduce, Reuse, Recycle" started as a public relations campaign by the container industry (Rogers 2005, 171; see also O'Lear 2010). It was intended to encourage people to consume. This widespread and persistent message, found on a recycling bin near you, is insidious: although we *could* reduce our consumption, it is also just as good to keep consuming—and then recycle. No harm done!

Green consumption goes hand in hand with modern social and technological systems that define industrialized society. As discussed in chapter 4, modernity is based on three key ideas: (1) that we can (and should) manage environmental systems through the use of science and technology; (2) that we can apply liberal-democratic values through appropriate institutions at national, international, and other scales of governance; and (3) that those combined mechanisms, science and technology and institutions of governance, should guide the management of environmental systems for the benefit of human societies (Glover 2006, 2015). These features of modern society may seem obvious. They seem to describe adequately the way the world works. The modern perspective, in effect, is a powerful discourse carried out in the forms of text and narrative, practice, ideology, and materiality. This way of thinking surrounds us, much like water surrounds a fish, and we do not tend to question how established and persistent perspectives crowd out other ways of knowing and interacting with environmental systems.

We can comment on each of these foundational assumptions of modernity. First, the modern view does not permit other ways of knowing or valuing the world. There are many versions of science, not to mention multiple, simultaneous cultural perspectives on the meaning and value of environmental systems. (Is this a forest, or is it a calculable amount of board feet of lumber?) Second, the modern framework does not ask who gets to establish the institutions—the social, political, and economic structures, rules, and practices—that guide decisions. Whose voices and views are left out when problems are prioritized and decisions are made? Third, the modern perspective does not question that environmental systems should be managed for the benefit of humans. This view is anthropocentric in its focus on human needs. A biocentric view, in contrast, understands humans as one aspect of a larger web of ecological relationships. How might the planet be different today if the well-being of landscapes, waterways, and other species was even close to as important as the well-being of humans? Western forms of science that purport to offer universal truths about the way in which the world works stabilize modernity as a discourse. Yet these so-called universal truths can only be partial truths and cannot universally represent all possible ways of understanding a situation.

Let's look at an example to demonstrate why and how it matters which science and technology is prioritized, who establishes institutions, and who makes decisions about the purpose of environmental systems. In the book *Concrete Revolution: Large Dams, Cold War Geopolitics, and the US Bureau of Reclamation* (2015), Christopher Sneddon looks at how the United States created a global network of large dams during the Cold War. At that time, the United States and the Soviet Union were vying for influence among less economically developed countries. The United States persuaded countries such as Lebanon, Ethiopia, and Thailand to construct large dams within their territories. The objective of this modernization of river basins was to consolidate power to a US-friendly entity within each country, to generate electricity, and to open these economies to US business interests. One of the important aspects in this development was the role of the US Bureau of Reclamation and technical experts. Individuals in the Bureau of Reclamation were trained in and promoted a utilitarian perspective of natural resources as having value only once they are redirected for economic purposes. River basins in these different settings had unique characteristics, but the application of modern technical and scientific expertise on river basin alteration, dam construction, and economic accounting to measure success made these diverse landscapes relatively uniform. Uniformity made these different systems easier to measure, assess, and manage. These river basins, then, shifted from providing diverse resources to different groups of people to providing a narrowly defined commodity controlled by an elite group of resource managers and government bureaucrats. Through the strategic application of technical and scientific expertise on dam construction, the United States established a network of political and economic alliances that also served to keep known elites in positions of power in these countries.

From a critical geopolitical perspective, this network of dams forms a material discourse. These artifacts on the landscape—repurposed river basins, industrial-scale dam and hydroelectric infrastructure, and altered ecosystems and local land use practices—reflect a particular view of the world and a set of political and economic priorities that were made material through the application of particular technical and scientific expertise. "Modernizing" river basins to maximize and control their economic value was a driving objective. Large dams demonstrate technological capacity and the ability to alter landscapes, divert water, and generate electricity. They also reflect the prioritization of certain forms of expertise over others. Alternative meanings or perceptions of river basins were not considered in this process. These dams, as a network, are a material discourse about the US political and economic agendas during the Cold War. They are a discourse about how the United

Nam Ngum Dam, Laos. Despite technical problems and questionable economic feasibility, since it was not located close to market demand for electricity, this dam was a top-priority project for the Eisenhower and Kennedy administrations due to the perception of Laos as a critical buffer between Communist China and other mainland Asia states (Sneddon 2015, 168–69).
Source: Chaoborus/Wikimedia

States established spatial relationships through which it extended its own power. They represent power in the ability to alter river basins, alter control over a resource, and alter relationships and power dynamics both within and between countries.

We can hold up the example of large dams and modernizing river basins as an example of the use of scientific expertise and technology to ask questions about who benefits from the application of these technologies, how do they alter environmental features, and what are the long-term implications. How does the application of these technologies alter relationships of power and control over environmental features? What are possible concerns that these technologies may have for generations not yet born? Who gets to decide if promoting a technology is in the best interest for humans or for environmental systems? Just because we have a technology to do something or to manipulate some aspect of the world does not necessarily mean that using that technology will lead to the best possible outcome. New technologies, such as carbon dioxide injection, may offer the possibility to improve how we do things, but they can also lock us in to ways of life that ultimately damage the environmental systems that make our lives possible. We would be wise to ask to what degree a technology might allow flexibility in future decision making and to what degree it might close down our options in the future.

"The Oceans Are Finally Getting the Attention They Deserve"

In recent years, we have seen much more information and public discussion on the state of the world's oceans. Oil spills and toxic dumping have polluted oceans and have had a negative impact on marine life. Vast masses of floating plastic and other garbage move with ocean currents or become trapped over stretches of ocean surface. Industrialized economies churning out wastes into waterways are increasing acidification levels of the oceans. Industrial-scale fishing is set to overwhelm the ability of fish populations to reproduce and threatens the viability of entire oceanic ecosystems. Coral reefs, the tropical rainforests of the ocean, are becoming bleached and weakened as ocean temperatures increase beyond the viability of many coral species. A growing imbalance of fresh water and salt water, due to ice cap melt on both poles of the planet, is altering ocean currents and associated atmospheric currents such as the jet stream. The oceans are changing, but the good news here seems to be that we are, at least, paying more attention to their plight.

This section of *The Washington Post* article states that "roughly 3 percent of the oceans are now safeguarded far from the 30 percent to 40 percent that many scientists claim is necessary for the seas' sustainability over the long term" (Dennis and Mooney 2016), but improvements have been made. By some calculations, global marine protected areas have increased by a factor of five since 2008, but even with ambitious international collaboration, it is unlikely that 10 percent of the world's oceans will have protected status by the year 2035 (Boonzaier and Pauly 2016). Even these numbers do not tell the whole story of marine conservation. Designating areas of the ocean as protected provides "a simple metric that is communicable and quantifiable, and it has been chosen by the international community as an indicator of conservation" (32). Yet these designations "could amount to no more than paper parks" (33) if they are not backed up with the means and intention to implement ecological goals. Data sets on marine protected areas can be inconsistent, out of date, and incomplete, leading to a lack of clarity not only in terms of how much area is being protected but also what, exactly, is being protected and how. Measurable, designated protected areas are an important step toward conserving ocean ecosystems, but there are multiple factors to consider. Other measures such as protection levels and objectives at different ocean depths, management and implementation activities, and outcomes of conservation efforts are more meaningful indicators of marine protection and preservation (Boonzaier and Pauly 2016, 33).

In this discussion about ocean management, it is helpful to return to a concept introduced in chapter 1; namely, the idea of the geographies of volume. The issue of marine protected areas is a lucid illustration of why it is important to think in terms of depth and volume, not just two-dimensional surface area. The familiar approach to territorial control emphasizes the management of borders around an area and what kinds of activities those borders contain, exclude, or allow across a border. Thinking in terms of three-dimensional volume, however, challenges us to think about multiple, simultaneous processes happening at different levels or depths. Work in urban geography, for instance, has considered vertical urbanisms (Harris 2015; see also Graham 2016) with attention to urban planning not just at the surface but underground (e.g., subways), in the airspace (skyscrapers and air traffic pathways), as well as uneven distributions of power in vertical, urban spaces (e.g., penthouses vs. slums). Additionally, we are familiar with two-dimensional maps that depict processes on a surface area, but how might we visualize three-dimensional processes? One approach would be to borrow cartographic methods from cave mapping that aims to show area as well as depth. If we think in terms of volume, we have a different perspective on how relationships of power create or play out in three-dimensional spaces. Marine protection areas, in this light, could be thought of in terms of volumes and multilayered processes and policies.

The oceans, in all their volume, not only need our attention, but they need different attention. The fact that the planet is changing challenges the very way that we need to think about marine conservation. We know that climate change and warming temperatures are causing Arctic ice to melt at unprecedented rates. Although this ice usually varies seasonally, we can see through various forms of scientific measures and visual images that, overall, Arctic ice is receding and becoming thinner. Three key points of concern emerge about the altered, unfrozen nature of considerable portions of the Arctic. First, the lack of ice is altering the continued well-being and life patterns of human societies and animal populations in the Arctic. Indigenous people who have relied on frozen ground and access to hunting and fishing areas are having to alter their ways of life and methods of economic livelihood. We have all heard about polar bears, not to mention other forms of wildlife, that are struggling to survive in the melting Arctic. Second, the waning ice cover is making more underground resources accessible. There has been much speculation and vying for control over possible subsurface fossil fuel reserves that might now be extractable. Third, the Northwest Passage through the Arctic is becoming navigable on a regular basis. It took from 1903 to 1906 for Roald Amundsen, a Norwegian explorer, to make the first successful recorded navigation of this route connecting the Atlantic and Pacific oceans. In 2007, the passageway was free of ice in the summer for the first time in recorded history. The *Crystal Serenity* cruise ship, with thirteen

Science, Imagery, and Understanding the Environment   157

decks, six restaurants, and a crew of six hundred people, took only thirty-two days to traverse the Northwest Passage in the summer of 2016. It is not just a route for ships that is becoming available but a doughnut hole of open, international waters (Council on Foreign Relations 2017) that has attracted fishing vessels from countries that have no legal claim to the Arctic (see map 5.1). With this drastically changing status, who gets to decide the fate of the Arctic? Will it become a frontier of first-come, first-served resource capture for countries or industries capable of getting there before anyone else?

A report by the International Union for the Conservation of Nature and Natural Resources (Speer et al. 2017) has called for the designation of some of the unique ecosystems in the Arctic Ocean to be recognized—and protected—with United Nations Educational, Scientific and Cultural Organization (UNESCO) World Heritage status. Areas such as the Bering Strait Ecoregion, some High Arctic archipelagoes, and the Great Siberian Polynya

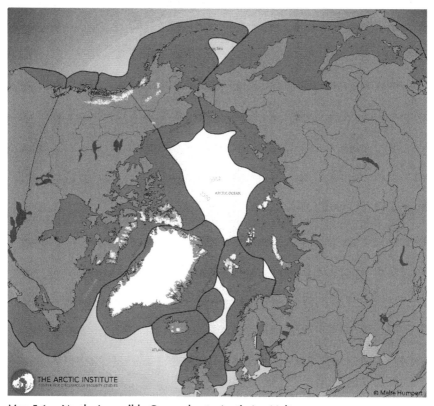

Map 5.1.   Newly Accessible Ocean due to Arctic Ice Melt
Source: The Arctic Institute, Center for Circumpolar Security Studies

arguably exemplify globally unique features of the Arctic Ocean and have Outstanding Universal Value (OUV). OUV does not aim to reflect cultural heritage but instead recognizes "the most unique and globally exceptional features in the Arctic" (12). The report takes an unusual approach:

> Recognizing that marine ecosystems almost always transcend national boundaries, an ecosystem approach was used to identify possible marine areas OUV rather than a country-by-country approach. An ecosystem approach focuses on identifying and describing ecologically significant features without regard to jurisdictional boundaries. This approach is more suitable to the dynamics of the marine environment and reflects more meaningful scales from an ecosystem perspective. (12)

This approach to marine protection defies more traditional and familiar approaches to international efforts to address environmental concerns. It illustrates the suggestion of Daniel Sarewitz (2004), discussed earlier in this chapter, to identify the values and objectives first and then find the appropriate scientific knowledge to achieve those ends.

The example of ecosystem-level marine protection efforts returns us to the question of what kind of scientific information is being used to support a particular discourse in the form of policy, practice, materiality, and identity. Shifting the conversation away from state-level risk and security to a focus on ecosystem-level concerns raises different kinds of questions: How is risk to an ecosystem defined differently than risks to states and state interests? What does security mean in an ecosystem context, and how is that security achieved? In addition, marine ecosystems are a particularly good example of why it is important to think in terms of volume and multiple layers of activity. Marine ecosystems exhibit not only horizontal interactions but also vertical interactions. To understand security and risk in the context of ecosystems, we need more than surface data. We need a more nuanced understanding of what is being secured, what is at risk, and how those concerns play out across a myriad of relationships. Establishing protected marine areas at the ocean's surface is indeed a necessary and important step in this direction, but it alone is insufficient to address impacts and implications of human-environment interactions regarding oceans and marine ecosystems operating below the surface.

A key theme for this chapter is how science serves to stabilize notions of security and risk. This is not to say that science itself is good or bad, but it is important to understand how different forms of science may be used to support particular objectives. We can see throughout these examples of positive news stories how particular forms of scientific information and knowledge are utilized to tell a certain story about human-environment relationships. There is a tendency to focus on carbon dioxide emission levels and measures rather than a wider array of atmospheric greenhouse gases. Calculations of potential wind and solar capacity do not reflect actual electricity generation and challenges of funding the renewable energy grid. International leadership on climate change tends to emphasize political goals and the "best available science" rather than agreed-upon ecological outcomes. Technological solutions, an example of modernist thinking in high-tech packaging, can distract attention away from benefits of reduced consumption. Emphasis on calculable areas of marine protection does not necessarily promote conservation outcomes below the surface. These are just a few examples of ways in which we can look more closely at how science can be used selectively to build specific arguments to avoid some form of risk or enhance security in some way.

This section of the chapter has focused on a small sample of issues from a single news story in a mainstream newspaper. Even within this limited selection of possible topics, the discussion has demonstrated how an environmental geopolitics approach can support a critical analysis of the use of scientific information in mainstream geopolitical narratives. As this section has demonstrated, almost any use of scientific information may be shown to be partial because the world, and the ways we understand it, are varied and complex. An environmental geopolitics approach, however, helps us to discern how any given portrayal of human-environment relationship usually prioritizes a particular understanding of the environment, considers only part of humans' role in the relationship, if humans' role is even considered at all, and how the spatial understanding of any given human-environment relationship may be limited, either intentionally or not.

Seeing Changes versus Making Changes

Gary Braasch (1945–2016) was a natural history photojournalist who devoted his life to documenting effects of climate change and using visual evidence to persuade people to take action. Braasch paid attention to trends in how photographs shape our understanding of environmental issues such as climate change (2013). Scientists have used visually simple depictions of scientific information to communicate about climate change. An early example is the graph of the steady increase of recorded temperatures since 1880. The famous Keeling Curve depicts an increase in atmospheric carbon dioxide since the late 1950s. The "hockey stick" graph shows a reconstruction of Northern Hemisphere temperature over the last millennium and the dramatically steep incline in temperature in the twentieth century. Braasch observed that dramatic and simple graphs could be more persuasive to public audiences because the detail and fluctuation of complex data associated with these processes tend to raise complicated questions.

Even more persuasive are images, particularly symbolic images such as polar bears adrift on icebergs in open water or scenes of floods, droughts, and bleached coral reefs, to name a few, that have become almost cliché through overuse. Two general categories of climate change imagery are *cause* and *solution* imagery. Cause imagery shows smokestacks, traffic jams, oil drilling sites, and fumes from tailpipes or industrial processes. Solution imagery tends to show fields of wind turbines or solar panels, or forms of green consumption, such as electric cars or sustainably sourced goods (Braasch 2013). Research on how people perceive images about climate change has shown that these images tend to reinforce two main ideas (O'Neill 2013). The first idea is that climate change is distant and remote from people's lived experience. Who has actually seen a polar bear in the wild? The second idea is that climate change is contested. Images of politicians, climate negotiations, or protests suggest that there is political controversy around climate change. Neither of these visual frames is particularly helpful in advancing a better understanding of climate change impacts in particular places, or how societies could work toward better outcomes.

Braasch (2013, 36) observed that "science and technology photography remains an important professional specialty and avenue for increased public understanding and involvement. Informed photography of climate change also covers energy sources, adaptation, and methods for reducing carbon emissions." More than encouraging people merely to see changes, Braasch argued that photojournalism could help people to make changes. Frightening images tend to have a "helplessness inducing effect." The more useful approach is to utilize positive imagery that is solution oriented and specific rather than general. Efforts to inform the public about climate change—or other human-environment concerns—"should be more inspiring and educational. Picturing a healthier and safer future can be empowering" (38).

It isn't just science that can serve to shape how we understand human-environment relationships as moving toward risk or security. Visual images can influence the way we think about human-environment relationships. More accurately, visual images can be integrated into preexisting perspectives about human-environment relationships, much as the image of Earth from space was used to make very different arguments about how society should think about planetary resources. Visual images can help us not only see what is happening, but they can also help us understand what we might do about it.

Seeing can be believing, and believing is often a first step toward taking action and making different decisions. But what about images that we do not see in newspapers, the evening news, or other mass media outlets? How do we learn about aspects of human-environment relationships that are difficult to capture in a photograph or that are difficult to represent with familiar forms of scientific data? It is important to understand that influential aspects of human-environment relationships are often invisible or made invisible to us. This point returns us to the concept—and reality—of slow violence. As discussed in chapter 3, slow violence helps us to understand what we cannot immediately see.

Science, Imagery, and Slow Violence
We might ask, how do we know slow violence when we see it? But that is just the point. Often, we do not see it. Unlike immediate, direct violence, slow violence can be difficult to visualize with images or even to measure through scientific metrics. How do we know to look at something or try to measure something if we are not even aware that it might be important? In policy circles, there is the concept of the "unknown unknown" or "unkunk" (Rosenbaum 2017, 23). An unknown unknown is a feature, process, or category of information that we do not know to consider until we are investigating a situation, and even then, it may not be clear what all of the components of the missing piece are. However, slow violence is more than mere missing information. Often, it entails overpowered or silenced perspectives that might otherwise have altered the outcome. Slow violence is evident in data that are not collected or considered; it is the photos and images that we do not or cannot see; it is the discourses—the texts, narratives, practices, materialities, and identities—that do not influence how decisions are made about how human-environment relationships unfold and change.

In his work, Galtung (1969, 168) defined violence as "the cause of the difference between the potential and the actual; between what could have been and what is." With an environmental geopolitics approach, we can inquire into "what could have been and what is" by focusing on security. Chapter 1 discussed how issues become securitized and prioritized for a response beyond normal politics. Not only must there be sufficient knowledge about a situation to persuade an audience that there is a security concern, but an appropriate authority must also be identified to take action. If a discourse enables action to alleviate the security threat, then slow violence could be avoided. However, in cases where slow violence becomes evident, we would probably find that the situation was not portrayed in terms of a security threat, an appropriate authority was not identified to ameliorate the situation, or the situation was not understood as a security concern for everyone involved. In other words, situations of slow violence are missed opportunities to identify and act on a security concern. Here, though, security does not necessarily refer to traditional forms of state-level interests. Such a limited definition of security could itself enable situations of slow violence to unfold within a state even while the state itself is rendered secure. A nuanced understanding of security that includes the well-being of individuals, societies, and ecosystems, for instance, could encourage a more careful consideration of pathways that do the most good and avoid the most harm.

Risk, also discussed in chapter 1, is the other side of security. Risk is necessarily something that has potential to happen in the future. Once risk happens, it becomes a current catastrophe. The unknown specificities of risk can amplify the apprehension and fear that influence our thinking. Questions about "what could have been and what is" shift to questions about "what might yet be" when we think in terms of risk. Situations of slow violence, like risk, are difficult to clearly identify, measure, and understand in all of their dimensions. When we hear or read discourses about risk—about dangers of emerging threats and likely disasters—it is important to take the discourses apart to see how they demonstrate the three key elements of environmental geopolitics. That is, how does a discourse of risk link elements of the environment, human activity, and power dynamics, and connections between and across places? How a discourse about risk is put together, what kinds of information are included, and how it portrays risk as a threat can shape whether or not, how, for whom, and where slow violence happens.

Conclusion

This chapter has introduced science and technology studies (STS) as both an academic field and as an approach to help us understand that *science* is not a black box but a wide variety of perspectives and expertise. The selective use of science or even some forms of scientific information can serve to stabilize particular discourses about human-environment relationships. Examining five positive news stories about environmental issues provided an opportunity to demonstrate how discourses may be dismantled to allow the consideration of additional kinds of information that spin a different story. Science itself is not bad or wrong, but it is important to be able to look at how it can be used selectively to promote a particular worldview. This point is particularly helpful when scientific information is used to support discourses about security and about risk. What is being secured and what might be at risk are questions that can be interpreted in different ways to promote different courses of action.

Visual images such as graphs of scientific data and photographs can also shape how we understand environmental features beyond our immediate, direct experience. Yet even these forms of information do not offer a complete or objective discourse about their subjects. Drawing on the critical stance of STS, we can examine these forms of documentation and communication as having no *true* meaning until they are positioned within a discourse and given meaning.

Environmental geopolitics makes three key observations about dominant, mainstream discourses about human-environment relationships. First, mainstream discourses about the environment rarely specify the role and meaning of the environment. Second, they tend to consider humans' role or agency selectively, if at all, and dynamics of power tend to be invisible. Third, these discourses pay little attention to spatial dimensions of human-environment relationships that occur unevenly in different places and are intertwined with local, political, and cultural geographies. This chapter has illustrated each of these points in its consideration of how selective use of science and information can shape how we understand environment-related security and risk. We can see these themes in different forms of discourse: narrative/textual, practice, material, and identity. Examples of discourse as narrative or text include the international agreements emerging from the Paris climate talks, policies about marine protected areas, and international efforts to develop a policy to ban the use of hydrofluorocarbons. Examples of discourse as practice include how the "doughnut hole" of Arctic waters made available by melting ice is being treated as a resource frontier for fishing and tourism; the development of technologies, such as carbon dioxide injection, over practices of reduced consumption; and the pursuit of photojournalism as a means to educate and empower people about environmental concerns. Examples of discourse as materiality include efforts to ground marine protection efforts on the unique characteristics of physical ecosystems; energy infrastructure that supports fossil fuel–based electricity generation versus infrastructure that could support a transition to renewable forms of electricity; and large dams as a material discourse reflecting Cold War politics and the prioritization of river basin modernization. Finally, examples of discourse as identity are demonstrated in instances where slow violence is experienced by marginalized, less powerful groups of people or by people rendered invisible by dominant discourses. Discourse as identity is also reflected in ways that people are given options as consumers rather than empowered as citizens. The argument made throughout this book is that once we can identify a discourse, we can question the underlying assumptions and the means by which it is stabilized. Only then can we reasonably analyze a discourse and consider other perspectives.

CHAPTER SIX

Building from Here

The first chapter of this book defined environmental geopolitics as a way to examine how environmental themes are used to support geopolitical arguments and realities. Environmental geopolitics offers a way to ask how *the environment* is brought into narratives, practices, and physical realities of power and place. The foundation of this approach is an understanding that geopolitics is not a map of reality, but a narrative about the way the world works from a particular perspective. Past and current geopolitical narratives present what appears at the time as an interpretation of obvious facts about the world. Geopolitical explanations about the world or some portion of it tend to reinforce ideas about who *we* are, what kinds of risks threaten our well-being and security, and what can or should be done about it. Geopolitics is a form of storytelling that situates groups of people, usually *Us* and *Them*, within geographic situations requiring actions (or inactions) in particular places to achieve a desirable end, usually for *Us*.

To be critical in an intellectual context is to question assumptions. Taking a critical orientation allows us to ask how things got to be the way they are as well as how they might be different. Environmental geopolitics, then, is a critical approach in its curiosity about human-environment relationships. It encourages us to think through *human*: How do we identify ourselves in certain ways, and how do we label, value, or make assumptions about other people? Environmental geopolitics is curious about *the environment*: What distinguishes natural features from humans, and in what ways are we intertwined with environmental features and our ideas about them? We often rely on science as a means to interpret environmental characteristics. We have developed methodologies and measures to analyze the environment—even the environment of our own bodies—but indicators and measures are often silent about the dynamics of power that have altered the many environments in which we live. Finally, environmental geopolitics is curious about human-environment interactions—Who decides how those interactions unfold, which aspects of these interactions are prioritized and which are obscured, and how do human-environment interactions draw from and shape particular places in different ways?

The image on the next page provides a visual analogy for human-environment interactions as discussed in this book. These apartment buildings in Milan, Italy, are referred to as a "vertical forest" because they integrate a significant number of trees in the exterior landscaping of a high-rise apartment building. At first glance, it might be easy to discern the human features (constructed building) from the environmental features (trees), but beyond that, the division is less clear. The building may be a human construction, but it requires materials drawn from somewhere in the environment. It is designed to support many trees, so the architecture itself necessarily takes into consideration the requirements of trees in terms of water, soil, sunlight, and longer-term issues such as root development. Are trees installed in a building the same as trees that are part of a diverse ecosystem that includes other plants, animals, and symbiotic relationships across species? That is, are the trees part of *nature* or part of something that is *human*? Would the building exist without the trees, and would the trees exist without the building? What does bringing trees into building design indicate about values? These vertical forest buildings are a visually obvious example of human-environment interactions, but our day-to-day lives are steeped in other, less obvious examples of human-environment interactions.

Environmental geopolitics aims to tease out nuances in mainstream claims and arguments about human-environment relationships, but of particular interest is how power and spatial dimensions come into play. Power and spatial dimensions of relationships are not always obvious, but questioning assumptions can help bring these elements to light. To that end, three observations have guided the discussion in this book and the focus on human-environment interactions:

1. The role and meaning of the environment are rarely specified.
2. Humans' role or agency in these situations tends to be considered selectively. In particular, dynamics of power remain invisible and uninvestigated.

Vertical forest buildings, Milan, Italy. A material example of human-environment interactions. A clear division is more difficult than it initially seems.
Source: iStock

3. Insufficient attention is paid to spatial dimensions of human-environment relationships that occur unevenly in different places and are intertwined with local, political, and cultural geographies.

Throughout these chapters, these questions have provided a starting point from which to examine geopolitical arguments about the environment. Examples have been drawn from an array of international contexts, industrial sectors, scholarly work, and current events. Most of these examples are mainstream arguments or understandings about human-environment relationships. Some may be so familiar that they go unquestioned, but that is precisely why it is useful to consider them carefully. The image of Earth from space that appears in chapter 1, for instance, may seem almost cliché to someone flipping through the book. However, when we pause to consider what meaning that image has for us and how we arrived at that understanding, it becomes apparent how we can be swept up into a narrative that is only one of many.

Discussions in these chapters have highlighted different dimensions of discourse. Academic analyses have tended to focus on discourse in the form of texts such as speeches, documents, and narrative, including literature, film, and cartoons. Throughout this book, however, we consider other forms of discourse, such as physical materialities, identity, and practice, to demonstrate the range and variety of ways in which geopolitical claims shape the world. Material discourses are the tangible things we create and build. They are the physical infrastructures that support or obstruct the means of life. Material discourses are evident in how societies draw from environmental resources in particular ways, and they are evident in altered landscapes resulting from the extraction, construction, and movement of things, and patterns of consumption and waste. Materialities indicate a great deal about how environmental features are valued and used as well as how they are preserved or disregarded. What are the underlying values and motivations of, for instance, a green tea plantation or a collection of ice cores, and how do these material discourses reflect power dynamics and human-environment relationships?

Discourse in the form of identity is evident in how people self-select into groups or label other people as cohesive groups. Identity discourses are evident in the construction of *Us* and *Them* not just around the world, but in our own country, community, family, and other social groups with which we identify. Identity also has to do with embodiment and how we understand our own experience or that of others. These discourses intertwine with how we interpret security and risk—Whose security and whose risk? They shape how we interact with other people and with the environment. Common-pool resource arrangements, discussed in chapter 3, rely on and reinforce the importance of collaborative efforts in which all participants play an important part. They require participants in these arrangements to embody a sense of cooperation for the benefit of sustaining a particular kind of relationship with an ecosystem. How we identify ourselves shapes how we interact with the world in other ways. When we think of ourselves as citizens, we tend to think in terms of rights that we can expect and responsibilities that we owe to society. When we think of ourselves as consumers, we are more likely to think in terms of responding to economic incentives, contending with economic constraints, or product preferences. How are those identities encouraged or manipulated by others in order to achieve particular ends? That is, how are discourses constructed that favor or strengthen certain identities over others? As consumers, we might not perceive greenwashing efforts that corporations or industries may use to present products in a favorable light, yet we understand that consuming green reinforces a positive identity. As consumers, we can also resist or reject certain products, industries, and identities encouraged through advertising in any number of venues. In terms of identifying as a citizen, does that identity contribute to feelings of empowerment and agency, or to a sense of being overwhelmed and helpless? Again, how are these identities formed, and how are they intertwined with particular places either implicitly or explicitly?

Discourses of practice are the ways in which people interact with each other and with the world. Practices are what people and societies do. They are created and legitimized by particular understandings of the world, our relationships with other people, and our environmental settings. Power in the form of the capacity to act and to resist weaves throughout these discourses. Sometimes power serves to promote and maintain established discourses; at other times, power serves to challenge the status quo and promote alternative perspectives. Images in chapter 1 of people marching for action on climate change illustrate practices of engagement and resistance. Other chapters have considered several examples of discourse as practice. Chapter 2 discussed government policies encouraging people either to have fewer children (as in China) or more children (as in Russia). Advances in technology in the form of fuel, irrigation, and pesticides have promoted changes in agricultural practice, products, productivity, and impact. Chapter 3 discussed why it matters that coal and petroleum are associated with different practices of extraction, political empowerment, transportation, and consumption. Chapter 4 considered different views on the appropriateness of applying military training and practices in situations of environmental instability. In all of these cases, there is value in examining practice—what people are doing, how they are engaging with or responding to an environmental setting, and the intended as well as unintended outcomes of those interactions.

All of these forms of discourse—narrative, materiality, identity, and practice—are interwoven. How we think of ourselves shapes how we interact with the world and the kinds of practices that we engage in either mindfully or mindlessly. Discourse also operates at societal and national levels. How we view and value the environment is evident in popular culture, legal norms, education priorities, transportation systems, shopping habits, leisure travel, and political preferences. Focusing on discourses, particularly over time and in different places, can help us to understand environmental geopolitics and the many forms and impacts of human-environment relationships. The value in studying discourses in multiple forms is that it becomes evident how these discourses are stabilized and legitimized.

Stabilizing Discourses with Science

There are many ways to stabilize a discourse in an effort to advance a particular view of the world. This book has considered three strategies that are frequently used to stabilize discourses about human-environment relationships. The first strategy is to use science to present a view of the world as fact. Discussions on the Enlightenment and modernity, in chapters 3 and 4 respectively, have provided useful historical context about the emergence of dominant forms of science understood by many to be a direct translation of the meaning of *nature*. Science in the form of empirical observation, organized information, instrumentation, and calculation may be asserted as raw knowledge about the world, but scientific measures and methodologies are steeped in human values and selective perspectives. Science may tell us many things about the world, but it cannot tell a full and complete story. Science is a way to interpret that which can be measured (or is thought to be important enough to measure), but for any given feature, there are dimensions we cannot measure or do not know to measure. For example, it is difficult to measure latent health effects that appear years after exposure to certain chemicals or a toxic environment. We can make educated speculations about possible latent health effects, or we can study known cases of delayed responses to various exposures, but it is difficult to study latent effects through controlled experimentation. This is part of the reason that slow violence in the form of delayed health effects can be particularly invisible and insidious: invisible because the effects are difficult to bring to light in time to limit damage, and insidious because by the time the effects are apparent, the damage has already been done. In another example about the limits of science, considerable research has assessed the changing composition of the atmosphere and implications for life systems on the planet. Scientists have measured, for instance, how levels of carbon dioxide in the atmosphere have changed over time. What it more difficult to discern are the sources of that carbon dioxide in terms of emissions for basic survival (burning coal for cooking) versus luxury emissions (such as driving an expensive vehicle for recreational purposes). Such political economy dimensions of atmospheric carbon dioxide reveal much about the inequities of who is benefitting the most from current arrangements. This is another example of a useful and meaningful phenomenon that is difficult to measure, so it is often overlooked or not considered in scientific assessments.

There have also been examples in this book of arguments presented as scientific fact intended to persuade people to think and act in certain ways. Malthus's graph showing the exponential increase of human population far exceeding more slowly increasing food resources is still referred to as universal fact. The graph is not based on actual data of population growth but on Malthus's own speculation of events happening in a particular historical context. Similarly, the $I = PAT$ equation appears as mathematical fact until we examine how these factors of environmental impact, human population, affluence, and technology might actually be related in particular places. These examples from chapter 2 illustrate how claims of scientific authority have influenced how people think and act in the world even though there is little scientific support for either of these claims to universal truths. We also examined the well-known graph of peak oil in chapter 2 as purportedly depicting scientific fact. On closer inspection, though, there are many assumptions underlying the understanding of a sharp drop-off in the availability of petroleum. Chapter 5 took a closer look at the interdisciplinary field of science and technology studies as a way to step back and assess practices and claims of science and the role they have in shaping society. In that chapter, a sample news story provided material to demonstrate ways in which scientific information is used selectively to shape a particular view of the world. This discussion suggested that although there may never be an entirely complete view of anything, there is value in questioning the facts and underlying assumptions of a scientific argument. Such an approach opens the possibility to consider alternative perspectives and dimensions to any particular situation, and it broadens our understanding as well as our options for response.

Stepping back from scientific claims to observe and inquire into how science—and scientists—operates allows an expanded view of science as more than *just the facts*. Science and technology studies helps us to think about whose facts, why these facts and not others, and what facts might we be missing because we might not know to look for them. Other facts might challenge the status quo and are therefore downplayed. As environmental geopolitics operationalizes curiosity about underlying assumptions, it is important to extend that curiosity to science, how it is being used, and what kinds of knowledge or viewpoints might be missing from the dominant perspective. Science has arrived at its current state through the actions, observations, and decisions of particular people who focused on particular things to measure and study. Other things that are deemed less important, less interesting, or less measurable do not receive the same amount of attention. Mainstream science in the United States and other Western societies has roots in Enlightenment thinking that worked well with capitalist expansion. Both of these modes of thought and practice separated people from the environment, and even people from people (*Us* and *Them*). Modernity emerged and further emphasized the ability of science and technology to divide and manage from an allegedly objective and rational viewpoint. On one hand, then, the scientific systems and information we use are imbued with human values. On the other hand, scientific information has no meaning in itself until it is drawn into preexisting, value-laden arguments. The presence or absence of petroleum, timber, or strategic minerals, for instance, have no meaning in themselves until these features are assigned value and importance within human systems. Environmental geopolitics encourages a critical stance that questions what kinds of science support a particular discourse about the world. From there, we might consider what other kinds of knowledge systems or ontologies could be useful in understanding and addressing human-environment dynamics.

Security, Risk, and Slow Violence

Two additional strategies to stabilize a discourse are like ends of a single spectrum: security and risk. A view of the world that explains how we can maintain or enhance our security can be appealing. Similarly, a view of the world that explains why something or someone poses a significant threat to our well-being can also be motivating. Geopolitical discourses that identify particular places, groups of people, or spatial processes likely to hasten or threaten our well-being can be persuasive because they appear to point to tangible aspects of the world over which we might exert control for our own ends. Throughout the book there have been several opportunities to ask, What is being secured and for whom? That question also entails a *where*. Where are well-being and power being secured, and at the same time, but perhaps given less attention, where will the well-being of people, species, or ecosystems be rendered less robust and worse off? An environmental geopolitical analysis of discourse can be particularly useful when it focuses attention on notions of risk or security. Some discourses assert that risk or security are associated with particular places, with the movement of things from place to place, or with people who either identify as a group associated with place (e.g., our national culture) or with people who are labeled because of where they are or what they are doing with spatial effect (e.g., transnational migrants). Discourses that purport to explain risk or security may explicitly or implicitly call for action, or they may suggest inaction. Environmental geopolitics assists in the unpuzzling of a discourse: What are the underlying values or goals? Who benefits from this view and where? How do aspects of the environment or environmental features play into this worldview? What is the call to action (or inaction) embedded in this discourse?

Just as environmental geopolitics questions discourses that claim to support security or minimize risk, it is also a useful way to examine what is meant by risk and security. Looking specifically at assumptions about the role and meaning of an environmental feature, at human agency and dynamics of power, and at spatial dimensions of a particular discourse advances a deeper understanding of what is being secured or threatened. Similarly, critical security studies question the notion of security as something that might be spatially contained or controlled through political power and military might. Scholarly work on risk examines what we can reliably know about something that may or may not happen in the future and how the perception of a potential threat is communicated and amplified. Environmental geopolitics draws on these bodies of knowledge and contributes a geographical perspective to see how a given discourse constructs security or risk as being associated with a particular place or spatial process.

Slow violence is another theme this book considers in terms of geopolitical discourse, particularly in chapters 3 and 5. Unlike more visually recognizable, immediate violence, slow violence can become apparent over time, disconnected from direct action. It can result unintentionally or through neglect. It may take the form of irreversible, negative impacts on ecosystems, human health and well-being, and lost capacity to thrive. Slow violence can be difficult to measure and quantify, so it evades attention and response. It can be tricky to visualize through familiar modes of illustration. Two images in chapter 3 depict different aspects of slow violence associated with industrial-scale palm oil plantations in Indonesia. The photo showing haze of smoke in Thailand all the way from the deforestation fires in Indonesia suggests the kinds of negative health impacts that will affect people even at a distance from the expansion of palm oil plantations. Less evident is the slow violence in the second image showing a palm oil plantation. The tidy rows of palms belie the destruction of ecosystems, human settlements, and animal communities that existed before the land was cleared. That destruction is more than slow; in some ways it is total. It is also ongoing and irreversible. How is it possible to measure, calculate, and assess what has been lost? Similarly, the map of oil spills in US waters (map 3.2) and the description of the damage done to ecosystems along the Alaska coastline from an oil spill that happened decades ago tell stories of ongoing struggle to recover and survive. In some ways, that neglectful violence has been done, but in other ways it persists where practices have not changed.

Slow violence may be associated with different forms of discourse such as practices that undermine the well-being of people and ecosystems. Slow violence tends to be linked to groups of people who are vulnerable because they happen to be in a particular place at a particular time or because they have relatively less power in society to defend themselves and their interests. In addition to these identities of vulnerable people, slow violence is also embodied—literally—in the diminished health, freedom, safety, and rights of groups of people who are exposed, marginalized, or powerless. The other side of slow violence are the people who make decisions and policies that allow destructive and neglectful practices in the interest of making certain gains without paying the full cost or having to take responsibility for negative effects, anticipated or not. Slow violence is material. Landscapes are created, destroyed, or otherwise altered in ways that harm people and ecosystems. On page 175 is a photo of the Farallon Islands, which are located about thirty miles off the coast of San Francisco, California. The islands appear lovely but are silent about the slow violence potentially unfolding under the surface. The US Atomic Energy Commission used this area as a dumpsite for low-level nuclear waste from 1946 to 1970. Nearly fifty thousand containers of radioactive waste were sunk here (shot with holes if they happened to float). Additionally, the wreckage of a ship used in the nuclear tests on the Bikini Atoll was towed to these islands, smoldering, and sunk. The effects of this nuclear waste on nearby areas have not been studied, so the degree and extent of lingering contamination are unknown. The area around these islands is now known as the Gulf of the Farallones National Marine Sanctuary and is a protected habitat for whales, seals, and great white sharks. This photo depicting slow violence reflects the notion that this kind of violence can be difficult to see, and therefore, it can be a challenge to study and understand.

Finally, slow violence is also evident in narrative—the ways in which we speak of people and describe their place in the world. Slow violence is evi-

Gulf of the Farallones National Marine Sanctuary. A picture of slow violence?
Source: *Atlas Obscura*/Wikimedia Commons (public domain)

dent in the absence of recognition of people and in ways ecosystems are not valued. The term *environmental externalities* refers to environmental impacts that are not quantified, valued, or assessed in the process of determining the cost of a particular item or action. Air pollution, for instance, is an environmental externality that is not captured in the price of a gallon of gas. That is, air pollution caused from burning that gallon of gas is not accounted for in the price of gas, but in the long run, air pollution is a cost to everyone. In the same way, slow violence is often glaring in the ways it is absent from conversations, policies, and debates, and in this way it can persist. The approach of environmental geopolitics, however, encourages the questioning of assumptions about discourses, and that includes questioning assumptions about what is not considered to be important in a given discourse.

Adjusting (Dis)Course

In Kalkar, Germany, in 1972, construction began on the SNR-300, the first large nuclear breeding reactor in the country. The reactor's unconventional design used plutonium fuel cooled by sodium. Despite the higher likelihood of catastrophe associated with this kind of reactor and after multiple delays, the project was eventually completed. The result was a state-of-the-art material discourse reflecting both the political context of the Cold War and scientific advancement in nuclear technology for civilian purposes. Authorities, however, decided not to fire up the reactor in part due to concern from people living in the area.

> Totally unused, the building was essentially one of the most expensive, complicated pieces of trash in the world. Among the more amazing facts about the unused reactor are its cost—20,000 individual houses could have been constructed with the money; its size—the total complex being some 80 soccer fields large, made of enough concrete to construct a highway from Amsterdam to Maastricht; and its complexity—with enough wire strung up in the complex to circle the entire global twice. (Atlas Obscura 2017)

The image of the cooling tower is colorful even in black and white, and it doesn't take much to picture the swing ride inside of it. This example of a repurposed nuclear facility provides a memorable and useful image for the closing comments of this book.

Wunderland in Kalkar, Germany. An unused nuclear power plant repurposed as an amusement park serves as a useful metaphor for the potential to rethink human-environment relationships.
Source: Koetjuh/Wikimedia (public domain)

The aim throughout this book has been to examine and question ways that we think about human-environment relationships by focusing on how environmental features are understood and portrayed, the role of human agency and dynamics of power, and geographies of human-environment interactions. Recognizing that different discourses or understandings about the world are reflected in what we say, do, and build allows a clearer view of how these understandings are stabilized and legitimized. How can we create new narratives about our relationship with environmental features? How might we change course despite the fact so much is invested in the status quo? If it is possible to see how a particular view of the world is stabilized by invoking particular scientific evidence or through calls to enhance security or avoid risk, then it is possible to consider new ways to construct human-environment relationships. Scientific knowledge and interpretations of security and risk certainly have relevance for this task, but how we interpret these fields and draw from them will likely need fresh perspectives. This is the challenge of environmental geopolitics: to create discourses—narratives, identities, practices, and materialities—that serve to avoid, diminish, and address processes of violence, slow or otherwise.

Part of this work will be to identify values and objectives first, and then determine the appropriate knowledge, incentives, and policies to bring us closer to those ends (Sarewitz 2004). That process will involve conversations and debates, and at its heart will be the communication of ideas and possibilities. Returning to the images on the front and back cover of this book, we see similar information portrayed in vastly different ways, and these presentations will appeal differently to different people. This point is helpful in thinking about how to communicate new ideas and alternative interpretations of familiar problems. How can we look at the same things in different ways through arts and sciences, mapping techniques (which are both art and science), stories, participation, teaching, writing, blogging, vlogging, voting, and consuming (or not consuming)? As individuals and groups (of various form and function), how can we adjust the structures within which society operates to open possibilities that might not otherwise exist? Geopolitical discourses change over time. How we view, value, and fear the world also changes depending on how discourses are stabilized or destabilized, promoted, disrupted, and reinterpreted.

These are questions for all of us to think through, and each of us can contribute in ways that have meaning for us. To provide definitive answers in a book would defeat the purpose of encouraging creative potential. Instead, the aim of this book has been to focus attention on how some familiar, dominant ways of thinking about human-environmental relationships have developed and why they persist. Once the inner workings of a discourse are recognized, it is possible to embark on the project of questioning the ways in which we think about the world toward reshaping discourse. The tools are available to foster new narratives, practices, fusions of identity, and material realities. It is up to us to use them.

References

Agamben, Giorgio. 2002. "Security and Terror." *Theory and Event* 5 (4): 585–602. Translated by Carolin Emcke.

Agnew, John. 2011. "Presidential Address: Waterpower: Politics and the Geography of Water Provision." *Annals of the Association of American Geographers* 101 (3): 463–76.

Agnew, John, and Luca Muscarà. 2012. *Making Political Geography*, 2nd ed. Lanham: Rowman & Littlefield.

Amuzegar, Jahangir. 1982. "Oil Wealth: A Very Mixed Blessing." *Foreign Affairs* 60 (4): 814–35.

Appleman, Philip. 1976. "Introduction." In *An Essay on the Principle of Population: Text, Sources, and Background Criticism*, ed. Philip Appleman, xi–xxvii. New York: W. W. Norton.

Ascher, William. 1999. *Why Governments Waste Natural Resources: Policy Failures in Developing Countries*. Baltimore: The Johns Hopkins University Press.

———. 2000. "Understanding Why Governments in Developing Countries Waste Natural Resources." *Environment* 42 (2): 8–18.

Atkinson, David, and Klaus Dodds. 2000. "Introduction: Geopolitical Traditions: A Century of Geopolitical Thought." In *Geopolitical Traditions: A Century of Geopolitical Thought*, ed. Klaus Dodds and David Atkinson, 1–24. London: Routledge.

Atkinson, David, Peter Jackson, David Sibley, and Neil Washbourne. 2005. "Introduction: Difference and Belonging." In *Cultural Geography: A Critical Dictionary of Key Concepts*, ed. David Atkinson, Peter Jackson, David Sibley, and Neil Washbourne, 89–90. London: I. B. Taurus.

Atlas Obscura. 2017. "Wunderland Kalkar." *http://www.atlasobscura.com/places/wunderland-kalkar*.

Auty, Richard M. 2001. *Resource Abundance and Economic Development*. New York: Oxford University Press.

Auty, Richard M., and Raymond French Mikesell. 1998. *Sustainable Development in Mineral Economies*. Oxford: Clarendon Press.

Baechler, Günther. 1999. "Environmental Degradation in the South as a Cause of Armed Conflict." In *Environmental Change and Security: A European Perspective*, ed. Alexander Carius and Kurt M. Lietzmann, 107–29. Berlin: Springer-Verlag.

Barnett, Jon. 2001. *The Meaning of Environmental Security: Ecological Politics and Policy in the New Security Era*. New York: Zed Books.

———. 2000. "Destabilizing the Environment-Conflict Thesis." *Review of International Studies* 26 (2): 271–88.

Barnett, Jon, and W. Neil Adger. 2009. "Environmental Change, Human Security, and Violent Conflict." In *Global Environmental Change and Human Security*, ed. Richard A. Matthew, Jon Barnett, Bryan McDonald, and Karen L. O'Brien, 119–36. Cambridge: The MIT Press.

Barry, Andrew. 2013. *Material Politics: Disputes along the Pipeline*. Malden: Wiley Blackwell.

Bassin, Mark. 1987. "Imperialism and the Nation State in Friedrich Ratzel's Political Geography." *Progress in Human Geography* 11: 473–95.

Beck, Ulrich. 1992. *Risk Society: Towards a New Modernity*. Translated by Mark Ritter. London: Sage Publications.

———. 2006. "Living in the World Risk Society." *Economy and Society* 35 (3): 329–45.

———. 2009. *World at Risk*. Translated by Ciaran Cronin. Cambridge: Polity Press.

Beckett, Margaret. 2006. Untitled speech on foreign policy and climate security given at the British Embassy, Berlin, 24 October.

Bijker, Wiebe E. 2001. "Understanding Technological Culture through a Constructivist View of Science, Technology, and Society." In *Visions of STS: Counterpoints in Science, Technology, and Society Studies*, ed. Stephen H. Cutcliffe and Carl Mitcham, 19–34. Albany: State University of New York Press.

Boonzaier, Lisa, and Daniel Pauly. 2016. "Marine Protection Targets: An Updated Assessment of Global Progress." *Oryx* 50 (1): 27–35.

Braasch, Gary. 2013. "Climate Change: Is Seeing Believing?" *Bulletin of the Atomic Scientists* 69 (6): 33–41.

Bridge, Gavin. 2010. "Geographies of Peak Oil: The Other Carbon Problem." *Geoforum* 41 (4): 523–30.

———. 2015. "Energy (In)Security: World-Making in an Age of Scarcity." *Geographical Journal* 181 (4): 328–39.

Brown, Lester R. 2012. *Full Planet, Empty Plates: The New Geopolitics of Food Scarcity*. New York: W. W. Norton & Company.

Buxton, Nick, and Ben Hayes, eds. 2016. *The Secure and the Dispossessed: How the Military and Corporations Are Shaping a Climate-Changed World*. London: Pluto Press.

Buzan, Barry, Ole Waever, and Jaap de Wilde. 1998. *Security: A New Framework for Analysis*. London: Lynne Rienner.

Capstick, Stuart, Lorraine Whitmarsh, Wouter Poortinga, Nick Pidgeon, and Paul Upham. 2015. "International Trends in Public Perceptions of Climate Change over the Past Quarter Century." *WIREs Climate Change* 6: 35–61.

Carson, Rachel. 1962. *Silent Spring*. Boston: Houghton Mifflin.

Castree, Noel. 2003a. "The Geopolitics of Nature." In *A Companion to Political Geography*, ed. John Agnew, Katharyne Mitchell, and Gerard Toal, 423–39. Malden: Blackwell Publishing.

———. 2003b. "Environmental Issues: Relational Ontologies and Hybrid Politics." *Progress in Human Geography* 27 (2): 203–11.

———. 2014a. "The Anthropocene and Geography I: The Back Story." *Geography Compass* 8/7: 436–49.

———. 2014b. "The Anthropocene and Geography II: Current Contributions." *Geography Compass* 8/7: 450–63.

———. 2014c. "The Anthropocene and Geography III: Future Directions." *Geography Compass* 8/7: 464–76.

Charlton, Joseph. 2013. "Skip Work, Have Sex: Russians Celebrate 'Day of Conception' as Sporting Community Continues to Criticize Putin's Anti-Gay Legislation." *Independent*, September 12, 2013. http://www.independent.co.uk/news/world/europe/skip-work-have-sex-russians-celebrate-day-of-conception-as-sporting-community-continues-to-criticise-8812840.html.

Chertow, Marian R. 2001. "The IPAT Equation and Its Variants." *Journal of Industrial Ecology* 4 (4): 13–29.

CNA (Center for Naval Analysis). 2007. *National Security and the Threat of Climate Change*. Alexandria, VA: The CNA Corporation. https://www.cna.org/cna_files/pdf/National%20Security%20and%20the%20Threat%20of%20Climate%20Change.pdf.

———. 2014. *National Security and the Accelerating Risks of Climate Change*. Alexandria, VA: The CNA Corporation. https://www.cna.org/cna_files/pdf/MAB_5-8-14.pdf.

Collier, Paul. 2000. "Doing Well Out of War: An Economic Perspective." In *Greed and Grievance: Economic Agendas in Civil War*, ed. David Malone and Mats Collier, 91–111. Boulder: Lynne Rienner.

Collier, Paul, and Anke Hoeffler. 2004. "Greed and Grievance in Civil War." *Oxford Economic Papers* 56: 563–95.

Commoner, Barry. 1971. *The Closing Circle: Nature, Man, and Technology*. New York: Alfred A. Knopf.

Council on Foreign Relations. 2017. *Arctic Imperatives: Reinforcing U.S. Strategy on America's Fourth Coast* (Independent Task Force Report No. 75). New York: Council on Foreign Relations.

Cox, Robert. 1981. "Social Forces, States and World Orders: Beyond International Relations Theory." *Millennium: Journal of International Studies* 10 (2): 126–55.

Crown Estate. 2017. "Offshore Wind Electricity." https://www.thecrownestate.co.uk/energy-minerals-and-infrastructure/offshore-wind-energy/.

Crutzen, Paul J., and Eugene F. Stoermer. 2000. "The Anthropocene." International Geosphere-Biosphere Programme (IGBP) *Global Change Newsletter* (May) 41: 17–18.

Dalby, Simon. 1990. *Creating the Second Cold War: The Discourse of Politics*. New York: Guilford Publications, Inc., and London: Pinter Publications.

———. 1999. "Threats from the South? Geopolitics Equity, and Environmental Security." In *Contested Grounds: Security and Conflict in the New Environmental Politics*, ed. Daniel Deudney and Richard A. Matthew, 155–85. Albany: State University of New York Press.

———. 2009. *Security and Environmental Change*. Malden: Polity Press.

———. 2013. "The Geopolitics of Climate Change." *Political Geography* 37: 38–47.

———. 2014. "Geographic Pedagogy in the Anthropocene." In Johnson and Morehouse (2014), 442–44.

de Seversky, Alexander P. 1942. *Victory through Air Power*. New York: Simon and Schuster.

De Soysa, Indra. 2002. "Paradise Is a Bazar? Greed, Creed and Governance in Civil War, 1989–1999." *Journal of Peace Research* 39 (4): 395–416.

Death, Carl, ed. 2014. *Critical Environmental Politics*. London: Routledge.

Deligiannis, Tom. 2012. "The Evolution of Environment-Conflict Research: Toward a Livelihood Framework." *Global Environmental Politics* 12 (1): 78–100.

Demeritt, David. 1994. "The Nature of Metaphors in Cultural Geography and Environmental History." *Progress in Human Geography* 18 (2): 163–85.

———. 2002. "What Is the 'Social Construction of Nature'? A Typology and Sympathetic Critique." *Progress in Human Geography* 26 (6): 767–90.

Dennis, Brady, and Chris Mooney. 2016. "It Wasn't Entirely Bad News. Here Are Five Positive Environmental Stories from 2016." *Washington Post*, December 28, 2016. https://www.washingtonpost.com/news/energy-environment/wp/2016/12/28/it-wasnt-entirely-bad-news-here-are-five-positive-environmental-stories-from-2016/?utm_term=.601249cbc255&wpisrc=nl_green&wpmm=1.

Detges, Adrian. 2017. *Climate and Conflict: Reviewing the Statistical Evidence, A Summary for Policy-Makers*. Berlin: Adelphi and the Federal Foreign Office. https://www.adelphi.de/en/publication/climate-and-conflict-reviewing-statistical-evidence.

Deudney, Daniel. 1991. "Environment and Security: Muddled Thinking." *Bulletin of Atomic Scientists* 47 (3): 22–29.

Diamond, Jared. 2005. *Collapse: How Societies Choose to Fail or Succeed*. New York: Viking Press.

Dietz, Thomas, Elinor Ostrom, and Paul C. Stern. 2003. "The Struggle to Govern the Commons." *Science* 302 (December): 1907–12.

Diez, Thomas, Franziskus von Lucke, and Zehra Wellmann. 2016. *The Securitisation of Climate Change: Actors, Processes and Consequences*. New York: Routledge.

Dillon, Michael. 2008. "Underwriting Security." *Security Dialogue* 39 (2–3): 309–32.

Dimick, Dennis. 2014. "As World's Population Booms, Will Its Resources Be Enough for Us?" *National Geographic*. http://news.nationalgeographic.com/news/2014/09/140920-population-11billion-demographics-anthropocene/.

Dittmer, Jason. 2005. "Captain America's Empire: Reflections on Identity, Popular Culture, and Post-9/11 Geopolitics." *Annals of the Association of American Geographers* 95 (3): 626–43.

———. 2015. "The Politics of Writing Global Space." *Progress in Human Geography* 39 (5): 668–69.

DoD (Department of Defense). 2010. Quadrennial Defense Review Report, February. http://www.comw.org/qdr/fulltext/1002QDR2010.pdf.

———. 2014a. *Department of Defense 2014 Climate Change Adaptation Roadmap*. Alexandria, VA: Office of the Deputy Under Secretary of Defense for Installations and Environment (Science & Technology Directorate). https://www.acq.osd.mil/eie/downloads/CCARprint_wForward_e.pdf.

———. 2014b. Quadrennial Defense Review Report, Department of Defense, March. http://archive.defense.gov/pubs/2014_Quadrennial_Defense_Review.pdf.

———. 2016. *DoD Directive 4715.21: Climate Change Adaptation and Resilience*. Office of the Under Secretary of Defense for Acquisition, Technology, and Logistics (Effective 14 January 2016). http://www.dtic.mil/whs/directives.

Dodds, Klaus. 1996. "The 1982 Falklands War and a Critical Geopolitical Eye: Steve Bell and the If . . . Cartoons." *Political Geography* 15 (6): 571–92.

———. 2001. "Political Geography III: Critical Geopolitics after Ten Years." *Progress in Human Geography* 25 (3): 469–84.

———. 2003. "Licensed to Stereotype: Geopolitics, James Bond and the Spectre of Balkanism." *Geopolitics* 8 (2): 125–56.

———. 2005. "Screening Geopolitics: James Bond and the Early Cold War Films (1962–1967)." *Geopolitics* 10 (2): 266–89.

Dodds, Klaus, Merje Kuus, and Joanne Sharp. 2013. "Introduction: Geopolitics and Its Critics." In *The Ashgate Research Companion to Critical Geopolitics*, ed. Klaus Dodds, Merje Kuus, and Joanne Sharp, 3–14. Burlington: Ashgate.

Dorling, Daniel, Mark Newman, and Anna Barford. 2008. *The Atlas of the Real World: Mapping the Way We Live*. New York: Thames & Hudson.

Dreyfus, Hubert L., and Paul Rabinow. 1983. *Michel Foucault: Beyond Structuralism and Hermeneutics*, 2nd ed. Chicago: The University of Chicago Press.

Dunning, Thad. 2005. "Resource Dependence, Economic Performance and Political Stability." *Journal of Conflict Resolution* 49 (4): 451–82.

Economist. 2015. "Fisheries: Drawing the Line." September 2, 2015.

———. 2016. "Why World Leaders Are Meeting to Discuss Hydrofluorocarbons." October 10, 2016. http://www.economist.com/blogs/economist-explains/2016/10/economist-explains-4.

———. 2017. "Briefing: Renewable Energy, A World Turned Upside Down." February 25, 2017. http://www.economist.com/news/briefing/21717365-wind-and-solar-energy-are-disrupting-century-old-model-providing-electricity-what-will.

Edkins, Jenny. 1999. *Poststructuralism and International Relations: Bringing the Political Back In*. London: Lynne Rienner.
Ehrlich, Paul R. 1968. *The Population Bomb*. New York: Ballantine Books.
Ehrlich, Paul R., and John. P. Holdren. 1971. "Impact of Population Growth." *Science* 171 (3977): 1212–17.
———. 1972. "A Bulletin Dialogue on *The Closing Circle*: Critique." *Bulletin of Atomic Scientists* 28 (5): 16–27.
Elden, Stuart. 2013. "Secure the Volume: Vertical Geopolitics and the Depth of Power." *Political Geography* 34: 35–51.
Ellsworth, William L. 2013. "Injection-Induced Earthquakes." *Science* 341 (6142): 1225942.
European Commission Climate Action. 2017. "Paris Agreement." https://ec.europa.eu/clima/policies/international/negotiations/paris_en.
Fairhead, James, Melissa Leach, and Ian Scoones. 2012. "Green Grabbing: A New Appropriation of Nature?" *Journal of Peasant Studies* 39 (2): 237–61.
Fearon, James D. 2004. "Why Do Some Civil Wars Last So Much Longer Than Others?" *Journal of Peace Research* 41: 275–303.
———. 2005. "Primary Commodity Exports and Civil War." *Journal of Conflict Resolution* 49 (4): 483–507.
Floyd, Rita. 2010. *Security and the Environment: Securitization Theory and US Environmental Security Policy*. Cambridge: Cambridge University Press.
Forsyth, Tim. 2008. "The Contentious World of Jared Diamond's *Collapse*." In *Contentious Geographies: Environmental Knowledge, Meaning, Scale*, ed. Michael K. Goodman, Maxwell T. Boykoff, and Kyle T. Evered, 27–38. Farnham: Ashgate.
Gallagher, Catherine. 1986. "The Body versus the Social Body in the Works of Thomas Malthus and Henry Mayhew." *Representations* 14 (Spring): 83–106.
Galtung, Johan. 1969. "Violence, Peace, and Peace Research." *Journal of Peace Research* 6 (3): 167–91.
Gelb, Alan. 1986. "Adjustment to Windfall Gains: A Comparative Analysis of Oil-Exporting Countries." In *Natural Resources and the Macroeconomy*, edited by J. Peter Neary and Sweder Van Wijnbergen, 54–93. Oxford: Basil Blackwell.
———. 1988. *Oil Windfalls: Blessing or Curse?* New York: Oxford University Press.
Gemenne, François. 2015. "The Anthropocene and Its Victims." In *The Anthropocene and the Global Environmental Crisis: Rethinking Modernity in a New Epoch*, ed. Clive Hamilton, Christophe Bonneuil, and François Gemenne, 168–74. New York: Routledge.
Gilbert, Emily. 2012. "The Militarization of Climate Change." *ACME An International E-Journal for Critical Geographies* 11 (1): 1–14.
Gillis, Justin. 2016. "In Zika Epidemic, a Warning on Climate Change." *New York Times*, February 20, 2016. http://www.nytimes.com/2016/02/21/world/americas/in-zika-epidemic-a-warning-on-climate-change.html.
Glantz, Michael H. 1998. "Creeping Environmental Problems in the Aral Sea Basin." In *Central Eurasian Water Crisis: Caspian, Aral, and Dead Seas*, ed. Iwao Kobori and Michael H. Glantz, 25–52. Tokyo: United Nations University Press.

Gleditsch, Nils Petter, Kathryn Furlong, Håvard Hegre, Bethany Lacina, and Taylor Owen. 2006. "Conflicts over Shared Rivers: Resource Scarcity or Fuzzy Boundaries?" *Political Geography* 25 (4): 361–82.

Gleick, Peter. 1991. "Environment and Security: The Clear Connections." *Bulletin of Atomic Scientists* 47 (3): 17–21.

———. 2014. "Water, Drought, Climate Change, and Conflict in Syria." *Weather, Climate, and Society* 6 (3): 331–40.

Glover, Leigh. 2006. *Postmodern Climate Change*. New York: Routledge.

———. 2015. "Postmodern Interpretations." In *Reframing Climate Change: Constructing Ecological Geopolitics*, ed. Shannon O'Lear and Simon Dalby, 14–30. New York: Routledge.

Goeminne, Gert. 2010. "Climate Policy Is Dead, Long Live Climate Politics!" *Ethics, Place and Environment* 13 (2): 207–14.

Graham, Stephen. 2016. *Vertical: The City from Satellites to Bunkers*. London: Verso.

Grandoni, Dino, and Paulina Firozi. 2017. "The United States and Syria Are Now the Only Two Countries out of the Paris Climate Accord." *Washington Post*, September 21, 2017. https://www.washingtonpost.com/news/powerpost/paloma/the-energy-202/2017/09/21/the-energy-202-the-united-states-and-syria-are-now-the-only-two-countries-out-of-the-paris-climate-accord/59c2dd0930fb04517665 0d96/?utm_term=.fd576a267cf7.

Gray, Leslie C., and William G. Moseley. 2005. "A Geographical Perspective on Poverty-Environment Interactions." *Geographical Journal* 171 (1): 9–23.

Gross, Matthias. 2016. "Risk as Zombie Category: Ulrich Beck's Unfinished Project on the 'Non-Knowledge' Society." *Security Dialogue* 47 (5): 386–402.

Haas, Peter M. 2002. "Constructing Environmental Conflicts from Resource Scarcity." *Global Environmental Politics* 2 (1): 1–11.

Hackett, Edward J., Olga Amsterdamska, Michael Lynch, and Judy Wajcman. 2008. "Introduction." In *The Handbook of Science and Technology Studies*, 3rd edition, ed. Edward J. Hackett, Olga Amsterdamska, Michael Lynch, and Judy Wajcman, 1–7. Cambridge: The MIT Press.

Hamilton, Clive, Christophe Bonneuil, and François Gemenne. 2015. "Thinking the Anthropocene." In *The Anthropocene and the Global Environmental Crisis: Rethinking Modernity in a New Epoch*, ed. Clive Hamilton, Christophe Bonneuil, and François Gemenne, 1–14. New York: Routledge.

Hansen, Lene. 2006. *Security as Practice: Discourse Analysis and the Bosnian War*. London: Routledge.

Haraway, Donna. 1988. "Situated Knowledges: The Science Question in Feminism and the Privilege of Partial Perspective." *Feminist Studies* 14 (3): 575–99.

Hardin, Garrett. 1968. "The Tragedy of the Commons." *Science* 162 (3859): 1243–48.

Harris, Andrew. 2015. "Vertical Urbanisms: Opening up Geographies of the Three-Dimensional City." *Progress in Human Geography* 39 (5): 601–20.

Harvey, David. 1996. *Justice, Nature & the Geography of Difference*. Cambridge: Blackwell.

Hemmingsen, Emma. 2010. "At the Base of Hubbert's Peak: Grounding the Debate on Petroleum Scarcity." *Geoforum* 41: 531–40.

Hildyard, Nicholas, Larry Lohmann, and Sarah Sexton. 2012. *Energy Security for Whom? For What?* Dorset: The Corner House. http://www.thecornerhouse.org.uk/sites/thecornerhouse.org.uk/files/Energy%20Security%20For%20Whom%20For%20What.pdf.

Holleman, Marybeth. 2014. "After 25 Years, Exxon Valdez Oil Spill Hasn't Ended." CNN Opinion Online, March 25, 2014. http://www.cnn.com/2014/03/23/opinion/holleman-exxon-valdez-anniversary/index.html.

Homer-Dixon, Thomas F. 1999. *Environment, Security and Violence*. Princeton: Princeton University Press.

Hommel, Demian, and Alexander B. Murphy. 2013. "Rethinking Geopolitics in an Era of Climate Change." *GeoJournal* 78 (3): 507–24.

Hornborg, Alf. 2015. "The Political Ecology of the Technocene: Uncovering Ecologically Unequal Exchange in the World-System." In *The Anthropocene and the Global Environmental Crisis: Rethinking Modernity in a New Epoch*, ed. Clive Hamilton, Christophe Bonneuil, and François Gemenne, 57–69. New York: Routledge.

Howarth, Robert W., Anthony Ingraffea, and Terry Engelder. 2011. "Natural Gas: Should Fracking Stop?" *Nature* 477 (7364): 271–75.

Howe, Joshua P. 2011. "History and Climate: A Road Map to Humanistic Scholarship on Climate Change." *Climatic Change* 105 (1): 357–63.

Hubbert, M. King. 1969. "Energy Resources." In *Resources and Man*, ed. P. Cloud, 157–242. San Francisco: W. H. Freeman.

Huber, Matthew T. 2011. "Enforcing Scarcity: Oil, Violence, and the Making of the Market." *Annals of the Association of American Geographers* 101 (4): 816–26.

Jasanoff, Sheila. 2012. *Science and Public Reason*. New York: Routledge.

Jasanoff, Sheila, Gerald E. Markle, James C. Petersen, and Trevor Pinch, eds. 1995. *Handbook of Science and Technology Studies*. Thousand Oaks: Sage.

Jasanoff, Sheila, and Brian Wynne. 1998. "Science and Decisionmaking." In *Human Choice and Climate Change Volume One: The Societal Framework*, ed. Steve Rayner and Elizabeth L. Malone, 1–77. Columbus: Battelle Press.

Johnson, Elizabeth, and Harlan Morehouse, eds. 2014. "After the Anthropocene: Politics and Geographic Inquiry for a New Epoch." *Progress in Human Geography* 38 (1): 1–18.

Johnston, Chris, Oliver Milman, and John Vidal. 2016. "Climate Change: Global Deal Reached to Limit Use of Hydrofluorocarbons." *The Guardian*, October 15, 2016. https://www.theguardian.com/environment/2016/oct/15/climate-change-environmentalists-hail-deal-to-limit-use-of-hydrofluorocarbons.

Johnston, R. J., Derek Gregory, Geraldine Pratt, and Michael Watts. 2000. *Dictionary of Human Geography*, 4th ed. Malden: Blackwell Publishing.

Jones, Martin, Rhys Jones, Michael Woods, Mark Whitehead, Deborah Dixon, and Matthew Hanna. 2015. *An Introduction to Political Geography: Space, Place and Politics*, 2nd ed. London: Routledge.

Jones, Peter, Daphne Comfort, and David Hillier. 2017. "Fracking for Shale in the UK: Risks, Reputation and Regulation." In *Handbook on Geographies of Technology*, ed. Barney Warf, 302–17. Cheltenham: Edward Elgar Publishing Limited.

Kaplan, Caren. 2006. "Mobility and War: The Cosmic View of US 'Air Power.'" *Environment and Planning A* 38: 395–407.

Karion, Anna, Colm Sweeney, Gabrielle Pétron, Gregory Frost, R. Michael Hardesty, Jonathan Kofler, Ben R. Miller, Tim Newberger, Sonja Wolter, Robert Banta, Alan Brewer, Ed Dlugokencky, Patricia Lang, Stephen A. Montzka, Russell Schnell, Pieter Tans, Michael Trainer, Robert Zamora, and Stephen Conley. 2013. "Methane Emissions Estimate from Airborne Measurements over a Western United States Natural Gas Field." *Geophysical Research Letters* 40 (16): 4393–97.

Karl, Terry Lynn. 1997. *The Paradox of Plenty: Oil Booms and Petro-States*. Berkeley: University of California Press.

———. 2000. "Crude Calculations: OPEC Lessons for the Caspian Region." In *Energy and Conflict in Central Asia and the Caucasus*, ed. Robert Ebel and Rajan Menon, 29–54. Lanham: Rowman & Littlefield.

Katz, Cindi. 1995. "Under the Falling Sky: Apocalyptic Environmentalism and the Production of Nature." In *Marxism in the Postmodern Age: Confronting the New World Order*, ed. Antonio Callari, Stephen Cullenberg, and Carole Biewener, 276–82. New York: The Guilford Press.

Kaufman, Asher. 2014. "Notes and Comments: Thinking Beyond Direct Violence." *International Journal of Middle East Studies* 46 (2): 441–46.

Kearns, Gerry. 1997. "The Imperial Subject: Geography and Travel in the Work of Mary Kingsley and Halford Mackinder." *Transactions of the Institute of British Geographers* 22 (4): 450–72.

———. 2009. *Geopolitics and Empire: The Legacy of Halford Mackinder*. Oxford: Oxford University Press.

Klare, Michael T. 2001. *Resource Wars: The Changing Landscape of Global Conflict*. New York: Henry Holt and Company.

———. 2004. *Blood and Oil: The Dangers and Consequences of America's Growing Dependency on Imported Petroleum*. New York: Henry Holt and Company.

Klein, Naomi. 2014. *This Changes Everything: Capitalism vs. The Climate*. New York: Simon & Schuster.

Koblitz, Neal. 1981. "Mathematics as Propaganda." In *Mathematics Tomorrow*, ed. Lynn Arthur Steen, 111–20. New York: Springer-Verlag.

Koubi, Vally, Gabriele Spilker, Tobias Böhmelt, and Thomas Bernauer. 2014. "Do Natural Resources Matter for Interstate and Intrastate Armed Conflict?" *Journal of Peace Research* 51 (2): 227–43.

Kovel, Joel. 2007. *The Enemy of Nature: The End of Capitalism or the End of the World?* 2nd ed. New York: Zed Books.

Kreft, Sonke, David Eckstein, and Inga Melchior. 2016. *Global Climate Risk Index 2017*. Berlin: Germanwatch e.V. https://germanwatch.org/en/12978.

Kuchinskaya, Olga. 2014. *The Politics of Invisibility: Public Knowledge about Radiation Health Effects after Chernobyl*. Cambridge: The MIT Press.

Labban, Mazen. 2010. "Oil in Parallax: Scarcity, Markets, and the Financialization of Accumulation." *Geoforum* 41: 541–52.

Latour, Bruno. 1993. *We Have Never Been Modern*. London: Harvester Wheatsheaf.

———. 2004. *Politics of Nature: How to Bring the Sciences into Democracy*. Cambridge: Harvard University Press.

Latour, Bruno, and Steve Woolgar. 1979. *Laboratory Life: The Social Construction of Scientific Facts*. Beverly Hills: Sage.

Le Billon, Philippe. 2001. "The Political Ecology of War: Natural Resources and Armed Conflicts." *Political Geography* 20 (5): 561–84.

———. 2007. "Geographies of War: Perspectives on 'Resource Wars.'" *Geography Compass* 1 (2): 163–82.

———. 2012. *Wars of Plunder: Conflicts, Profits and the Politics of Resources*. New York: Columbia University Press.

Lefebvre, Henri. 1991. *The Production of Space*. Translated by Donald Nicholson-Smith. Malden: Blackwell Publishing.

Lehman, Jessi, and Sara Nelson. 2014. "Experimental Politics in the Anthropocene." In Johnson and Morehouse (2014), 444–47.

Linton, Jamie. 2010. *What Is Water? The History of a Modern Abstraction*. Vancouver: University of British Columbia Press.

Litfin, Karen. 1997. "The Gendered Eye in the Sky: A Feminist Perspective on Earth Observation Satellites." *Frontiers* 18 (2): 26–47.

Loftus, Alex. 2014. "Water (In)security: Securing the Right to Water." *Geographical Journal* 181 (4): 350–56.

———. 2015. "Violent Geographical Abstractions." *Environment and Planning D: Society and Space* 33 (2): 366–81.

Lohmann, Larry. 2005. "Malthusianism and the Terror of Scarcity." In *Making Threats: Biofears and Environmental Anxieties*, ed. Betsy Hartmann, Banu Subramaniam, and Charles Zerner, 81–98. Lanham: Rowman & Littlefield.

Longhurst, Robyn. 2005. "The Body." In *Cultural Geography: A Critical Dictionary of Key Concepts*, ed. David Atkinson, Peter Jackson, David Sibley, and Neil Washbourne, 91–96. London: I. B. Taurus.

Lövbrand, Eva, and Johannes Stripple. 2011. "Making Climate Change Governable: Accounting for Carbon as Sinks, Credits, and Personal Budgets." *Critical Policy Studies* 5 (2): 187–200.

Lujala, Päivi, Nils Petter Gleditsch, and E. Gilmore. 2005. "A Diamonds Curse? Civil War and a Lootable Resource." *Journal of Conflict Resolution* 49 (4): 538–62.

MacKenzie, Donald. 1990. *Inventing Accuracy: A Historical Sociology of Nuclear Missile Guidance*. Cambridge: The MIT Press.

———. 2009. "Making Things the Same: Gases, Emission Rights and the Politics of Carbon Markets." *Accounting, Organizations and Society* 34: 440–55.

Mackinder, Halford J. 1919. *Democratic Ideals and Reality: A Study in the Politics of Reconstruction*. New York: Henry Holt and Company.

Malthus, Thomas Robert. 1993a. "An Essay on the Principle of Population (1798)." In *An Essay on the Principle of Population: Text, Sources, and Background Criticism*, ed. Philip Appleman, 15–129. New York: W. W. Norton & Company Inc.

———. 1993b. "An Essay on the Principle of Population: From the Revised Edition (1803)." In *An Essay on the Principle of Population: Text, Sources, and Background Criticism*, ed. Philip Appleman, 130–42. New York: W. W. Norton & Company Inc.

Mamadouh, Virginie, and Gertjan Dijkink. 2006. "Geopolitics, International Relations and Political Geography: The Politics of Geopolitical Discourse (Introduction to Special Issue of *Geopolitics: The Politics of Geopolitical Discourse*)." *Geopolitics* 11 (3): 349–66.

Marzec, Robert P. 2015. *Militarizing the Environment: Climate Change and the Security State*. Minneapolis: University of Minnesota Press.

McKibben, Bill. 2017. "The New Battle Plan for the Planet's Climate Crisis." *Rolling Stone*. February 9, 2017.

Meierding, Emily. 2013. "Climate Change and Conflict: Avoiding Small Talk about the Weather." *International Studies Review* 15 (2): 185–203.

Meng, Q. Y., and R. W. Bentley. 2008. "Global Oil Peaking: Responding to the Case for 'Abundant Supplies of Oil.'" *Energy* 33: 1179–84.

Mitchell, Timothy. 2009. "Carbon Democracy." *Economy and Society* 38 (3): 399–432.

———. 2011. *Carbon Democracy: Political Power in the Age of Oil*. New York: Verso Books.

Monmonier, Mark S. 1996. *How to Lie with Maps*, 2nd edition. Chicago: University of Chicago Press.

Mooney, Chris. 2016. "World Bank: The Way Climate Change Is Really Going to Hurt Us Is through Water." *Washington Post*, May 3, 2016. https://www.washingtonpost.com/news/energy-environment/wp/2016/05/03/world-bank-the-way-climate-change-is-really-going-to-hurt-us-is-through-water/.

Moore, Anna W., and Nicholas A. Perdue. 2014. "Imagining a Critical Geopolitical Cartography." *Geography Compass* 8 (12): 892–901.

Morton, Oliver. 2008. *Eating the Sun: How Plants Power the Planet*. New York: HarperCollins Publishers.

———. 2015. "The Music of Science/The Wizardry of Geoengineering." *Economist* 1843 (November/December). https://www.1843magazine.com/the-music-of-science/the-wizardry-of-geoengineering.

Müller, Martin. 2008. "Reconsidering the Concept of Discourse for the Field of Critical Geopolitics: Towards Discourse as Language and Practice." *Political Geography* 27: 322–38.

Murphy, Alexander B., org. ed. 2004. "Is There a Politics to Geopolitics?" *Progress in Human Geography* 28 (5): 619–40.

Myers, Norman. 1993. *Ultimate Security: The Environmental Basis of Political Stability*. New York: W.W. Norton & Company.

Nally, David. 2015. "Governing Precarious Lives: Land Grabs, Geopolitics, and 'Food Security.'" *Geographical Journal* 181 (4): 340–49.

Nandy, Ashis. 1988. *Science, Hegemony and Violence: A Requiem for Modernity*. Tokyo: The United Nations University.

NIC (National Intelligence Council). 2016. *Implications for US National Security of Anticipated Climate Change*. Office of the Director of National Intelligence. September 21, 2016. https://www.dni.gov/index.php/newsroom/reports-and-publications/214-reports-publications-2016/1415-implications-for-us-national-security-of-anticipated-climate-change.

Nixon, Rob. 2011. *Slow Violence and the Environmentalism of the Poor*. Cambridge: Harvard University Press.

O'Brien, Karen, Siri Eriksen, Lynn P. Nygaard, and Ane Schjolden. 2007. "Why Different Interpretations of Vulnerability Matter in Climate Change Discourses." *Climate Policy* 7 (1): 73–88.

O'Lear, Shannon R. M. 1996. "Using Electronic Mail (E-mail) Surveys for Geographic Research: Lessons from a Survey of Russian Environmentalists." *Professional Geographer* 48 (2): 213–22.

———. 1999. "Networks of Engagement: Electronic Communication and Grassroots Environmental Activism in Kaliningrad." *Geografiska Annaler* 81: 165–78.

———. 2005. "Resource Concerns for Territorial Conflict." *GeoJournal* 64 (4): 297–306.

———. 2010. *Environmental Politics: Scale and Power*. New York: Cambridge University Press.

———. 2016. "Climate Science and Slow Violence: A View from Political Geography and STS on Mobilizing Technoscientific Ontologies of Climate Change." *Political Geography* 52: 4–13.

O'Lear, Shannon, and Simon Dalby. 2015. "Reframing the Climate Change Discussion." In *Reframing Climate Change: Constructing Ecological Geopolitics*, ed. Shannon O'Lear and Simon Dalby, 1–13. New York: Routledge.

O'Lear, Shannon, and Paul F. Diehl. 2011. "The Scope of Resource Conflict: A Model of Scale." *Whitehead Journal of Diplomacy and International Relations* 12 (1): 27–37.

O'Lear, Shannon, and Angela Gray. 2006. "Asking the Right Questions: Environmental Conflict in the Case of Azerbaijan." *Area* 38 (4): 390–401.

O'Neill, Saffron J. 2013. "Image Matters: Climate Change Imagery in US, UK and Australian Newspapers." *Geoforum* 49: 10–19.

Ó Tuathail, Gearóid. 1996. *Critical Geopolitics: The Politics of Writing Global Space*. Minneapolis: University of Minnesota Press.

Obama, Barack. 2016. *Presidential Memorandum–Climate Change and National Security*. September 21, 2016. Office of the Press Secretary, The White House. https://www

.whitehouse.gov/the-press-office/2016/09/21/presidential-memorandum-climate-change-and-national-security.

Oels, Angela. 2005. "Rendering Climate Change Governable: From Biopower to Advanced Liberal Government?" *Journal of Environmental Policy & Planning* 7 (3): 185–207.

———. 2012. "From the 'Securitization' of Climate Change to the 'Climatization' of the Security Field: Comparing Three Theoretical Perspectives." In *Climate Change, Human Security and Violent Conflict: Challenges for Societal Stability*, ed. Michael Scheffran Brzoska, Jürgen Schilling, Janpeter Link, P. Michael Brauch, and Hans Günter, 185–205. Berlin: Springer-Verlag.

———. 2013. "Rendering Climate Change Governable by Risk: From Probability to Contingency." *Geoforum* 45: 17–29.

Olson, Mancur. 1963. "Rapid Economic Growth as a Destabilizing Force." *Journal of Economic History* 23 (4): 529–52.

Oreskes, Naomi, and Erik M. Conway. 2010. *Merchants of Doubt: How a Handful of Scientists Obscured the Truth on Issues from Tobacco Smoke to Global Warming*. New York: Bloomsbury Press.

Ostrom, Elinor. 1999. "Coping with Tragedies of the Commons." *Annual Review of Political Science* 2 (1): 493–535.

———. 2008. "The Challenge of Common-Pool Resources." *Environment* 50 (4): 8–20.

Ostrom, Elinor, Joanna Burger, Christopher B. Field, Richard B. Norgaard, and David Policansky. 1999. "Revisiting the Commons: Local Lessons, Global Challenges." *Science* 284 (April): 278–82.

Ostrom, Elinor, Roy Gardner, and James Walker. 1994. *Rules, Games, and Common-Pool Resources*. Ann Arbor: The University of Michigan Press.

Parenti, Christian. 2011. *Tropic of Chaos: Climate Change and the New Geography of Violence*. New York: Nation Books.

Paterson, Matthew, and Johannes Stripple. 2012. "Virtuous Carbon." *Environmental Politics* 21 (4): 563–82.

Peoples, Columba, and Nick Vaughan-Williams. 2015. *Critical Security Studies: An Introduction*, 2nd edition. London: Routledge.

Philo, C. 1992. "Foucault's Geography." *Environment and Planning D: Society and Space* 10: 137–61.

———. 2015. "(In)secure Environments and the Domination of Nature: Introduction to Themed Section." *Geographical Journal* 181 (4): 322–27.

Philpott, Tom. 2013. "The Real Reason Kansas Is Running Out of Water." *Grist*, September 4, 2013. http://grist.org/food/the-real-reason-kansas-is-running-out-of-water/.

Pickett, Nathaniel Ray. 2016. "The Chornobyl Disaster and the End of the Soviet Union." In Матеріали міжнародної наукової конференції "Крах радянської імперії: Анатомія катастрофи" [Materials from the International Academic

Conference "Collapse of the Soviet Empire: Anatomy of a Catastrophe"], ed. I. P. Borys. Nizhyn, Ukraine: Mykola Gogol Nizhyn State University.

Poole, Robert. 2008. *Earthrise: How Man First Saw the Earth*. New Haven: Yale University Press.

President's Air Policy Commission. 1948. *Survival in the Air Age*. Washington: U.S. Government Printing Office.

Rappert, Brian, and Brian Balmer. 2007. "Rethinking 'Secrecy' and 'Disclosure': What Science and Technology Studies Can Offer Attempts to Govern WMD Threats." In *Technology and Security: Governing Threats in the New Millennium*, ed. Brian Rappert, 45–65. New York: Palgrave Macmillan.

Reiz, Nicole, and Shannon O'Lear. 2016. "Spaces of Violence and (In)justice in Haiti: A Critical Legal Geography Perspective on Rape, UN Peacekeeping, and the United Nations Status of Forces Agreement." *Territory, Politics and Governance* 4: 453–71.

Richardson, Tanya, and Gisa Weszkalnys. 2014. "Introduction: Resource Materialities." *Anthropological Quarterly* 87 (1): 5–30.

Robbins, Paul. 2004. *Political Ecology: A Critical Introduction*. Malden: Blackwell Publishing.

———. 2007. *Lawn People: How Grasses, Weeds, and Chemicals Make Us Who We Are*. Philadelphia: Temple University Press.

Robbins, Paul, and Sara H. Smith. 2016. "Baby Bust: Towards Political Demography." *Progress in Human Geography* 41 (2): 199–219.

Rogers, Heather. 2005. *Gone Tomorrow: The Hidden Life of Garbage*. New York: The New Press.

Rosenbaum, Walter A. 2017. *Environmental Politics and Policy*, 10th Edition. Thousand Oaks: CQ Press.

Ross, Eric B. 1998. *The Malthus Factor: Poverty, Politics and Population in Capitalist Development*. New York: St. Martin's Press.

———. 2000. *Briefing: The Malthus Factor: Poverty, Politics and Population in Capitalist Development*. Dorset: The Corner House. http://www.thecornerhouse.org.uk/sites/thecornerhouse.org.uk/files/20malth.pdf.

Ross, Michael. 2006. "A Closer Look at Oil, Diamonds, and Civil War." *Annual Review of Political Science* 9: 265–300.

Rubinstein, Justin L., and Alireza Babaie Mahani. 2015. "Myths and Facts on Wastewater Injection, Hydraulic Fracturing, Enhanced Oil Recovery, and Induced Seismicity." *Seismological Research Letters* 86 (4): 1060–67.

Sack, Robert David. 1986. *Human Territoriality: Its Theory and History*. New York: Cambridge University Press.

Sagan, Carl. 1994. "With Science on Our Side." *Washington Post*, January 9, 1994. https://www.washingtonpost.com/archive/entertainment/books/1994/01/09/with-science-on-our-side/9e5d2141-9d53-4b4b-aa0f-7a6a0faff845/?utm_term=.9ddc117e05d2.

Sarewitz, Daniel. 2004. "How Science Makes Environmental Controversies Worse." *Environmental Science & Policy* 7 (5): 385–403.

Sassen, Saskia. 2013. "Land Grabs Today: Feeding the Disassembling of National Territory." *Globalizations* 10 (1): 25–46.

Sayer, Derek. 1997. *The Violence of Abstraction: The Analytic Foundations of Historical Materialism*. Malden: Basil Blackwell.

Scanlan, Stephen J. 2013. "Feeding the Planet or Feeding Us a Line? Agribusiness, 'Grainwashing,' and Hunger in the World Food System." *International Journal of Sociology of Agriculture and Food* 20 (3): 357–82.

Scanlan, Stephen J., J. Craig Jenkins, and Lindsey Peterson. 2010. "The Scarcity Fallacy." *Contexts* 9: 34–39.

Schäfer, Mike S., Jürgen Scheffran, and Logal Penniket. 2015. "Securitization of Media Reporting on Climate Change? A Cross-National Analysis in Nine Countries." *Security Dialogue* 47 (1): 76–96.

Schwartz, Peter, and Doug Randall. 2003. *An Abrupt Climate Change Scenario and Its Implications for United States National Security*. Pasadena: California Institute of Technology/Jet Propulsion Lab.

Scott, James C. 1998. *Seeing Like a State: How Certain Schemes to Improve the Human Condition Have Failed*. New Haven: Yale University Press.

Selby, Jan, Omar S. Dahi, Christiane Fröhlich, and Mike Hulme. 2017a. "Climate Change and the Syrian Civil War Revisited." *Political Geography* 60: 232–44.

———. 2017b. "Climate Change and the Syrian Civil War Revisited: A Rejoinder." *Political Geography* 60: 253–55.

Selchow, Sabine. 2016. "The Paths Not (Yet) Taken: Ulrich Beck, the 'Cosmopolized World' and Security Studies." *Security Dialogue* 47 (5): 369–85.

Sen, Amartya. 1981. *Poverty and Famines: An Essay on Entitlement and Deprivation*. New York: Oxford University Press.

Sismondo, Sergio. 2008. "Science and Technology Studies and an Engaged Program." In *The Handbook of Science and Technology Studies, Third Edition*, ed. Edward J. Hackett, Olga Amsterdamska, Michael Lynch, and Judy Wajcman, 13–31. Cambridge: The MIT Press.

Slovic, Paul. 2016. "Understanding Perceived Risk: 1978–2015." *Environment: Science and Policy for Sustainable Development* 58 (1): 25–29.

Smaje, Chris. 2013. "Global Hunger: Three Christmas Ghost Stories." Statistics-Views. Chichester: John Wiley & Sons Limited. http://www.statisticsviews.com/details/feature/5650081/Global-Hunger-Three-Christmas-Ghost-Stories.html.

Smith, Neil. 1984. *Uneven Development: Nature, Capital, and the Production of Space*. New York: Blackwell.

———. 1996. "The Production of Nature." In *FutureNatural: Nature, Science, Culture*, ed. George Robertson, Melinda Mash, Lisa Tickner, Jon Bird, Barry Curtis, and Tim Putnam, 35–54. New York: Routledge.

———. 2003. *American Empire: Roosevelt's Geographer and the Prelude to Globalization*. Berkeley: University of California Press.

Sneddon, Christopher. 2015. *Concrete Revolution: Large Dams, Cold War Geopolitics, and the US Bureau of Reclamation*. Chicago: The University of Chicago Press.

Speer, Lisa, Regan Nelson, Robbert Casier, Maria Gavrilo, Cecilie von Quillfeldt, Jesse Cleary, Patrick Halpin, and Patricia Hooper. 2017. *Natural Marine World Heritage in the Arctic Ocean, Report of an Expert Workshop and Review Process.* Gland: International Union for Conservation of Nature and Natural Resources.

Spiegel-Rösing, Ina, and Derek de Solla Price. 1977. *Science, Technology, and Society: A Cross-Disciplinary Perspective.* Beverly Hills: Sage Publications.

Steffen, Will, Paul J. Crutzen, and John R. McNeill. 2007. "The Anthropocene: Are Humans Now Overwhelming the Great Forces of Nature?" *Ambio* 36 (8): 614–21.

Swyngedouw, Erik. 1999. "Modernity and Hybridity: Nature, *Regeneracionismo*, and the Production of the Spanish Waterscape, 1890–1930." *Annals of the Association of American Geographers* 89 (3): 443–65.

———. 2010a. "Apocalypse Forever? Post-Political Populism and the Spectre of Climate Change." *Theory, Culture & Society* 27 (2–3): 213–32.

———. 2010b. "Trouble with Nature: 'Ecology as the New Opium for the Masses.'" In *The Ashgate Research Companion to Planning Theory: Conceptual Challenges for Spatial Planning*, ed. Jean Hillier and Patsy Healey, 299–318. Burlington: Ashgate.

Thrift, Nigel. 2000. "It's the Little Things." In *Geopolitical Traditions: A Century of Geopolitical Thought*, ed. Klaus Dodds and David Atkinson, 380–87. London: Routledge.

Toset, Hans Petter Wollebaek, Nils Petter Gleditsch, and Håvard Hegre. 2000. "Shared Rivers and Interstate Conflict." *Political Geography* 19 (8): 971–96.

Trombetta, Maria Julia. 2008. "Environmental Security and Climate Change: Analysing the Discourse." *Cambridge Review of International Affairs* 21 (4): 585–602.

United Nations, Department of Economic and Social Affairs, Population Division. 2015. *World Population Prospects: The 2015 Revision, Key Findings and Advance Tables.* Working Paper No. ESA/WP.241. http://esa.un.org/unpd/wpp/publications/files/key_findings_wpp_2015.pdf.

US Department of Energy. 2016. *Wind and Solar Data and Projections from the U.S. Energy Information Administration: Past Performance and Ongoing Enhancements.* Washington: U.S. Department of Energy. https://www.eia.gov/outlooks/aeo/supplement/renewable/pdf/projections.pdf.

US Energy Information Administration. 2015. "First Offshore Wind Farm in the United States Begins Construction." http://www.eia.gov/todayinenergy/detail.php?id=22512#tabs_SpotPriceSlider-2.

Waever, Ole. 1995. "Securitization and Desecuritization." In *On Security*, ed. Ronnie D. Lipschutz, 46–86. New York: Columbia University Press.

Wakefield, Stephanie. 2014. "The Crisis Is the Age." In Johnson and Morehouse (2014), 450–52.

Walker, R. B. J. 1987. "The Concept of Security and International Relations Theory." Working Paper No. 3; Series edited by James M. Skelly. First Annual Conference on Discourse, Peace, Security and International Society. Ballyvaughn, Ireland, August 9–16, 1987.

Wapner, Paul. 2014. "Climate Suffering." *Global Environmental Politics* 14 (2): 1–6.

Watson, Elizabeth E. 2010. "Part I: Types of Determinist Environmental Thinking." *Progress in Human Geography* 34 (1): 101–5.

Watts, Michael, and Nancy Peluso. 2014. "Resource Violence." In *Critical Environmental Politics*, ed. Carl Death, 184–97. New York: Routledge.

Weber, Elke U., and Paul C. Stern. 2011. "Public Understanding of Climate Change in the United States." *American Psychologist* 66 (4): 315–28.

Weisman, Alan. 2013. *Countdown: Our Last, Best Hope for a Future on Earth?* New York: Little, Brown and Company.

Werrell, Caitlin E., and Francesco Femia, eds. 2017. *Epicenters of Climate and Security: The New Geostrategic Landscape of the Anthropocene*. Washington, DC: The Center for Climate and Security. https://climateandsecurity.org/epicenters/.

Westing, Arthur H. 1984. *Environmental Warfare: A Technical, Legal, and Policy Appraisal*. London: Taylor & Francis.

Whatmore, Sarah. 2002. *Hybrid Geographies: Natures Cultures Spaces*. London: Sage.

World Business Council for Sustainable Development. 2009. *Facts and Trends: Water, Version 2*. http://www.wbcsd.org/Pages/EDocument/EDocumentDetails.aspx?ID=137&NoSearchContextKey=true.

Yearley, Steven. 2008. "Nature and the Environment in Science and Technology Studies." In *The Handbook of Science and Technology Studies, Third edition*, ed. Edward J. Hackett, Olga Amsterdamska, Michael Lynch, and Judy Wajcman, 921–47. Cambridge: The MIT Press.

Yuen, Eddie. 2012. "The Politics of Failure Have Failed: The Environmental Movement and Catastrophism." In *Catastrophism: The Apocalyptic Politics of Collapse and Rebirth*, ed. Sasha Lilley, David McNally, Eddie Yuen, and James Davis, 15–43. Oakland: PM Press.

Yusoff, Kathryn. 2009. "Excess, Catastrophe, and Climate Change." *Environment and Planning D: Society and Space* 27 (6): 1010–29.

Zalik, Anna. 2010. "Oil 'Futures': Shell's Scenarios and the Social Constitution of the Global Oil Market." *Geoforum* 41: 553–64.

Žižek, Slavoj. 1991. *Looking Awry: An Introduction to Jacques Lacan through Popular Culture*. Cambridge: The MIT Press.

Index

Page references for figures are italicized.

abundance. *See* resource abundance
adaptation, 110, 127, 129, 130, 131, 160
affluence, 31. *See also* I = PAT
Africa, water consumption in, 43, 46–47, 48, 52
agency. *See* human agency; resource: agency of
agribusiness, 60–61
agriculture: high-tech/industrial, 27, 30, 40, 62, 89; increased demand for agricultural land, 79; mechanical revolution in, 33; technological solutions for, 50, 61; water subsidies for, 49, 55. *See also* commodity; Green Revolution
air power, 11–12
Alaska, USA, 12, 96, 174
Anthropocene, 24–25, 62, 78, 110, 139
Apollo 17. *See* Earth, image from space
Aral Sea, 45–46
Arctic: fossil fuel exploration in, 156; ice melts, 109, 156, *157*; Indigenous communities, 156; passage through, 156; polar projection map, *12*; protection of ecosystem, 158
atmosphere: altering of, 115, 119, 140, 144, 145; greenhouse gas in, 142–43; heat-trapping potential of, 143, 144. *See also* carbon dioxide; greenhouse gas
Atomic Energy Commission (US), 174

baby bust. *See* population decline
biofuel, 40, 89, 90
biological reductionism, 10. *See also* environmental determinism
Borlaug, Norman, 30
Boserup, Esther, 30
Brandalism, *107*
Britain. *See* United Kingdom
Bureau of Reclamation (US), 153

capitalism, 50, 84, 116; as cause of climate change, 115, 117, 126; and control of nature, 84; questioning of, 117–19

197

carbon democracy, 79
carbon dioxide (CO_2), 62, 116, 119, 159; emissions, 142, 143, 144, 171; measurement of, 144; storage, 150; tCO2e, tonne of carbon dioxide equivalent, 144; trading, 131, 144–45. *See also* greenhouse gas
carrying capacity, 33
causation science, 119
cause imagery, 160
Center for Climate & Security, 105
Center for Naval Analysis (CNA Corporation), 47, 108, 109
Chernobyl, Ukraine, 66, 95–96
China: demographic policy, 39; water consumption in, 43, 46–47, 48, 55
chlorofluorocarbons (CFCs), 66, 142–43
civil violence. *See* violence
classical geopolitics, 9–13, 14, 20
climate change: adaptation, 130–31; causes of, 115, 126; and conflict, 122–23; and dynamics of power, 117; global view of, 123; imagery, 159–61; impacts of, 105, 106, 109–10, 111, 112, 114, 121, 122, 123, 127, 156, 160; in the media, 103; and national security, 105, 108, 112–13, 121–22, 123; resilience, 127, 131; responses to, 115–17, 118, 126, 132, 150; and risk, 107, 108, 109, 112, 113, 121, 123, 132; risk management, 111, 126–27; and security, 106–8, 110, 121, 125, 128–29, 130–31; skepticism of, 98, 118–19; as threat multiplier, 47, 108, 109, 122; and water, 43–44
climate change policy (US), 110–13
climate modeling, 118
climate science, 119, 134
climate security, 6, 8, 104–5, 107–8, 132; discourses of, 113–20, 124, 128–29; as military issue, 103, 108–9, 121, 128; as practice, 107, 125–26; responding with science, 118; spatialization of, 107, 117, 120–24
climate skeptics. *See* climate change: skepticism
climate suffering, 101
critical geopolitics, 9, 14–18, 19, 105, 153
coal, 8; externalities of, 88–89, 98; as resource complex, 79–80
co-constructivist approach, 139, 140
Cold War, 66–67, 104; infrastructure projects during, 153, 176
collaboration. *See* common-pool resources
colonization, 79, 115; and commodities, 66; legacy of, 40, 42, 62. *See also* imperial expansion
commodity: crop, 40, 45–46, 49, 89; as driver of conflict, 72; export, 71; management of, 71, 153; pricing, 58; resource, 6, 59, 66, 71, 72, 99, 153. *See also* agriculture
common-pool resources, 91–93
commons, 41, 92
Conference of the Parties (COP 21), 106, *107*, 148
conflict: armed/violent, 81–83, 91, 93, 100; and climate change, 109, 122–23; prevention, 127; quantification of, 81–82, 100, 123; and resource abundance, 71–72; and resource scarcity, 69–71, 93; as social process, 82–83. *See also* resource conflict; slow violence
consumerism/consumption: impacts of, 7, 31; as discourse, 18; green, 126, 151, 152, 160; reducing, 35, 116, 145, 151–52, 159, 163
COP21. *See* Conference of the Parties
Copenhagen School, 124–26. *See also* securitization

critical geopolitics, 14–15, 18, 105
critical security studies, 3, 104, 124, 173
critical theory, 20

demographic policy, 38–39. *See also* population decline; population growth
Department of Defense (US), 108–10, 121; policy on climate change, 110–113
determinism, 40–42, 52, 57. developing countries, 42, 55, 72, 104, 108, 143, 153
diamonds. *See* conflict: and resource abundance
diesel. *See* biofuel
discourse analysis, 14–16, 19. *See also* embodiment; materiality; practice
disease, 33, 109; Zika virus, 123

Earth, image from space, 22–23, 137, 160, 168
earthquakes, injection-induced. *See* hydraulic fracturing
ecological fallacy, 70
ecology, apolitical, 85
economic: competitiveness, 112; decline, 43; development, 30–31, 42, 49, 51; growth, 47, 50, 51, 58, 117, 126, 142; incentives, 38, 117, 147; inequality, 40, 42, 50, 124; productivity, 32; stability, 48; system, 55, 57, 74, 75, 77, 83, 115,117, 152; wealth, 11, 13
ecosystem, 45, 51, 68, 95, 128, 129, 158, 166; alteration of, 96, 98, 139, 153,174; services, 6, 84, 98; value of, 117, 157–58, 175
effect science, 119
electricity, 132; generation of, 47, 88, 148, 153, 159; infrastructure, 148, 153, *154*, 163. *See also* energy

embodiment, 16–18, 23–24, 37, 61, 66, 74, 86, 168
emissions. *See* greenhouse gas
enclosure, 34, 35, 52, 59, 87, 89, 129–30
energy, 50, 55, 57, 66, 77, 79, 87, 93, 116, 142, 145–48, *151*, 160. *See also* electricity
Energy Information Administration (US), 145
energy security, 8, 65, 86–89, 108
England, eighteenth century, 34–35, 87
Enlightenment, the, 84–85, 91, 93, 95, 100, 172
entitlement, 38, 69
Environment and Conflicts Project (ENCOP), 70
environment, meaning of, 6, 21
environmental: determinism, 10–11, 99; discrimination, 70; externalities, 98, 175; movement, 22–23; policy, 134; value, 73
environmental security, 19, 21, 65–67, 104–5, 141
environmentality, 129
ethanol, 40, 55. *See also* biofuel
Europe, 40, 43, 47, 52, 66, 79–80, 115
Exxon Valdez oil spill, 96

Farallon Islands, CA, 174
fertility rate, 38, 39, 51
financialization of resources, 58, 79
food, 2, 27, 34, 40, 60
Food and Water Watch, 49
food insecurity, 60–61, 101
food scarcity, 30, 60–62
food security, 89–91, 108, 112, 123
food supply, 28, 29, 30, 32, 33–34, 35, 39–40, 60, 61, 122
food systems, 61, *151*
fossil fuel. *See* oil
Foucault, Michel, 14–15
fracking. *See* hydraulic fracturing

France, 48
fresh water. *See* water

Ganges River, 43, 44, 45
genetically modified organisms (GMOs), 49
geographies of volume, 8, 155–56
Germany, 11, 128–29, 175–76
Global Carbon Project, 142
Global Climate Risk Index, 106
global warming. *See* climate change
god trick of science/objectivity, 13, 140. *See also* science
grainwashing, 60–62
Green Revolution, 30, 50
greenhouse gas, 115, 117, 127, 142–44, 148–50, 159

Haushofer, Karl, 11
health, 87, 95, 112, 118, 122–23. *See also* disease
Heartland Theory, 11
High Plains Aquifer, 49
homeland security, 130. *See also* national security
Hubbert's Peak, 56, 57, 59
human agency, 6–7, 18, 25, 49, 115, 117, 119, 147–48
hydraulic fracturing, 87–88, 142
hydroelectric dams, 153–54
hydrofluorocarbons (HFCs), 142–43

I = PAT, 28, 29–32, 171
identity, 17, 66, 86, 94, 168–69
imperial expansion, 10, 11, 65, 66, 89
India, 11, 43–45, 46, 47, 48, 55, 101, 132
insecure environments, 85, 86, 89
Intergovernmental Panel on Climate Change (IPCC), 112, 118, 127
International Monetary Fund (IMF), 89
International Union for the Conservation of Nature and Natural Resources, 157

jatropha. *See* biofuel

Kansas, USA, 48–49
Keeling Curve, 159
Kjellén, Rudolph, 10

laborers, 34–36, 38, 80
land acquisition, 89–91. *See also* enclosure
land tenure, 87
Lebensraum, 10, 11
liquid petroleum. *See* oil

Mackinder, Sir Halford, 11–12, 14, 65
Mali, 48
Malthus, Thomas Robert, 28–30, 32–33, 34
Malthusian thinking, 28, 30, 32–36, 40, 41–42, 43, 50, 52, 55, 56–57, 59, 60, 62, 63, 69, 70, 87, 92, 101; binaries in, 36–37; critiques of, 36–40, 50–51
marine conservation, 155–56, 158. *See also* oceans
materiality, 16, 18, 24, 38, 39, 50, 61, 66, 74, 90, 142, 148, 153, 163, 167, 168, 174, 175–76
methane. *See* greenhouse gas
Middle East, 43, 46–47
migration, 38, 122, 127
military. *See* United States military
mining. *See* coal
modernity, 76, 115–119, 139, 152, 170, 172
modernization, 60, 153
Montreal Protocol, 143. *See also* chlorofluorocarbons

National Defense Authorization Act, US, 108
national security, 47, 103, 105, 108, 112–13, 118, 121–23, 129–30
natural gas. *See* greenhouse gas
naturalization of knowledge, 12–13

natural resources, 83–84, 110, 111, 117, 153
natural security, 129–30
nature, 21, 22, 23, 32, 59, 76–78, 83–85, 89, 91, 98, 115, 129–30, 137, 139, 149, 166, 170
Nicaragua, 106
nonknowledge, 133–34
North America, 43, 47, 48, 52
Norway, 71, *114*
Northwest Passage, 156–57
nuclear disaster, 3, 66, 95
nuclear reactor, 175–76
nuclear waste, 174

oil, 58, 71, 72, 73, 79, 80–81, 86–89, 94; pipeline, 16, 58; spill, 96, 97, 155, 174
oil scarcity, 28, 56–59
oceans, 6, 7–8, 119, 155–56, *157*, 158
organic theory of the state, 10, 11
Outstanding Universal Value (OUV), 158
overpopulation, 36, 48, 50
ozone layer, 66, 142–43

palm oil, 67, 68, 173–74
Paris Climate Accord, 106, 148
Paris Climate Conference, 148–49
peak oil, 56–59, 79, 171
pesticides, 30, 33, 40, 169
petroleum, 66, 79–80. *See also* oil
photojournalism, 160, 163
photovoltaics. *See* solar energy
policy, 71, 81, 85, 90–91, 108, 110–11, 113, 117, 118, 119, 127–28, 138, 140, 144, 149
pollution, 7, 30, 87, 115, 175
Poor Laws, 34
population decline, 38, 39, 50–51
population dynamics, 37–39, 41
population growth, 23, 27–32, 32–37, 38, 39, 40–42, 43, 44, 45, 47, 50, 51, 55, 57, 59, 61, 109, 171

postpolitical, 7, 85
poverty, 37–38, 50–51, 82. *See also* welfare
poverty reduction, 127
power: appropriate use of, 140; consolidation of, 72, 153; disparities in, 42, 86, 94, 98, 156; dynamics of, 6–7, 18, 36, 40, 63, 77, 80, 91, 99–100, 117–118, 140, 166; and environmental features, 74–75, 79–80; and space, 11, 13, 14–15, 16, 18, 58, 154
practice: as discourse, 14, 17–18, 24, 38, 50, 59, 61, 74, 86, 90, 125, 142, 163, 169–70; as prevention, 125–26
Presidential Memo on climate change, 112–13, 115, 118, 121–22, 126
private property, 35, 36, 41, 81
public health. *See* health

radiation exposure. *See* Chernobyl
Ratzel, Freidrich, 10, 13
renewable energy, 87, 145–48, 160. *See also* electricity
resilience, 131
resource: access to, 38, 42, 50, 52, 65, 69, 85, 90, 92, 93, 156; agency of, 52, 55, 73–74, 99; complex, 77, 79, 99; curse, 72; determinism, 68, 73, 86, 99; environments, 78–79; lootable, 74–75; overuse of, 6, 41, 42, 51, 59, 92; securing of, 59, 66–67, 84, 85–86, 87, 91, 110; as social process, 75–81, 99; social relations of, 74, 77; valuation of, 59, 68, 73, 74, 75, 78, 82, 84–85, 98, 99, 117, 126, 153; volume, 58; wars, 66
resource abundance, 62, 68, 69–72, 73, 74, 77, 99
resource characteristics, 68, 74–75, 80, 99
resource conflict, 6, 12, 44, 65, 66, 68, 69–75, 82, 85–87, 100–101

resource management, 23, 24, 28, 58, 59, 72, 74, 75, 77, 83, 86, 91–93, 94, 130, 135, 153–54, 168
resource scarcity, 24, 27, 30, 32, 35, 36, 59, 61–62, 69–72, 73, 77, 82, 98. *See also* food scarcity; oil scarcity; water scarcity
risk, 16, 24, 29, 30, 32, 35, 96, 121, 128, 158, 160, 162, 168; at-risk places, 46, 47; conceptualization of, 3, 9, 12, 132–33; discourses of, 52, 55, 107, 136, 162, 173; environmental, 2, 5, 19, 25, 43–44, 66, 99, 104, 105, 136, 141; management, 110, 111, 126–27; measurement of, 5, 133, 136; mitigation, 108–9; nonknowledge, 133–34; perception, 5, 98; society, 3, 125, 132; spatial aspects of, 3, 12–13, 24, 107, 121, 141, 173. *See also* security
Russia, 11, 39, 95. *See also* Soviet Union

Saudi Arabia, 56, 58
scarcity, 2, 35, 43, 58–59, 63, 65, 68, 69–70, 73, 81, 93. *See also* food scarcity; resource scarcity; water scarcity
science, 33, 91, 112, 115, 116–18, 136–37, 138–40, 142, 149, 160, 170
Science and Technology Studies (STS), 137–40, 149, 171
security, 2, 3, 7, 17, 27, 32, 36, 47, 62, 66–67, 83, 87, 99, 105, 108, 121, 124, 125–26, 128–29, 133, 136; climatization of, 127; discourses of, 25, 104, 107, 109, 130–32, 161–62, 168, 173; ecosystem, 158; protocol, 17; spatial aspects of, 13, 24. *See also* food security; environmental security; water security
securitization, 3, 66, 77–78, 124–26
shale gas. *See* hydraulic fracturing

signal value, 5
slow violence, 68, 93–98, 161–62, 170, 173–75
Smith, Adam, 35
Social Darwinism, 10–11
socionature, 76, 80, 99
solar power. *See* renewable energy
solution imagery, 160
South America, 52, 55
Southeast Asia, 52, 55
Soviet Union: collapse of, 39, 66, 96; infrastructure and planning, 45–46; response to Chernobyl, 95–96
speaking truth to power, 140
speech move, 124–25, 126
subsistence rights, 34, 35
Syria, 122

tCO2e. *See* carbon dioxide
threat multiplier, 5, 44, 47, 108, 122
tobacco industry, 96, 98
Toronto Group, 69–70
Tragedy of the Commons, 41, 92. *See also* determinism
Transnational Institute, Amsterdam, 131
Trump, Donald, 103, 106, 148

United Kingdom (UK), 65–66, 108, 146
United Nations (UN), 17, 50, 51, 119; Convention on the Law of the Sea, 24; Framework Convention on Climate Change (UNFCCC), 106; UNESCO, 157
United States (US), 22, 49, 66, 81, 103, 106, 112, 122, 148, 153; military, 12, 103, 104, 108–9, 111, 121, 128, 129; oil supply, 56–57; renewal energy in, 145–47; water consumption in, 48, 55
unknown unknown, 161
urban geography, 156

urbanization, 109
Utopian theory, eighteenth century, 32, 36

vertical forest, 166
vertical urbanisms, 156
violence, 4, 17, 70, 80, 85, 94, 140, 161, 177. *See also* conflict; slow violence

water: agency of, 52, 55, 73; consumption patterns, 48, 54, 55; infrastructure, 76, 86, 153–54; management of, 86; seasonality, 45; social construction of, 76–77; supply, 27–28, 44, 49, 53, 55, 105; waste, 49
water scarcity, 27, 43, 45–48, 52, 55, 59
water security, 85–86, 108, 123
welfare system, 34–35
wind power. *See* renewable energy
World Bank, 43, 47–48
World Trade Organization, 89
Wunderland Kalkar, *176*

Zika virus. *See* disease

About the Author

Shannon O'Lear is a Professor with appointments in the Geography and Atmospheric Science Department and the Environmental Studies Program at the University of Kansas. She is currently the Director of the Center for Global and International Studies. She is a political geographer focused on environmental issues with regional expertise in the South Caucasus. She has taught courses on environmental policy, environmental geopolitics, political geography, geopolitics of Russia and Eurasia, geography of genocide, and introductory human geography. She has published her work on the Nagorno-Karabakh conflict in the South Caucasus, territorial conflict, resource conflict, borders, environmental security, and genocide. Her coedited volume, *Reframing Climate Change: Constructing Ecological Geopolitics*, was published in 2015, and her book, *Environmental Politics: Scale and Power*, was published in 2010. She received her BA and MA degrees from the University of Colorado at Boulder and holds a PhD in geography from Syracuse University.

HUMAN GEOGRAPHY IN THE TWENTY-FIRST CENTURY
ISSUES AND APPLICATIONS
Series Editor: Barney Warf, University of Kansas

Human geography is increasingly focused on real-world problems. Applying geographic concepts to current global concerns, this series focuses on the urgent issues confronting us as we move into the new century. Designed for university-level geography and related multidisciplinary courses such as area studies, global issues, and development, these textbooks are richly illustrated and include suggestions for linking to related Internet resources. The series aims to help students to better understand, integrate, and apply common themes and linkages in the social and physical sciences and in the humanities, and, by doing so, to become more effective problem solvers in the challenging world they will face.

Boundaries of Faith: Geographical Perspectives on Religious Fundamentalism
    by Roger W. Stump
Six Billion Plus: World Population in the Twenty-First Century, Second Edition
    by K. Bruce Newbold
Popular Culture, Geopolitics, and Identity
    by Jason Dittmer
Bordering and Ordering the Twenty-First Century: Understanding Borders
    by Gabriel Popescu
Placing Animals: An Introduction to the Geography of Human-Animal Relations
    by Julie Urbanik
Global Information Society: Technology, Knowledge, and Mobility
    by Mark I. Wilson, Aharon Kellerman, and Kenneth E. Corey
Imprinting Ethnicity: Segregation, Placemaking, and the Articulations of Difference
    by David H. Kaplan